Robert Graves

ROBERT GRAVES
COMPLETE POEMS
Volume II

Robert Graves Programme
General Editor: Patrick J.M. Quinn

Centenary Selected Poems
edited by Patrick J.M. Quinn

Collected Writings on Poetry
edited by Paul O'Prey

Complete Short Stories
edited by Lucia Graves

Complete Poems I
edited by Beryl Graves and Dunstan Ward

Complete Poems II
edited by Beryl Graves and Dunstan Ward

The White Goddess:
A Historical Grammar of Poetic Myth
edited by Grevel Lindop

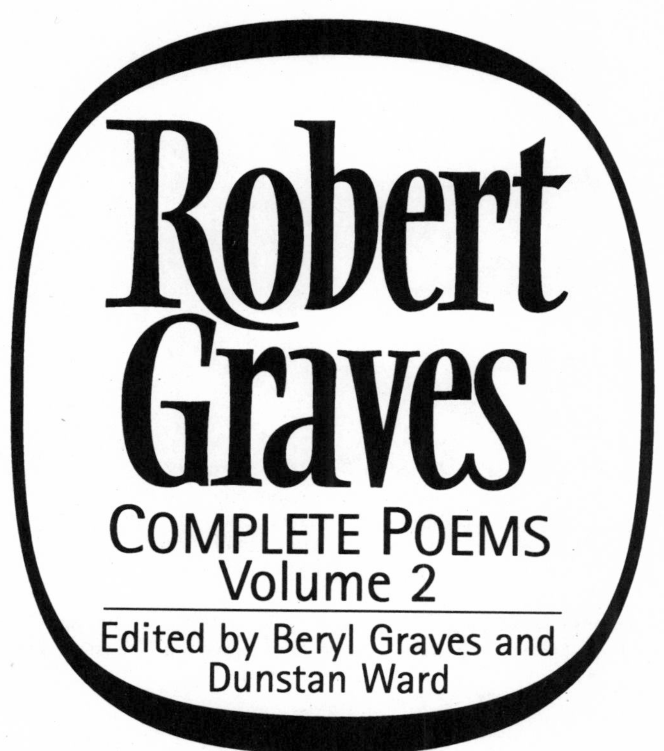
Robert
Graves
COMPLETE POEMS
Volume 2
Edited by Beryl Graves and
Dunstan Ward

CARCANET

First published in Great Britain in 1997 by
Carcanet Press Limited
4th Floor, Conavon Court
12-16 Blackfriars Street
Manchester M3 5BQ

A CIP catalogue record for this book
is available from the British Library

ISBN 1 85754 261 4

The publisher acknowledges financial assistance
from the Arts Council of England.

Set in 10pt Meridien by Bryan Williamson, Frome
Printed and bound in England by SRP Ltd, Exeter

CONTENTS

ACKNOWLEDGEMENTS

The editors wish to thank the following institutions for enabling us to examine manuscript materials, and for permission to quote from them: the Henry W. and Albert A. Berg Collection, New York Public Library, Astor, Lennox and Tilden Foundations; the Bodleian Library, Oxford; the Poetry/Rare Books Collection, University Libraries, State University of New York at Buffalo; the St John's College Robert Graves Trust, Oxford; the Morris Library, Southern Illinois University at Carbondale; the Harry Ransom Humanities Research Center, the University of Texas at Austin; the University of Victoria, British Columbia, Canada; the Beinecke Rare Book and Manuscript Library, Yale University. As with Volume I, we are indebted to the Curator of the Poetry/Rare Books Collection, SUNY at Buffalo, Professor Robert J. Bertholf, for his aid and encouragement, and to Dr Michael Basinski, Assistant Curator.

Many others have helped us in the preparation of this volume; in particular, we should like to thank Mrs Elizabeth Chilver; Señora Elena Lambea and Mr William Graves; Mr Richard Perceval Graves; and Mrs Stella Irwin. Information was kindly provided by the Irish Georgian Society and the Kinsey Institute, Bloomington, Indiana.

We are especially grateful to Ms Lucia Graves for her continued assistance with research.

Dunstan Ward is pleased to have the opportunity to acknowledge a research grant from the British Academy to visit libraries and collections in the United States, and the support of the University of London's British Institute in Paris.

The understanding and professionalism of our editor, Dr Robyn Marsack, have again been much appreciated.

INTRODUCTION

The years spanned by the 285 poems in this volume, 1927-1959, divide into two main periods. The first is defined by Robert Graves's association with Laura Riding, the American poet in whom he identified the 'Sovereign Muse'. After the break in 1939, the relationship that led to his second marriage establishes the other period, in which the White Goddess becomes the central presence.

If, as he afterwards affirmed, Graves was 'learning all the time' while he was with Riding,[1] these were also years of drama and upheaval: the end of his first marriage; Riding's attempted suicide; departure from England in 1929, after writing his classic autobiography *Good-bye to All That*; seven years in Mallorca where, for all that is positive in his diary, their life together 'grew more and more painful';[2] then, uprooted by the Spanish Civil War, exile in England, Switzerland and France; finally, 'the horror of her parting'.[3]

In contrast, the following two decades – despite World War II, in which his eldest son, David, was killed – brought Graves stability, with his remarriage and another family of four children, and his return in 1946, after six years in Devon, to his Mallorcan home in the mountain village of Deyá.

During the first period Graves's poetry did not reach a large readership. Besides being geographically isolated, he had virtually ceased contributing to periodicals and anthologies,[4] and of the six books before 1938, four were limited editions amounting to just 740 copies; even Heinemann's *Poems 1926-1930* was published in an edition of only 1000.

The 1938 *Collected Poems* was 'selective rather than collective',[5] like *Poems (1914-26)* and the succeeding volumes in 1948, 1955 and 1959. 'A volume of collected poems should form a sequence of the intenser moments of the poet's spiritual autobiography,' Graves believed;[6] in suppressing (and occasionally restoring) his

---

1 Graves to Gertrude Stein, n.d. [Feb.(?) 1946]; *SL 1*, p.341. For the bibliographical notes and abbreviations, see pp.257-9.

2 Graves to Gertrude Stein, 28 Jan. 1946; *SL 1*, p.337.

3 See the note on 'Theseus and Ariadne' (*P38-45*).

4 See the note on *CP38*.

5 *GTAT29*, p.439; see the note on *P14-26*, *Complete Poems*, Volume I.

6 *PS51*, 'Foreword', p.viii.

poems, and reordering them in their sections – from 1938 designated simply by a roman numeral[7] – he was reshaping, with the canon, his life 'story'.[8]

The next phase was his most creative, in prose and verse alike.[9] 'These last years [. . .] with Beryl', he wrote, 'have been the happiest of my life and I have done my best work in them.'[10] The rigour he had achieved in his poetry was now combined with a renewed lyricism, as revealed in *Work in Hand* (1942) and *Poems 1938-1945*. From 'a sudden overwhelming obsession'[11] in 1944 emerged *The White Goddess*, eventually published (through the perceptiveness of T.S. Eliot) in 1948 – a whole system of thought and belief within which lifelong poetic preoccupations could find their place.

The Goddess pervades Graves's poetry: anticipated in the early work, she is prefigured while he is in the service of an exacting Muse; then celebrated by the poet as her mythologist and, increasingly, her devotee; and in his mid-fifties he experiences again her inspiration and apparent betrayal – a pattern that was to continue and dominate the future.

The favourable critical reception of *Poems 1938-1945* marked a turning-point in Graves's reputation.[12] In the 1950s the number of his poems in periodicals climbed back to the level of the early 1920s; paperback editions in 1957 and 1958 made his poetry widely available; lecture tours in America and television appearances swelled his audience. By the end of the decade he had become a celebrity, receiving – or refusing – awards and honours. Yet his later verse caused him some disquiet; when he wrote the last poem in this volume he was wondering whether he had reached his 'menopause'.[13] But if his major poetic achievement was behind him, his most prolific years still lay ahead.

---

[7] As were the chapters in *GTAT29*.

[8] *PS51*, p.ix. Like Volume I, this volume of the *Complete Poems* lists the contents of the *Collected Poems* in the notes, and summarizes the publication history of the individual poems.

[9] As well as three volumes of poetry (and two selections), eleven prose books were published in the 1940s.

[10] See footnote 2, above.

[11] *WG61*, pp.488/479.

[12] See the note on *P38-45*.

[13] See the notes on *S* and 'Around the Mountain' (*S*).

The arrangement of the poems in this volume corresponds to the first editions of Graves's books of verse, and follows the order within them. 'From' before the title of a book (e.g. 'From *Poems 1926-1930*') indicates that poems already included in an earlier book have been omitted; the complete contents are given in the notes.

In accordance with Graves's practice, this edition prints the latest texts of the poems. It compares these, in the notes, with the versions in the first editions. (His extensive revisions during composition, between periodical and book publication, and in the course of reprintings would require a full-scale variorum edition.)

The poems appear in the last version that Graves published, with further revisions incorporated. Anomalies and misprints have been corrected in the light of manuscripts and previous printings, as reported in the notes (under 'Emendations'). When an earlier variant in wording or punctuation has been adopted, it has been checked wherever possible against manuscripts and proofs.

Where Graves republished a poem with substantive revisions, the principal differences between the version in the first edition of the volume of verse concerned and the last version are recorded in the notes, as follows: all changes in wording are given, with omitted lines or stanzas; punctuation changes are given when they involve a change in sense; the main modifications in layout and typography are also indicated. Revisions intervening between first and last book publication, though studied in the course of preparing this edition, are noted only exceptionally, as are manuscript and periodical variants.

In the case of one poem that Graves last published in a children's book, for which he revised and to some extent adapted it, the changes are recorded but the preceding version has been printed.

The notes also give background information on the poems, with quotations from and/or references to other poems, letters, and prose works.

The poems have been printed flush left, as in *Collected Poems 1975*. Some details of punctuation – the use of single quotation marks (double for quotations within them), punctuation relative to quotation marks and italics – have been normalized in line with Graves's later practice; and some inconsistent spelling has been altered (though the earlier use of the hyphenated form of certain words – 'to-day', 'to-morrow' – has been respected, as in the *Collected Poems*). Inconsistencies in the capitalization of titles in capitals-and-lower-case in the contents lists have been removed.

Where required, line numbers have been inserted in poems of over thirty lines which are not in stanzas, to make reference easier.

An asterisk after the title of a poem indicates a note at the back of the volume.

From POEMS (1914-27)

(1927)

NINE ADDITIONAL POEMS: 1927

THE PROGRESS*

There is a travelling fury in his feet
(Scorn for the waters of his native spring)
Which proves at last the downfall of this king:
Shame will not let him sound the long retreat.

Tormented by his progress he displays
An open flank to the swarmed enemy
Who, charging through and through, set his pride free
For death's impossible and footless ways.

HELL*

Husks, rags and bones, waste-paper, excrement,
Denied a soul whether for good or evil
And casually consigned to unfulfilment,
Are pronged into his bag by the great-devil.

Or words repeated, over and over and over,
Until their sense sickens and all but dies,
These the same fellow like a ghoulish lover
Will lay his hands upon and hypnotize.

From husks and rags and waste and excrement
He forms the pavement-feet and the lift-faces;
He steers the sick words into parliament
To rule a dust-bin world with deep-sleep phrases.

When healthy words or people chance to dine
Together in this rarely actual scene,
There is a love-taste in the bread and wine,
Nor is it asked: 'Do you mean what you mean?'

But to their table-converse boldly comes
  The same great-devil with his brush and tray,
To conjure plump loaves from the scattered crumbs,
  And feed his false five thousands day by day.

THE FURIOUS VOYAGE*

So, overmasterful, to sea!
But hope no distant view of sail,
No growling ice, nor weed, nor whale,
Nor breakers perilous on the lee.

Though you enlarge your angry mind
Three leagues and more about the ship
And stamp till every puncheon skip,
The wake runs evenly behind.

And it has width enough for you,
This vessel, dead from truck to keel,
With its unmanageable wheel,
A blank chart and a surly crew,

In ballast only due to fetch
The turning point of wretchedness
On an uncoasted, featureless
And barren ocean of blue stretch.

O JORROCKS, I HAVE PROMISED*

Sprung of no worthier parentage than sun
In February, and fireside and the snow
Streaked on the north side of each wall and hedge,
And breakfast late, in bed, and a tall puppy
Restless for sticks to fetch and tussle over,
And Jorrocks bawling from the library shelf,
And the accumulation of newspapers

And the day-after-judgement-day to face –
This poem (only well bred on one side,
Father a grum, mother a lady's maid)
Asked for a style, a place in literature.
So, since the morning had been wholly spoilt
By sun, by snow, breakfast in bed, the puppy,
By literature, a headache and their headaches;
Throwing away the rest of my bad day
I gave it style, let it be literature
Only too well, and let it talk itself
And me to boredom, let it draw lunch out
From one o'clock to three with nuts and smoking
While it went talking on, with imagery,
Why it was what it was, and had no breeding
But waste things and the ambition to be real;
And flattered me with puppy gratitude.
I let it miss the one train back to town
And stay to tea and supper and a bed
And even bed-in-breakfast the next morning.
More thanks.
The penalty of authorship;
Forced hospitality, an impotence
Expecting an impossible return
Not only from the plainly stupid chance
But from impossible caddishness, no less.
I answered leading questions about Poe
And let it photograph me in the snow
And gave it a signed copy of itself
And 'the nursery money-box is on the shelf,
How kind of you to give them each a penny.'

O Jorrocks I have promised
To serve thee to the end,
To entertain young Indians,
The pupils of my friend,
To entertain Etonians
And for their sake combine
The wit of T.S. Eliot,
The grace of Gertrude Stein.
Be thou forever near me
To hasten or control,
Thou Literary Supplement,

Thou Guardian of my soul.
I shall not fear the battle
While thou art by my side,
Nor wander from the pathway
If thou shalt be my guide.
Amen.

LOST ACRES*

These acres, always again lost
By every new ordnance-survey
And searched for at exhausting cost
Of time and thought, are still away.

They have their paper-substitute –
Intercalation of an inch
At the so-many-thousandth foot –
And no one parish feels the pinch.

But lost they are, despite all care,
And perhaps likely to be bound
Together in a piece somewhere,
A plot of undiscovered ground.

Invisible, they have the spite
To swerve the tautest measuring-chain
And the exact theodolite
Perched every side of them in vain.

Yet, be assured, we have no need
To plot these acres of the mind
With prehistoric fern and reed
And monsters such as heroes find.

Maybe they have their flowers, their birds,
Their trees behind the phantom fence,
But of a substance without words:
To walk there would be loss of sense.

GARDENER*

Loveliest flowers, though crooked in their border,
And glorious fruit, dangling from ill-pruned boughs –
Be sure the gardener had not eye enough
To wheel a barrow between the broadest gates
Without a clumsy scraping.

Yet none could think it simple awkwardness;
And when he stammered of a garden-guardian,
Said the smooth lawns came by angelic favour,
The pinks and pears in spite of his own blunders,
They nudged at this conceit.

Well, he had something, though he called it nothing –
An ass's wit, a hairy-belly shrewdness
That would appraise the intentions of an angel
By the very yard-stick of his own confusion,
And bring the most to pass.

TO A CHARGE OF DIDACTICISM

Didactic, I shall be didactic
   When I have hit on something new
Else dons unborn will be didactic
   On undidacticism too.

Didactic, they will be didactic
   With 'excellently's' and 'absurd's':
Let me make sure that they're didactic
   On my own words on my own words.

THE PHILATELIST-ROYAL*

The Philatelist-Royal
Was always too loyal
To say what he honestly
Thought of Philately.

Must it rank as a Science?
Then he had more reliance,
(As he told the Press wittily),
In Royal Philately
Than in all your geologies,
All your psychologies,
Bacteriologies,
Physics and such.
It was honester, much,
Free of mere speculations
And doubtful equations,
So therefore more true
From a pure science view
Than other school courses:
For Nature's blind forces
Here alone, they must own,
Played no meddlesome part.
It was better than Art:
It enforced education,
It strengthened the nation
In the arts of mensuration
And colour-discrimination,
In cleanliness, in hope,
In use of the microscope,
In mercantile transactions,
In a love of abstractions,
In geography and history:
It was a noble mystery.
So he told them again
That Philately's reign,
So mild and humane,
Would surely last longer,
Would surely prove stronger
Than the glory of Greece,
Than the grandeur of Rome.

It brought goodwill and peace
Wherever it found a home.
It was more democratic,
More full, more ecstatic,
Than the Bible, the bottle,
The Complete Works of Aristotle,
And worthierer and betterer
And etceterier and etcetera.

The Philatelist-Royal
Was always too loyal
To say what he honestly
Thought of Philately.

SONG: TO BE LESS PHILOSOPHICAL*

Listen, you theologians,
Give ear, you rhetoricians,
Hearken, you Aristotelians:
Of the Nature of God, my song shall be.

Our God is infinite,
Your God is infinite,
Their God is infinite,
Of infinite variety.

God, he is also finite,
God, she is also definite,
He, she; we, they; you, each and it –
Of finite omnipresence.

He is a bloody smart sergeant
And served in the Royal Artillery:
For gallantly exposing his person
He won the Victoria Cross.

She is also divorced,
From a Russian count in exile,
And paints a little and sings a little –
And won a little prize in Paris.

It has also the character of a soap
And may be employed quite freely
For disinfecting cattle trucks
And the very kine in the byre.

You are also mad, quite mad,
To imagine you are not God.
Goddam it, aren't you a Spirit,
And your ministers a flaming fire?

We are also gradually tending
To be less philosophical,
We talk through hats more personally,
With madness more divine.

They are a very smart Goddam Cross
With the character of a soap, a little:
They disinfect more personally,
To be less philosophical.

Each is a very smart Paris hat
And may be divorced quite freely,
Freely, freely in the Royal Artillery,
To be each less philosophical.

POEMS 1929

(1929)

SICK LOVE*

O Love, be fed with apples while you may,
And feel the sun and go in royal array,
A smiling innocent on the heavenly causeway,

Though in what listening horror for the cry
That soars in outer blackness dismally,
The dumb blind beast, the paranoiac fury:

Be warm, enjoy the season, lift your head,
Exquisite in the pulse of tainted blood,
That shivering glory not to be despised.

Take your delight in momentariness,
Walk between dark and dark – a shining space
With the grave's narrowness, though not its peace.

IN NO DIRECTION*

To go in no direction
   Surely as carelessly,
Walking on the hills alone,
   I never found easy.

Either I sent leaf or stick
   Twirling in the air,
Whose fall might be prophetic,
   Pointing 'there',

Or in superstition
   Edged somewhat away
From a sure direction,
   Yet could not stray,

Or undertook the climb
   That I had avoided
Directionless some other time,
   Or had not avoided,

Or called as companion
   An eyeless ghost
And held his no direction
   Till my feet were lost.

IN BROKEN IMAGES*

He is quick, thinking in clear images;
I am slow, thinking in broken images.

He becomes dull, trusting to his clear images;
I become sharp, mistrusting my broken images.

Trusting his images, he assumes their relevance;
Mistrusting my images, I question their relevance.

Assuming their relevance, he assumes the fact;
Questioning their relevance, I question the fact.

When the fact fails him, he questions his senses;
When the fact fails me, I approve my senses.

He continues quick and dull in his clear images;
I continue slow and sharp in my broken images.

He in a new confusion of his understanding;
I in a new understanding of my confusion.

THIEF*

To the galleys, thief, and sweat your soul out
With strong tugging under the curled whips,
That there your thievishness may find full play.
Whereas, before, you stole rings, flowers and watches,
Oaths, jests and proverbs,
Yet paid for bed and board like an honest man,
This shall be entire thiefdom: you shall steal
Sleep from chain-galling, diet from sour crusts,
Comradeship from the damned, the ten-year-chained –
And, more than this, the excuse for life itself
From a craft steered toward battles not your own.

WARNING TO CHILDREN*

Children, if you dare to think
Of the greatness, rareness, muchness,
Fewness of this precious only
Endless world in which you say
You live, you think of things like this:
Blocks of slate enclosing dappled
Red and green, enclosing tawny
Yellow nets, enclosing white
And black acres of dominoes,
Where a neat brown paper parcel
Tempts you to untie the string.
In the parcel a small island,
On the island a large tree,
On the tree a husky fruit.
Strip the husk and pare the rind off:
In the kernel you will see
Blocks of slate enclosed by dappled
Red and green, enclosed by tawny
Yellow nets, enclosed by white
And black acres of dominoes,
Where the same brown paper parcel –
Children, leave the string alone!
For who dares undo the parcel

Finds himself at once inside it,
On the island, in the fruit,
Blocks of slate about his head,
Finds himself enclosed by dappled
Green and red, enclosed by yellow
Tawny nets, enclosed by black
And white acres of dominoes,
With the same brown paper parcel
Still unopened on his knee.
And, if he then should dare to think
Of the fewness, muchness, rareness,
Greatness of this endless only
Precious world in which he says
He lives – he then unties the string.

DISMISSAL*

If you want life, there's no life here.
   Whatever trust you held for me
Or I for you in some such year,
   Is ended as you see.
I forced this quarrel; it was not
   So much disgust with all you did
As sudden doubt of whom and what
   My easy friendship hid;
   I carefully offended.
It would be best if you too broke
Acquaintance, with a monstrous look,
   Rather than stay to temporize
   Or steal away with brimming eyes
Like old friends in a book.
So if a man of you can be
   Regretful of the time that's gone
He must now imperturbably
   Accept this antic kick from one
   Who used to be his father's son
   Discreet in blind devotion.

GUESSING BLACK OR WHITE*

Guessing black or white,
  Guessing white, guessing black.
Guessing black or white.
  Guessing white, guessing black.

His mother was a terrier bitch,
His father a Dalmatian,
  Guessing black or white:
Not black because white
Because black because white;
Not white because black
Because white because black,
  Guessing black or white.

His mother was from Renfrew,
His father was a Zulu,
  Guessing black or white:
Not black because black
Because white because white;
Not white because white
Because black because black,
  Guessing black or white.

His mother was a domino,
His father was a dice-box,
  Guessing black or white:
Not white because white
Because white because white;
Not black because black
Because black because black,
  Guessing black or white.

HECTOR

The persons in the thought, like shapes, waver.
Not to forget them, forge a history
Of squarenesses and narrownesses, saying
'Thus ticket Hector with his fishing-rod
To the dungeon of the ticket Princess came,
Gave her a ticket.' Or what you will.
The shapes are neither this nor that,
Not Hectors and princesses, rods and dungeons,
Nor indeed shapes but, as I say, persons
Who look 'remember me and know me',
And so are lost under the many tickets.
But what the devil to do with ticket Hector
Who is no more person than he was a squareness
Or squareness was a shape? He stands, mock-Hector,
Fishing with his forged rod through the false grille
From the false moat outside the forged dungeon,
(The ticket princess standing by) –
The dull what's left of ticketing a ticket.
Let them close-ticket at their princely leisure
To please what girls and boys may read the myth.
The persons in the thought are long dead.

AGAINST KIND*

Become invisible by elimination
  Of kind in her, she none the less persisted
  Among kind with no need to find excuses
For choosing this and not some alien region.

Invisibility was her last kindness:
  She might have kept appearance, had she wished;
  Yet to be seen living against all kind,
That would be monstrous; she permitted blindness.

She asked and she permitted nothing further,
  She went her private and eventless way
  As uncompanioning as uncompanioned;
And for a while they did not think to mourn her.

But soon it vexed them that her name still stood
  Plain on their registers, and over-simple,
  Not witnessed to by laundry, light or fuel,
Or even, they wondered most, by drink and food.

They tried rebuttal; it was not for long:
  Pride and curiosity raised a whisper
  That swelled into a legend and the legend
Confirmed itself in terror and grew strong.

It was not that they would prefer her presence
  To her room (now hating her), but that her room
  Could not be filled by any creature of kind,
It gaped; they shook with sudden impotence.

Sleeplessness and shouting and new rumours
  Tempted them nightly; dulness wore their days;
  They waited for a sign, but none was given;
She owed them nothing, they held nothing of hers.

They raged at her that being invisible
  She would not use that gift, humouring them
  As Lilith, or as an idiot poltergeist,
Or as a Gyges turning the ring's bezel.

She gave no sign; at last they tumbled prostrate
  Fawning on her, confessing her their sins;
  They burned her the occasion's frankincense,
Crying 'Save, save!', but she was yet discrete.

And she must stay discrete, and they stay blind
  Forever, or for one time less than ever –
  If they, despaired and turning against kind,
Become invisible too, and read her mind.

MIDWAY*

Between insufferable monstrosities
And exiguities insufferable,
Midway is man's own station. We no longer
Need either hang our heads or lift them high
But for the fortunes of finance or love.
We have no truck either with the forebeings
Of Betelgeux or with the atom's git.
Our world steadies: untrembling we renew
Old fears of earthquakes, adders, floods, mad dogs
And all such wholesomes. Nothing that we do
Concerns the infinities of either scale.
Clocks tick with our consent to our time-tables,
Trains run between our buffers. Time and Space
Amuse us merely with their rough-house turn,
Their hard head-on collision in the tunnel.
A dying superstition smiles and hums
'Abide with me' – God's evening prayer, not ours.
So history still is written and is read:
The eternities of divine commonplace.

CABBAGE PATCH*

Green cabbage-wit, only by trying,
  Flew as bird-wit;
But flocking for the season's flying,
Restless perching and prying,
  Could not content it.

As lightning-wit therefore it struck
  And split the rocks indeed,
Fusing their veins, but in the instant's luck
  Was spilt by its own speed.

Back therefore to green cabbage-wit
In the old plot with glass and grit.
Tenth-in-the-line for kings and cabbages
Has honourable privileges
For which no rocks are split.

THE CASTLE*

Walls, mounds, enclosing corrugations
Of darkness, moonlight on dry grass.
Walking this courtyard, sleepless, in fever;
Planning to use – but by definition
There's no way out, no way out –
Rope-ladders, baulks of timber, pulleys,
A rocket whizzing over the walls and moat –
Machines easy to improvise.
No escape,
No such thing; to dream of new dimensions,
Cheating checkmate by painting the king's robe
So that he slides like a queen;
Or to cry, 'Nightmare, nightmare!'
Like a corpse in the cholera-pit
Under a load of corpses;
Or to run the head against these blind walls,
Enter the dungeon, torment the eyes
With apparitions chained two and two,
And go frantic with fear –
To die and wake up sweating by moonlight
In the same courtyard, sleepless as before.

WELSH INCIDENT*

'But that was nothing to what things came out
From the sea-caves of Criccieth yonder.'
'What were they? Mermaids? dragons? ghosts?'
'Nothing at all of any things like that.'
'What were they, then?'
'All sorts of queer things,
Things never seen or heard or written about,
Very strange, un-Welsh, utterly peculiar
Things. Oh, solid enough they seemed to touch,
Had anyone dared it. Marvellous creation,
All various shapes and sizes, and no sizes,
All new, each perfectly unlike his neighbour,
Though all came moving slowly out together.'

'Describe just one of them.'
                                        'I am unable.'
'What were their colours?'
                                        'Mostly nameless colours,
Colours you'd like to see; but one was puce
Or perhaps more like crimson, but not purplish.
Some had no colour.'
                                'Tell me, had they legs?'
'Not a leg nor foot among them that I saw.'
'But did these things come out in any order?
What o'clock was it? What was the day of the week?
Who else was present? How was the weather?'
'I was coming to that. It was half-past three
On Easter Tuesday last. The sun was shining.
The Harlech Silver Band played *Marchog Jesu*
On thirty-seven shimmering instruments,
Collecting for Caernarvon's (Fever) Hospital Fund.
The populations of Pwllheli, Criccieth,
Portmadoc, Borth, Tremadoc, Penrhyndeudraeth,
Were all assembled. Criccieth's mayor addressed them
First in good Welsh and then in fluent English,
Twisting his fingers in his chain of office,
Welcoming the things. They came out on the sand,
Not keeping time to the band, moving seaward
Silently at a snail's pace. But at last
The most odd, indescribable thing of all,
Which hardly one man there could see for wonder,
Did something recognizably a something.'
'Well, what?'
                        'It made a noise.'
                                                'A frightening noise?'
'No, no.'
                'A musical noise? A noise of scuffling?'
'No, but a very loud, respectable noise –
Like groaning to oneself on Sunday morning
In Chapel, close before the second psalm.'
'What did the mayor do?'
                                        'I was coming to that.'

BACK DOOR

For bringing it so far, thank you,
Though they seem very light ones, thank you;
Who gave you my address and rank?
It may prove so-so in the end;
That would depend on what else stays so.
Easy to blend all together
But the devil to know whether or not
And how to keep it fresh in taste:
They hang on the air like rot
And are blown to waste in the end.
Still this, I own, seems steady, thanks,
Four or five of them already,
Just what the store-rooms need.
For bringing it so far, thanks.
I recognized your pranks at once, indeed
Almost before I heard the gate slam.
Of course, it's all a gamble really:
First it's the finding, then the picking,
Then the minding, then the dressing,
Guessing them over the awkward stage,
(I was in the trade myself, you see,
When I was on the stage;
I had several made for me
When I was in the trade,
When I was on the stage),
Then it's those naked-light instructions
That the muctions plaster up,
Destruction take them,
In the room where the stuff's folded
On which the whole lay's laid.
Always the same, these crews, these crows –
Lousy! Not interested? No? The shame!
Then how much must I owe you?
Many thanks, again, many francs,
Many pranks, many thanks, again.
Good day!

FRONT DOOR SOLILOQUY*

'Yet from the antique heights or deeps of what
Or which was grandeur fallen, sprung or what
Or which, beyond doubt I am grandeur's grandson
True to the eagle nose, the pillared neck,
(Missed by the intervening generation)
Whom large hands, long face, and long feet sort out
From which and what, to wear my heels down even,
To be connected with all reigning houses,
Show sixteen quarterings or sixty-four
Or even more, with clear skin and eyes clear
To drive the nails in and not wound the wood,
With lungs and heart sound and with bowels easy:
An angry man, heaving the sacks of grain
From cart to loft and what and what and which
And even thus, and being no Rousseauist,
Nor artists-of-the-world-unite, or which,
Or what, never admitting, in effect,
Touch anything my touch does not adorn –
Now then I dung on my grandfather's doorstep,
Which is a reasonable and loving due
To hold no taint of spite or vassalage
And understood only by him and me –
But you, you bog-rat-whiskered, you psalm-griddling,
Lame, rotten-livered, which and what canaille,
You, when twin lackeys, with armorial shovels,
Unbolt the bossy gates and bend to the task,
Be off, work out your heads from between the railings,
Lest we unkennel the mastiff and the Dane –
This house is jealous of its nastiness.'

ANAGRAMMAGIC*

Anagrammatising
TRANSUBSTANTIATION,
Slyly deputising
For old Copopulation
SIN SAT ON A TIN TAR TUB
And did with joy his elbows rub.

Art introseduced him
To females dull and bad,
Flapper flappings, limb-slim,
From his blonde writing-pad,
The river-girlgling drained of blood –
Post-card flower of kodak mud.

By such anagrammagic
And mansturbantiation
They fathered then this tragic
Lustalgia on the nation,
And after that, and after that,
ON A TIN SIN TUB ART SAT.

VISION IN THE REPAIR-SHOP*

Be sure the crash was worse than ever.
In, flying out, collapsed with music;
Out, flying in, roared up in flames.
The blast was non-continuous.
But what matter? The force generated
At every point of impact
Was, you remarked, dispersed for other uses.
In this you saw the well-geared mind
Of the garage-man-in-chief,
Prime corpse of each new speed-track,
Who by unequalled salesmanship
Engines a car for every son and daughter
In a city of twelve millions –
What prettier traffic-block imaginable

Lasting, day in, day out, for centuries,
While life flows easily down the gutters
Or swings in the air on ropes,
And you and I, stuffing this cotton-wool
Closer into our ears, from habit,
Lie in plaster of Paris on our backs
And drink the drip of many radiators?

NATURE'S LINEAMENTS*

When mountain rocks and leafy trees
And clouds and things like these,
With edges,

Caricature the human face,
Such scribblings have no grace
Nor peace –

The bulbous nose, the sunken chin,
The ragged mouth in grin
Of cretin.

Nature is always so: you find
That all she has of mind
Is wind,

Retching among the empty spaces,
Ruffling the idiot grasses,
The sheep's fleeces.

Whose pleasures are excreting, poking,
Havocking and sucking,
Sleepy licking.

Whose griefs are melancholy,
Whose flowers are oafish,
Whose waters, silly,
Whose birds, raffish,
Whose fish, fish.

SEA SIDE*

Into a gentle wildness and confusion,
Of here and there, of one and everyone,
Of windy sandhills by an unkempt sea,
Came two and two in search of symmetry,
Found symmetry of two in sea and sand,
In left foot, right foot, left hand and right hand.

The beast with two backs is a single beast,
Yet by his love of singleness increased
To two and two and two and two again,
Until, instead of sandhills, see, a plain
Patterned in two and two, by two and two –
And the sea parts in horror at a view
Of rows of houses coupling, back to back,
While love smokes from their common chimney-stack
With two-four-eight-sixteenish single same
Re-registration of the duple name.

WM. BRAZIER*

At the end of Tarriers' Lane, which was the street
We children thought the pleasantest in Town
Because of the old elms growing from the pavement
And the crookedness, when the other streets were straight,
[They were always at the lamp-post round the corner,
Those pugs and papillons and in-betweens,
Nosing and snuffling for the latest news]
Lived Wm. Brazier, with a gilded sign,
'Practical Chimney Sweep'. He had black hands,
Black face, black clothes, black brushes and white teeth;
He jingled round the town in a pony-trap,
And the pony's name was Soot, and Soot was black.
But the brass fittings on the trap, the shafts,
On Soot's black harness, on the black whip-butt,
Twinkled and shone like any guardsman's buttons.
Wasn't that pretty? And when we children jeered:
'Hello, Wm. Brazier! Dirty-face Wm. Brazier!'

He would crack his whip at us and smile and bellow,
'Hello, my dears!' [If he were drunk, but otherwise:
'Scum off, you damned young milliners' bastards, you!']

Let them copy it out on a pink page of their albums,
Carefully leaving out the bracketed lines.
It's an old story – f's for s's –
But good enough for them, the suckers.

A FORMER ATTACHMENT*

And glad to find, on again looking at it,
It meant even less to me than I had thought –
You know the ship is moving when you see
The boxes on the quayside slide away
And become smaller – and feel a calm delight
When the port's cleared and the coast out of sight,
And ships are few, each on its proper course,
With no occasion for approach or discourse.

RETURN FARE*

And so to Ireland on an Easter Tuesday
To a particular place I could not find.
A sleeping man beside me in the boat-train
Sat whistling Liliburlero in his sleep;
Not, I had thought, a possible thing, yet so.
And through a port-hole of the Fishguard boat,
That was the hospital-boat of twelve years back,
Passengered as before with doubt and dying,
I saw the moon through glass, but a waning moon –
Bad luck, self-doubtful, so once more I slept.
And then the engines woke me up by stopping.
The piers of the quay loomed up. So I went up.
The sun shone rainily and jokingly,
And everyone joked at his own expense,

And the priest declared 'nothing but fishing tackle,'
Laughing provokingly. I could not laugh.
And the hard cackling laughter of the men
And the false whinnying laughter of the girls
Grieved me. The telegraph-clerk said, grieving too,
'St Peter, he's two words in the Free State now,
So that's a salmon due.' I paid the fish.
And everyone I asked about the place
Knew the place well, but not its whereabouts,
And the black-shawled peasant woman asked me then,
Wasn't I jaded? And she grieved to me
Of the apple and the expulsion from the garden.
Ireland went by, and went by as I saw her
When last I saw her for the first time
Exactly how I had seen her all the time.
And I found the place near Sligo, not the place,
So back to England on the Easter Thursday.

SINGLE FARE*

By way of Fishguard, all the lying devils
Are back to Holy Ireland whence they came.
Each took a single fare: which cost them less
And brought us comfort. The dumb devils too
Take single fares, return by rail to Scotland
Whence they came. So the air is cool and easy.
And if, in some quarter of some big city,
A little Eire or a little Scotland
Serves as a rallying-point for a few laggards,
No matter, we are free from taint of them.
And at the fire-side now (drinking our coffee),
If I ask, 'But to what township did they book,
Those dumb devils of Scotland?' you will answer:
'There's the Bass Rock, once more a separate kingdom,
Leagued with Ireland, the same cold grey crag
Screamed against by the gulls that are all devils.'
And of the Irish devils you will answer:
'In Holy Ireland many a country seat
Still stands unburned – as Cooper's Hill, Lisheen,

Cloghan Castle, or Killua in County Galway –
For the devils to enter, unlock the library doors
And write love-letters and long threatening letters
Even to us, if it so pleases them.'

IT WAS ALL VERY TIDY*

When I reached his place,
The grass was smooth,
The wind was delicate,
The wit well timed,
The limbs well formed,
The pictures straight on the wall:
It was all very tidy.

He was cancelling out
The last row of figures,
He had his beard tied up in ribbons,
There was no dust on his shoe,
Everyone nodded:
It was all very tidy.

Music was not playing,
There were no sudden noises,
The sun shone blandly,
The clock ticked:
It was all very tidy.

'Apart from and above all this,'
I reassured myself,
'There is now myself.'
It was all very tidy.

Death did not address me,
He had nearly done:
It was all very tidy.

They asked, did I not think
It was all very tidy?

I could not bring myself
To laugh, or untie
His beard's neat ribbons,
Or jog his elbow,
Or whistle, or sing,
Or make disturbance.
I consented, frozenly,
He was unexceptionable:
It was all very tidy.

A SHEET OF PAPER

Then was blank expectation,
Was happening without incident,
Was thinking without images,
Was speaking without words,
Was being without proof,
Happiness not signalized,
Sorrow without cause,
And place for nothing further.

Now is a sheet of paper,
A not blank expectation,
A happening, but with incident,
A thinking, but with images,
A speaking, but with words,
A being, over-proved,
A report of happiness,
A cause for sorrow,
Place for the signature
And for the long post-script.

TEN POEMS MORE

(1930)

THE READER OVER MY SHOULDER*

You, reading over my shoulder, peering beneath
My writing arm – I suddenly feel your breath
  Hot on my hand or on my nape,
So interrupt my theme, scratching these few
Words on the margin for you, namely you,
  Too-human shape fixed in that shape: –

All the saying of things against myself
And for myself I have well done myself.
  What now, old enemy, shall you do
But quote and underline, thrusting yourself
Against me, as ambassador of myself,
  In damned confusion of myself and you?

For you in strutting, you in sycophancy,
Have played too long this other self of me,
  Doubling the part of judge and patron
With that of creaking grind-stone to my wit.
Know me, have done: I am a proud spirit
  And you for ever clay. Have done!

HISTORY OF THE WORD*

The Word that in the beginning was the Word
For two or three, but elsewhere spoke unheard,
Found Words to interpret it, which for a season
Prevailed until ruled out by Law and Reason
Which, by a lax interpretation cursed,
In Laws and Reasons logically dispersed;
These, in their turn, found they could do no better
Than fall to Letters and each claim a letter.
In the beginning then, the Word alone,
But now the various tongue-tied Lexicon
In perfect impotence the day nearing
When every ear shall lose its sense of hearing
And every mind by knowledge be close-shuttered –
But two or three, that hear the Word uttered.

INTERRUPTION*

If ever against this easy blue and silver
Hazed-over countryside of thoughtfulness,
Far behind in the mind and above,
Boots from before and below approach trampling,
Watch how their premonition will display
A forward countryside, low in the distance –
A picture-postcard square of June grass;
Will warm a summer season, trim the hedges,
Cast the river about on either flank,
Start the late cuckoo emptily calling,
Invent a rambling tale of moles and voles,
Furnish a path with stiles.
Watch how the field will broaden, the feet nearing,
Sprout with great dandelions and buttercups,
Widen and heighten. The blue and silver
Fogs at the border of this all-grass.
Interruption looms gigantified,
Lurches against, treads thundering through,
Blots the landscape, scatters all,
Roars and rumbles like a dark tunnel,
Is gone.
                The picture-postcard grass and trees
Swim back to central: it is a large patch,
It is a modest, failing patch of green,
The postage-stamp of its departure,
Clouded with blue and silver, closing in now
To a plain countryside of less and less,
Unpeopled and unfeatured blue and silver,
Before, behind, above.

SURVIVAL OF LOVE

We love, and utterly,
Unnaturally:
From nature lately
By death you freed me,
Yourself free already.

Proof that we are unnatural:
This purposeful
And straining funeral,
Nature's unnatural,
Now become unfunereal.

And indeed merriest when
The gasp and strain
Will twitch like pain,
Clouding the former brain
Of us, the man and woman.

NEW LEGENDS*

Content in you,
Andromeda serene,
Mistress of air and ocean
And every fiery dragon,
Chained to no cliff,
Asking no rescue of me.

Content in you,
Mad Atalanta,
Stooping unpausing,
Ever ahead,
Acquitting me of rivalry.

Content in you
Who made King Proteus marvel,
Showing him singleness
Past all variety.

Content in you,
Niobe of no children,
Of no calamity.

Content in you,
Helen, foiler of beauty.

SAINT*

This Blatant Beast was finally overcome
And in no secret tourney: wit and fashion
Flocked out and for compassion
Wept as the Red Cross Knight pushed the blade home.

The people danced and sang the paeans due,
Roasting whole oxen on the public spit;
Twelve mountain peaks were lit
With bonfires; yet their hearts were doubt and rue.

Therefore no grave was deep enough to hold
The Beast, who after days came thrusting out,
Wormy from rump to snout,
His yellow cere-cloth patched with the grave's mould.

Nor could sea hold him: anchored with huge rocks,
He swelled and buoyed them up, paddling ashore
As evident as before
With deep-sea ooze and salty creaking bones.

Lime could not burn him, nor the sulphur fire:
So often as the good Knight bound him there,
With stink of singeing hair
And scorching flesh the corpse rolled from the pyre.

In the city-gutter would the Beast lie
Praising the Knight for all his valorous deeds:
'Ay, on those water-meads
He slew even me. These death-wounds testify.'

The Knight governed that city, a man shamed
And shrunken: for the Beast was over-dead,
With wounds no longer red
But gangrenous and loathsome and inflamed.

Not all the righteous judgements he could utter,
Nor mild laws frame, nor public works repair,
Nor wars wage, in despair,
Could bury that same Beast, crouched in the gutter.

A fresh remembrance-banquet to forestall,
The Knight turned hermit, went without farewell
To a far mountain-cell;
But the Beast followed as his seneschal,

And there drew water for him and hewed wood
With vacant howling laughter; else all day
Noisome with long decay
Sunning himself at the cave's entry stood.

Would bawl to pilgrims for a dole of bread
To feed the sick saint who once vanquished him
With spear so stark and grim;
Would set a pillow of grass beneath his head,
Would fetch him fever-wort from the pool's brim –
And crept into his grave when he was dead.

TAP ROOM*

Believe me not a dolt: I would invent
No proverbs; but considering them
I need to state them:

Beauty impracticable,
Strength undemonstrable;
Lives without end await them.

Yet know me able and quick
To force an ending. How?
Finding a dolt to have begun them.

Finding him where?
On Halfpenny Island where they milk the cats.
Where may that lie?
Near Farthing Island where they milk mice.

How shall he have begun them?
O how indeed, but
Cracking the nut against the hammer.
What nut? Why, sir, the nut . . .

Believe me not a dolt: I have invented
No proverbs . . .

THE TERRACED VALLEY*

In a deep thought of you and concentration
I came by hazard to a new region:
The unnecessary sun was not there,
The necessary earth lay without care –
For more than sunshine warmed the skin
Of the round world that was turned outside-in.

Calm sea beyond the terraced valley
Without horizon easily was spread,
As it were overhead,
Washing the mountain-spurs behind me:
The unnecessary sky was not there,
Therefore no heights, no deeps, no birds of the air.

Neat outside-inside, neat below-above,
Hermaphrodizing love.
Neat this-way-that-way and without mistake:
On the right hand could slide the left glove.
Neat over-under: the young snake
Through an unyielding shell his path could break.
Singing of kettles, like a singing brook,
Made out-of-doors a fireside nook.

But you, my love, where had you then your station?
Seeing that on this counter-earth together
We go not distant from each other;
I knew you near me in that strange region,

So searched for you, in hope to see you stand
On some near olive-terrace, in the heat,
The left-hand glove drawn on your right hand,
The empty snake's egg perfect at your feet –

But found you nowhere in the wide land,
And cried disconsolately, until you spoke
Immediate at my elbow, and your voice broke
This trick of time, changing the world about
To once more inside-in and outside-out.

OAK, POPLAR, PINE*

The temple priests though using but one sign
For TREE, distinguish poplar, oak and pine:
Oak, short and spreading – poplar, tall and thin –
Pine, tall, bunched at the top and well inked in.
Therefore in priestly thought all various trees
Must be enrolled, in kind, as one of these.
The fir, the cedar and the deodar
Are pines, so too the desert palm-trees are;
Aspens and birches are of poplar folk
But chestnut, damson, elm and fig are oak.
All might be simple, did the priests allow
That apple-blossom dresses the oak bough,
That dates are pines-cones; but they will not so,
Well taught how pine and oak and poplar grow:
In every temple-court, for all to see
Flourishes one example of each tree
In tricunx. Your high-priest would laugh to think
Of oak boughs blossoming in pagan pink,
Or numerous cones, hung from a single spine,
Sticky yet sweeter than the fruit of vine,
(For vine's no tree; vine is a creeping thing,
Cousin to snake, that with its juice can sting).
Confront your priest with evident apple-blossom;
Will faith and doubt, conflicting, heave his bosom?
Force dates between his lips, will he forget
That there's no date-palm in the alphabet?

Turn apostate? Even in secret? No,
He'll see the blossom as mere mistletoe.
The dates will be as grapes, good for his needs:
He'll swallow down their stones like little seeds.
And here's no lie, no hypocritic sham:
Believe him earnest-minded as I am.
His script has less, and mine more, characters
Than stand in use with lexicographers.
They end with palm, I see and use the sign
For tree that is to palm as palm to pine,
As apple-bough to oak-bough in the spring:
It is no secrecy but a long looking.

ACT V, SCENE 5*

You call the old nurse and the little page
To act survivors on your tragic stage –
You love the intrusive extra character.
'But where's the tragedy,' you say, 'if none
Remains to moralize on what's been done?
There's no catharsis in complete disaster.
Tears purge the soul – the nurse's broken line:
"O mistress, pretty one, dead!" the page's whine:
"Thou too? Alas, fond master!"'

No purge for my disgusted soul, no tears
Will wash away my bile of tragic years,
No sighs vicariously abate my rancour –
If nurse and page survive, I'd have them own
Small sorrow to be left up-stage alone,
And on the bloodiest field of massacre
Either rant out the anti-climax thus:
''A's dead, the bitch!' 'So's Oscar! Joy for us!'
Then fall to rifling pocket, belt and purse
With corky jokes and pantomime of sin;
Or let the feud rage on, page against nurse –
His jewelled dirk, her thund'rous rolling-pin.

SONG: LIFT-BOY*

Let me tell you the story of how I began:
I began as the boot-boy and ended as the boot-man,
With nothing in my pockets but a jack-knife and a button,
With nothing in my pockets but a jack-knife and a button,
With nothing in my pockets.

Let me tell you the story of how I went on:
I began as the lift-boy and ended as the lift-man,
With nothing in my pockets but a jack-knife and a button,
With nothing in my pockets but a jack-knife and a button,
With nothing in my pockets.

I found it very easy to whistle and play
With nothing in my head or my pockets all day,
With nothing in my pockets.

But along came Old Eagle, like Moses or David;
He stopped at the fourth floor and preached me Damnation:
'Not a soul shall be savèd, not one shall be savèd.
The whole First Creation shall forfeit salvation:
From knife-boy to lift-boy, from ragged to regal,
Not one shall be savèd, not you, not Old Eagle,
No soul on earth escapeth, even if all repent –'
So I cut the cords of the lift and down we went,
With nothing in our pockets.

From POEMS 1926-1930

(1931)

BROTHER*

It's odd enough to be alive with others,
But odder still to have sisters and brothers:
To make one of a characteristic litter –
The sisters puzzled and vexed, the brothers vexed and bitter
That this one wears, though flattened by abuse,
The family nose for individual use.

BAY OF NAPLES

The blind man reading Dante upside-down
And not in Braille frowned an admiring frown;
He sniffed, he underscored the passage read,
'One nose is better than both eyes,' he said.
'Here's a strong trace of orange-peel and sweat
And palate-scrapings on the rock, still wet,
And travellers' names carved on the sappy tree –
Old Ugolino's grief! Sublime!' said he.

FLYING CROOKED*

The butterfly, a cabbage-white,
(His honest idiocy of flight)
Will never now, it is too late,
Master the art of flying straight,
Yet has – who knows so well as I? –
A just sense of how not to fly:
He lurches here and here by guess
And God and hope and hopelessness.
Even the aerobatic swift
Has not his flying-crooked gift.

REASSURANCE TO THE SATYR

The hairs of my beard are red and black mingled,
With white now frequent in the red and black.
My finger-nails, see here, are ill-assorted;
My hands are not a pair, nor are my brows;
My nose is crooked as my smile.

'How?' says the Satyr. 'Dare I trust a monster
Who cannot match his left hand with his right,
Who wears three several colours in his beard?'
Satyr, the question is well asked.

Nevertheless I am as trustworthy
As any shepherd in this wide valley.
I touch the doubtful with the left hand first,
Then with the right, under right brow and left
Peer at it doubtfully.
I am red-bearded wild, white-bearded mild,
Black-bearded merry.

And what the other shepherds know but singly
And easily at the first sight or touch
(Who follow a straight nose and who smile even)
I know with labour and most amply:
I know each possible lie and bias
That crookedness can cozen out of straightness.
Satyr, you need not shrink.

SYNTHETIC SUCH*

'The sum of all the parts of Such –
   Of each laboratory scene –
Is Such.' While Science means this much
   And means no more, why, let it mean!

But were the science-men to find
   Some animating principle
Which gave synthetic Such a mind
   Vital, though metaphysical –

To Such, such an event, I think
   Would cause unscientific pain:
Science, appalled by thought, would shrink
   To its component parts again.

DRAGONS

These ancient dragons not committed yet
To any certain manner,
To any final matter,
Ranging creation recklessly,
Empowered to overset
Natural form and fate,
Freaking the sober species,
Smoothing rough accident to be
Level in a long series
And, each new century,
Forging for God a newer signet –
To these wild monsters boasting
Over and over
Their unchecked tyranny,
The only not a monster
In a small voice calling
Answered despitefully:
'Dragons, you count for nothing:
You are no more than weather,
The year's unsteadfastness
To which, now summer-basking,
To which, now in distress
Midwinter-shivering,
The mind pays no honour.'

THE NEXT TIME*

And that inevitable accident
   On the familiar journey – roughly reckoned
By miles and shillings – in a cramped compartment
   Between a first hereafter and a second?

And when we passengers are given two hours,
   The wheels failing once more at Somewhere-Nowhere,
To climb out, stretch our legs and pick wild flowers –
   Suppose that this time I elect to stay there?

TO WHOM ELSE?

(1931)

LARGESSE TO THE POOR*

I had been God's own time on travel
From stage to stage, guest-house to guest-house,
And at each stage furnished one room
To my own comfort, hoping God knows what,
Most happy when most sure that no condition
Might ever last in God's own time –
Unless to be death-numb, as I would not.

Yet I was always watchful at my choices
To change the bad at least for a no worse,
And I was strict nowhere to stay long.
In turn from each new home passing
I locked the door and pocketed the key,
Leaving behind goods plainly mine
(Should I return to claim them legally)
Of which I kept particular register –
In nightly rooms and chattels of the occasion
I was, to my own grief, a millionaire.

But now at last, out of God's firmament,
To break this endless journey –
Homeless to come where that awaits me
Which in my mind's unwearying discontent
I begged as pilgrim's due –
To fling my keys as largesse to the poor,
The always travel-hungry God-knows-who,
With, 'Let them fatten on my industry
Who find perfection and eternity
In might-be-worse, a roof over the head,
And any half-loaf better than no bread,
For which to thank God on their knees nightly.'

THE FELLOE'D YEAR*

The pleasure of summer was its calm success
Over winter past and winter sequent:
The pleasure of winter was a warm counting,
'Summer comes again, when, surely.'
This pleasure and that pleasure touched
In a perpetual spring-with-autumn ache,
A creak and groan of season,
In which all moved,
In which all move yet – I the same, yet praying
That the twelve spokes of this round-felloe'd year
Be a fixed compass, not a turning wheel.

TIME*

The vague sea thuds against the marble cliffs
And from their fragments age-long grinds
Pebbles like flowers.

Or the vague weather wanders in the fields,
And up spring flowers with coloured buds
Like marble pebbles.

The beauty of the flowers is Time, death-grieved;
The pebbles' beauty too is Time,
Life-wearied.

It is easy to admire a blowing flower
Or a smooth pebble flower-like freaked
By Time and vagueness.

Time is Time's lapse, the emulsive element coaxing
All obstinate locks and rusty hinges
To loving-kindness.

And am I proof against that lovesome pair,
Old age and childhood, twins in Time,
In sorrowful vagueness?

And will I not pretend the accustomed thanks:
Humouring age with filial flowers,
Childhood with pebbles?

ON RISING EARLY*

Rising early and walking in the garden
Before the sun has properly climbed the hill –
His rays warming the roof, not yet the grass
That is white with dew still.

And not enough breeze to eddy a puff of smoke,
And out in the meadows a thick mist lying yet,
And nothing anywhere ill or noticeable –
Thanks indeed for that.

But was there ever a day with wit enough
To be always early, to draw the smoke up straight
Even at three o'clock of an afternoon,
To spare dullness or sweat?

Indeed, many such days I remember
That were dew-white and gracious to the last,
That ruled out meal-times, yet had no more hunger
Than was felt by rising a half-hour before breakfast,
Nor more fatigue – where was it that I went
So unencumbered, with my feet trampling
Like strangers on the past?

ON DWELLING

Courtesies of good-morning and good-evening
From rustic lips fail as the town encroaches:
Soon nothing passes but the cold quick stare
Of eyes that see ghosts, yet too many for fear.

Here I too walk, silent myself, in wonder
At a town not mine though plainly coextensive
With mine, even in days coincident:
In mine I dwell, in theirs like them I haunt.

And the green country, should I turn again there?
My bumpkin neighbours loom even ghostlier:
Like trees they murmur or like blackbirds sing
Courtesies of good-morning and good-evening.

ON NECESSITY

Dung-worms are necessary. And their certain need
Is dung, more dung, much dung and on such dung to feed.
And though I chose to sit and ponder for whole days
On dung-worms, what could I find more to tell or praise
Than their necessity, their numbers and their greed
To which necessity in me its daily tribute pays?

THE FOOLISH SENSES*

Feverishly the eyes roll for what thorough
Sight may hold them still,
And most hysterically strains the throat
At the love song once easy to sing out
In minstrel serfdom to the armoured ill –
Let them cease now.

The view is inward, foolish eye: your rolling
Flatters the outward scene
To spread with sunset misery. Foolish throat,
That ill was colic, love its antidote,
And beauty, forced regret of who would sing
Of loves unclean.

No more, senses, shall you so confound me,
Playing your pageants through
That have outlived their uses in my mind –
Your outward staring that is inward blind
And the mad strummings of your melancholy,
Let them cease now.

DEVILISHLY PROVOKED*

Devilishly provoked
  By my officious pen –
Where I demand one word
  It scrawls me nine or ten;
But each surviving word
  Resentfully I make
Sweat for those nine or ten
  I blotted for its sake.

And even more provoked
  By my officious heart
Whose emblems of desire
  From every corner start:
So little joy I find
  In their superfluous play
I curse the spell that drives
  My only love away.

THE LEGS

There was this road,
And it led up-hill,
And it led down-hill,
And round and in and out.

And the traffic was legs,
Legs from the knees down,
Coming and going,
Never pausing.

And the gutters gurgled
With the rain's overflow,
And the sticks on the pavement
Blindly tapped and tapped.

What drew the legs along
Was the never-stopping,
And the senseless, frightening
Fate of being legs.

Legs for the road,
The road for legs,
Resolutely nowhere
In both directions.

My legs at least
Were not in that rout:
On grass by the roadside
Entire I stood,

Watching the unstoppable
Legs go by
With never a stumble
Between step and step.

Though my smile was broad
The legs could not see,
Though my laugh was loud
The legs could not hear.

My head dizzied, then:
I wondered suddenly,
Might I too be a walker
From the knees down?

Gently I touched my shins.
The doubt unchained them:
They had run in twenty puddles
Before I regained them.

OGRES AND PYGMIES*

Those famous men of old, the Ogres –
They had long beards and stinking arm-pits,
They were wide-mouthed, long-yarded and great-bellied
Yet not of taller stature, Sirs, than you.
They lived on Ogre-Strand, which was no place
But the churl's terror of their vast extent,
Where every foot was three-and-thirty inches
And every penny bought a whole hog.
Now of their company none survive, not one,
The times being, thank God, unfavourable
To all but nightmare shadows of their fame;
Their images stand howling on the hill
(The winds enforced against those wide mouths),
Whose granite haunches country-folk salute
With May Day kisses, and whose knobbed knees.

So many feats they did to admiration:
With their enormous throats they sang louder
Than ten cathedral choirs, with their grand yards
Stormed the most rare and obstinate maidenheads,
With their strong-gutted and capacious bellies
Digested stones and glass like ostriches.
They dug great pits and heaped huge mounds,
Deflected rivers, wrestled with the bear
And hammered judgements for posterity –
For the sweet-cupid-lipped and tassel-yarded
Delicate-stomached dwellers
In Pygmy Alley, where with brooding on them
A foot is shrunk to seven inches
And twelve-pence will not buy a spare rib.
And who would judge between Ogres and Pygmies –
The thundering text, the snivelling commentary –
Reading between such covers he will marvel
How his own members bloat and shrink again.

TO WHOM ELSE?*

To whom else other than,
To whom else not of man
Yet in human state,
Standing neither in stead
Of self nor idle godhead,
Should I, man in man bounded,
Myself dedicate?

To whom else momently,
To whom else endlessly,
But to you, I?
To you who only,
To you who mercilessly,
To you who lovingly,
Plucked out the lie?

To whom else less acquaint,
To whom else without taint
Of death, death-true?
With great astonishment
Thankfully I consent
To my estrangement
From me in you.

AS IT WERE POEMS*

I

In the legend of Reynard the Fox, Isegrim the Wolf, Grymbart the Brock, Tybert the Cat, Cuwart the Hare, Bellyn the Ram, Baldwin the Ass, Rukenawe the She-Ape and the rest of that company, where was I?

I was in the person of Bruin the Bear. And through the spite of Reynard and my own greed and credulity I left behind my ears and the claws of my fore-feet wedged in the trunk of a honey-tree.

In the legend of Troy where was I?

I was in the person of Ajax the son of Telamon. And Odysseus cheated me of the prize of dead Achilles' arms. For he suborned Trojan captives to testify that it was he who of us all had done their city the most harm. Angered by this, I drove Troy's whole forces single-handed from the field. But he covertly disposed slaughtered sheep in the place of the dead men that I had strewn behind me and so fastened on me the name of madman.

In the legend of Robin Hood and his Merry Men, where was I?

I would prefer to be written down for the Sheriff of Nottingham, Robin's enemy. But the natural truth is that I played the part of jolly Friar Tuck. I took and gave great buffets. I was the gross fool of the greenwood.

In the legend of Jesus and his companions, where was I?

I was not Jesus himself, I was not John the Baptist, nor Pontius Pilate, nor Judas Iscariot, nor even Peter. I was Lazarus sickening again in old age long after the Crucifixion, and knowing that this time I could not cheat death.

In the legend of Tobit, where was I?

I was not old Tobit himself, nor his kinsman Raguel, nor Sarah, Raguel's daughter, nor the angel Raphael, nor the devil Asmodaeus. I was Tobias, in sight of the towers of Ecbatana, with the gall, heart and liver of the fish in a pouch by my side.

In the legend of that Lucius whom a witch of Thessaly turned into a dumb ass and who after many cruel adventures was restored to human shape by the intervention of the goddess Isis, where was I?

I was that impassioned ass in the gold trappings.

In the legend of Isis, of Python the destroyer, and of Osiris yearly drowned, where was I?

I was the drowned Osiris.

II

A sick girl went from house to house fitting people into legends of her own making. For you and for me she made a legend of the Christ and of King West the Shepherd and of the Golden Seal of Solomon long hidden in a cave of a hill at Jerusalem. You were the Christ-Woman and I was King West and she was Queen East with whom King West takes ship to Palestine: to find the Golden Seal. You as of old nursed the souls of the dead; she and I led the living.

But you reasoned with the sick girl: in the legend of the Christ there is no room for a sequel, it is a page covered with writing on both sides. Whoever would take the story further must find a clean page.

And I scolded angrily: Jesus, the Christ-Man, was a timid plagiarist. He made no new legends but said over the old ones, fitting himself into them. He was the Child foretold by Isaiah and the other prophets. Born at Bethlehem, equivocally of the seed of David, riding through Zion in prophesied glory on an ass's colt, stiffnecked to eschew love that he might be duly rejected and despised, busying himself vexatiously with the transgressions of others – he was true to the smallest articles of the legend and was drawn at last miserably to a well-documented death.

III

And how shall I call you, between the name concealed in the legends and that open name by which reason calls you and in which you reasonably answer – your name to whosoever would not have his fellow levelheads say, 'Look, he is mad, he is talking with a familiar spirit'?

'Call me,' you say, 'by my open name, so that you do not call upon any of those false spirits of the legends, those names of travesty. For in my open name I am jealous for my hinder name, that it should not be belied in drunken mystifications: am I not the most levelheaded of all your fellows? So let my open name be my closed name, and my closed name, my open name.'

To which I answer, 'And so the names of the travesty vanish into a single name against the meddling of men with the unchangeable import of the name: Isis, the secrecy of the import.

In Egypt she was the holy name of the year of holy months: she was known to her priests as the invisible removed one, and to her people as the manifoldly incomprehensible. Every new moon crowned her with its peculiar head-dress – a rose, a star, an ear of barley, the horns of a goat: and she became the Moon itself, the single head of variety, Hecate by name. And Lilith, the owl of wisdom, because her lodges were held in stealthy darkness. At length the priests themselves forgot whom they meant in Isis. They even confounded her with the cowish Demeter, the blind force of Nature, and made her wife to Osiris.

'Now let all the false goddesses sprung from Isis – Pallas, Diana, Juno, Ceres and the rest – return to Isis, the greatly unnamed and greatly unseen and greatly unspoken with. Had but a single man seen her in Egypt, face to face, and known her for herself, then she would have been human woman, for other men to pass by and not know.

'So likewise Osiris was myself greatly meddling, Osiris the triple-named. He was Apollo in bright strength who dries up the floods. He was Dionysus, the growth of the vine. And he was Pluto, the dead man of the pit, the flooded Egypt to which life ever returns. Every year he rose again from the dead, but every year returned to the dead again. For she was only Isis, a closed name.'

ON PORTENTS*

If strange things happen where she is,
So that men say that graves open
And the dead walk, or that futurity
Becomes a womb and the unborn are shed,
Such portents are not to be wondered at,
Being tourbillions in Time made
By the strong pulling of her bladed mind
Through that ever-reluctant element.

From POEMS 1930-1933

(1933)

THE BARDS*

The bards falter in shame, their running verse
Stumbles, with marrow-bones the drunken diners
Pelt them for their delay.
It is a something fearful in the song
Plagues them – an unknown grief that like a churl
Goes commonplace in cowskin
And bursts unheralded, crowing and coughing,
An unpilled holly-club twirled in his hand,
Into their many-shielded, samite-curtained,
Jewel-bright hall where twelve kings sit at chess
Over the white-bronze pieces and the gold;
And by a gross enchantment
Flails down the rafters and leads off the queens –
The wild-swan-breasted, the rose-ruddy-cheeked
Raven-haired daughters of their admiration –
To stir his black pots and to bed on straw.

ULYSSES*

To the much-tossed Ulysses, never done
   With woman whether gowned as wife or whore,
Penelope and Circe seemed as one:
She like a whore made his lewd fancies run,
   And wifely she a hero to him bore.

Their counter-changings terrified his way:
   They were the clashing rocks, Symplegades,
Scylla and Charybdis too were they;
Now angry storms frosting the sea with spray
   And now the lotus island's drunken ease.

They multiplied into the Sirens' throng,
   Forewarned by fear of whom he stood bound fast
Hand and foot helpless to the vessel's mast,
Yet would not stop his ears: daring their song
   He groaned and sweated till that shore was past.

One, two and many: flesh had made him blind,
  Flesh had one pleasure only in the act,
Flesh set one purpose only in the mind –
Triumph of flesh and afterwards to find
  Still those same terrors wherewith flesh was racked.

His wiles were witty and his fame far known,
Every king's daughter sought him for her own,
  Yet he was nothing to be won or lost.
  All lands to him were Ithaca: love-tossed
He loathed the fraud, yet would not bed alone.

DOWN, WANTON, DOWN!

Down, wanton, down! Have you no shame
That at the whisper of Love's name,
Or Beauty's, presto! up you raise
Your angry head and stand at gaze?

Poor bombard-captain, sworn to reach
The ravelin and effect a breach –
Indifferent what you storm or why,
So be that in the breach you die!

Love may be blind, but Love at least
Knows what is man and what mere beast;
Or Beauty wayward, but requires
More delicacy from her squires.

Tell me, my witless, whose one boast
Could be your staunchness at the post,
When were you made a man of parts
To think fine and profess the arts?

Will many-gifted Beauty come
Bowing to your bald rule of thumb,
Or Love swear loyalty to your crown?
Be gone, have done! Down, wanton, down!

THE PHILOSOPHER*

Three blank walls, a barred window with no view,
A ceiling within reach of the raised hands,
A floor blank as the walls.

And, ruling out distractions of the body –
Growth of the hair and nails, a prison diet,
Thoughts of escape –

Ruling out memory and fantasy,
The distant tramping of a gaoler's boots,
Visiting mice and such,

What solace here for a laborious mind!
What a redoubtable and single task
One might attempt here:

Threading a logic between wall and wall,
Ceiling and floor, more accurate by far
Than the cob-spider's.

Truth captured without increment of flies:
Spinning and knotting till the cell became
A spacious other head

In which the emancipated reason might
Learn in due time to walk at greater length
And more unanswerably.

THE SUCCUBUS*

Thus will despair
In ecstasy of nightmare
Fetch you a devil-woman through the air,
  To slide below the sweated sheet
And kiss your lips in answer to your prayer
  And lock her hands with yours and your feet with her feet.

Yet why does she
Come never as longed-for beauty
Slender and cool, with limbs lovely to see,
   (The bedside candle guttering high)
And toss her head so the thick curls fall free
   Of halo'd breast, firm belly and long, slender thigh?

Why with hot face,
With paunched and uddered carcase,
Sudden and greedily does she embrace,
   Gulping away your soul, she lies so close,
Fathering brats on you of her own race?
   Yet is the fancy grosser than your lusts were gross?

NOBODY*

Nobody, ancient mischief, nobody,
Harasses always with an absent body.

Nobody coming up the road, nobody,
Like a tall man in a dark cloak, nobody.

Nobody about the house, nobody,
Like children creeping up the stairs, nobody.

Nobody anywhere in the garden, nobody,
Like a young girl quiet with needlework, nobody.

Nobody coming, nobody, not yet here,
Incessantly welcomed by the wakeful ear.

Until this nobody shall consent to die
Under his curse must everyone lie –

The curse of his envy, of his grief and fright,
Of sudden rape and murder screamed in the night.

DANEGELD

When I ceased to be a child
  I had great discontent
With a not-me unreconciled
  To what I thought and meant.

Some told me this, or that, or this –
  No counsel was the same:
Some preached God's holy purposes,
  Some used the Devil's name.

I made my truce with foreignness,
  As seemed the easiest plan:
The curious hauntings should express
  A me complete as man.

But this enlargement only spelt
  To see and yet be blind –
A pirate flesh allowed Danegeld
  By an unready mind.

Had I but held my truth apart
  And granted greed no say
In what I saw, deep in my heart,
  Must be my body way!

TRUDGE, BODY!*

Trudge, body, and climb, trudge and climb,
But not to stand again on any peak of time:
Trudge, body!

I'll cool you, body, with a hot sun, that draws the sweat,
I'll warm you, body, with ice-water, that stings the blood,
I'll enrage you, body, with idleness, to do
And having done to sleep the long night through:
Trudge, body!

But in such cooling, warming, doing or sleeping,
No pause for satisfaction: henceforth you make address
Beyond heat to the heat, beyond cold to the cold,
Beyond enraged idleness to enraged idleness.
With no more hours of hope, and none of regret,
Before each sun may rise, you salute it for set:
Trudge, body!

MUSIC AT NIGHT

Voices in gentle harmony
Rise from the slopes above the midnight sea,
And every sound comes true and clear,
And the song's old:
It charms the wisest ear –

Night and the sea and music bind
Such forced perfection on the darkened mind
That, ah now, with that dying fall
All truth seems told
And one light shines for all –

The Moon, who from the hill-top streams
On each white face and throat her absent beams.
The song-enchanted fellows send
Their chords of gold
Rippling beyond time's end.

They link arms and all evils fly:
The flesh is tamed, the spirit circles high.
Each angel softly sings his part
Not proud, not bold,
Dream-ecstasied in heart.

But lamp-light glitters through the trees:
Lamp-light will check these minor harmonies,
And soon the busy Sun will rise
And blaze and scold
From the same hill-top skies.

WITHOUT PAUSE*

Without cause and without
Pause blankness follows, turning
Man once more into
An autumn elm or
Ash in autumn mist,
His arms upraised, no
Heart or head, moreover
Nothing heard but now
This constant dropping always
Of such heavy drops
Distilled on finger-tips
From autumn mist and
Nowhere immanence or end
Or pause or cause,
But all is blankness
Seeming headache, yet not
Headache, yet not heartache:
Wanting heart and head,
The tree man – false,
Because the angry sap
Has faded down again
To tree roots dreading
Cold, and these abandoned
Leaves lie fallen flat
To make mould for
The pretty primroses that
Spring again in Spring
With little faces blank,
And sap again then
Rising proves the pain
Of Spring a fancy
Not attempted, no: so,
Until the frantic trial,
Blankness only made for
Pondering and tears against
That sudden lurch-away.

THE CLOCK MAN*

The clocks are ticking with good will:
   They make a cheerful sound.
I am that temporizer still
   Who sends their hands around,
By fresh experiments with birth and age
Teasing the times each time to further courage.

You who are grateful for your birth
   To hours that ticked you free
(And gratefully relapse to earth)
   Your thanks are due to me –
Which I accept, inured to shame, and mock
My vows to timelessness, sworn with the clock.

THE COMMONS OF SLEEP

That ancient common-land of sleep
Where the close-herded nations creep
   On all fours, tongue to ground –
Be sure that every night or near
I, sheep-like too, go wandering there
   And wake to have slept sound.

How comfortable can be misrule
Of dream that whirls the antic spool
   Of sense-entangling twist,
Where proud in idiot state I sit
At skirmish of ingenious wit,
   My nape by fairies kissed.

'From the world's loving-cup to drink,
In sleep, can be no shame,' I think.
   'Sleep has no part in shame.'
But to lie down in hope to find
Licence for devilishness of mind –
   Will sleeping bear the blame?

For at such welcome dream extends
Its hour beyond where sleeping ends
   And eyes are washed for day,
Till mind and mind's own honour seem
That nightmare dream-within-the-dream
   Which brings the most dismay.

Then lamps burn red and glow-worm green
And naked dancers grin between
   The rusting bars of love.
Loud and severe the drunken jokes
Go clanging out in midnight strokes.
   I weep: I wake: I move.

WHAT TIMES ARE THESE?

Against the far slow fields of white,
A cloud came suddenly in sight
   And down the valley passed,
Compact and grey as bonfire smoke –
This one cloud only, like a joke,
   It flew so fast.

And more: the shape, no inexact
Idle half-likeness but a fact
   Which all my senses knew,
Was a great dragon's and instead
Of fangs it had the scoffing head
   Of an old Jew.

What times are these that visions bear
So plainly down the morning air
   With wings and scales and beard?
I stared, and quick, a swirl of wind
Caught at his head: he writhed and thinned,
   He disappeared.

The last that stayed were the wide wings
And long tail barbed with double stings:
These drifted on alone
Over the watch-tower and the bay
So out to open sea, where they
Did not fade soon.

I knew him well, the Jew, for he
Was honest Uncle Usury
Who lends you blood for blood:
His dragon's claws were keen and just
To bleed the body into dust,
As the bond stood.

What times are these – to be allowed
This ancient vision of grey cloud
Gone in a casual breath?
The times of the torn dragon-wing
Still threatening seaward and the sting
Still poised for death.

From COLLECTED POEMS

(1938)

THE CHRISTMAS ROBIN*

The snows of February had buried Christmas
Deep in the woods, where grew self-seeded
The fir-trees of a Christmas yet unknown,
Without a candle or a strand of tinsel.

Nevertheless when, hand in hand, plodding
Between the frozen ruts, we lovers paused
And 'Christmas trees!' cried suddenly together,
Christmas was there again, as in December.

We velveted our love with fantasy
Down a long vista-row of Christmas trees,
Whose coloured candles slowly guttered down
As grandchildren came trooping round our knees.

But he knew better, did the Christmas robin –
The murderous robin with his breast aglow
And legs apart, in a spade-handle perched:
He prophesied more snow, and worse than snow.

CERTAIN MERCIES*

Now must all satisfaction
Appear mere mitigation
Of an accepted curse?

Must we henceforth be grateful
That the guards, though spiteful,
Are slow of foot and wit?

That by night we may spread
Over the plank bed
A thin coverlet?

That the rusty water
In the unclean pitcher
Our thirst quenches?

That the rotten, detestable
Food is yet eatable
By us ravenous?

That the prison censor
Permits a weekly letter?
(We may write: 'We are well.')

That, with patience and deference,
We do not experience
The punishment cell?

That each new indignity
Defeats only the body,
Pampering the spirit
With obscure, proud merit?

THE CUIRASSIERS OF THE FRONTIER*

Goths, Vandals, Huns, Isaurian mountaineers,
Made Roman by our Roman sacrament,
We can know little (as we care little)
Of the Metropolis: her candled churches,
Her white-gowned pederastic senators,
The cut-throat factions of her Hippodrome,
The eunuchs of her draped saloons.

Here is the frontier, here our camp and place –
Beans for the pot, fodder for horses,
And Roman arms. Enough. He who among us
At full gallop, the bowstring to his ear,
Lets drive his heavy arrows, to sink
Stinging through Persian corslets damascened,
Then follows with the lance – he has our love.

The Christ bade Holy Peter sheathe his sword,
Being outnumbered by the Temple guard.
And this was prudence, the cause not yet lost
While Peter might persuade the crowd to rescue.
Peter renegued, breaking his sacrament.
With us the penalty is death by stoning,
Not to be made a bishop.

In Peter's Church there is no faith nor truth,
Nor justice anywhere in palace or court.
That we continue watchful on the rampart
Concerns no priest. A gaping silken dragon,
Puffed by the wind, suffices us for God.
We, not the City, are the Empire's soul:
A rotten tree lives only in its rind.

CALLOW CAPTAIN

The sun beams jovial from an ancient sky,
  Flooding the round hills with heroic spate.
A callow captain, glaring, sword at thigh,
  Trots out his charger through the camp gate.
Soon comes the hour, his marriage hour, and soon
  He fathers children, reigns with ancestors
Who, likewise serving in the wars, won
  For a much-tattered flag renewed honours.

A wind ruffles the book, and he whose name
  Was mine vanishes; all is at an end.
Fortunate soldier: to be spared shame
  Of chapter-years unprofitable to spend,
To ride off into reticence, nor throw
  Before the story-sun a long shadow.

THE STRANGER

He noted from the hill top,
Fixing a cynic eye upon
The stranger in the distance
Up the green track approaching,
She had a sure and eager tread;
He guessed mere grace of body
Which would not for unloveliness
Of cheek or mouth or other feature
Retribution pay.

He watched as she came closer,
And half-incredulously saw
How lovely her face also,
Her hair, her naked hands.
Come closer yet, deception!
But closer as she came, the more
Unarguable her loveliness;
He frowned and blushed, confessing slowly,
No, it was no cheat.

To find her foolish-hearted
Would rid his baffled thought of her;
But there was wisdom in that brow
Of who might be a Muse.
Then all abashed he dropped his head:
For in his summer haughtiness
He had cried lust at her for whom
Through many deaths he had kept vigil,
Wakeful for her voice.

THE SMOKY HOUSE

He woke to a smell of smoke.
  The house was burning.
His room-mates reassured him:
  'Smouldering, not burning.'

'Break no window,' they warned,
'Make no draught:
Nobody wants a blaze.'
Choking, they laughed

At such a stubborn fellow
Unresigned to smoke,
To sore lungs and eyes –
For them a joke –

Yet who would not consent,
At a cry or curse,
That water on the smoulder
Made the smoke worse.

VARIABLES OF GREEN*

Grass-green and aspen-green,
Laurel-green and sea-green,
Fine-emerald-green,
And many another hue:
As green commands the variables of green
So love my loves of you.

THE GOBLET

From this heroic skull buried
Secretly in a tall ant-castle,
Drawn out, stripped of its jawbone, blanched
In sun all the hot summer,
Mounted with bands of hammered gold,
The eye-holes paned with crystal –
From this bright skull, a hero's goblet now,
What wine is to drink?

A dry draught, medicinal,
Not the sweet must that flowed
Too new between these lips
When here were living lips,
That pampered tongue
When here was tasting tongue.

But who shall be the drinker?
That passionate man, his rival
In endless love and battle,
Who overcame him at the end?
Or I, the avenging heir? I taste
Wine from a dead man's head
Whose griefs were not my own?

If I this skull a goblet made
It was a pious duty, nothing more.
Here is clean bone, and gold and crystal,
So may the ghost sigh gratitude
To drink his death, as I would mine.

FIEND, DRAGON, MERMAID*

The only Fiend, religious adversary,
Ceased in the end to plague me, dying
By his own hand on a scarred mountain-top
Full in my sight. His valedictory
Was pity for me as for one whose house,
Swept and garnished, now lay open
As hospice for a score of lesser devils:
I had no better friend than him, he swore.
His extreme spasms were of earthquake force –
They hurled me without sense on the sharp rocks;
The corpse, ridiculous – that long, thin neck,
Those long, thin, hairy legs, the sawdust belly –
This same was Hell's prince in his prime,
And lamed me in his fall.

Next of the ancient dragon I was freed
Which was an emanation of my fears
And in the Fiend's wake followed always.
An acid breeze puffed at his wings: he flew
Deathward in cloudy blue and gold, frightful,
Yet showing patches of webbed nothingness
Like soap-bubbles before they burst –
Which was a cause for smiling.
Furious, he glared: 'Confess, my dragon glory
Was a resplendency that seared the gaze –
All else mere candle-light and glowing ember!'

The mermaid last, with long hair combed and coiled
And childish-lovely face, swam slowly by.
She called my name, pleading an answer,
Yet knew that though my blood is salty still
It swings to other tides than the old sea.
'Greedy mermaid, are there no mariners
To plunge into green water when you sing,
That you should stretch your arms for me?
Fain to forget all winds and weathers
And perish in your beauty?' So she turned
With tears, affecting innocence:
'Proud heart, where shall you find again
So kind a breast as pillow for your woes,
Or such soft lips? Your peace was my love's care.'
'Peace is no dream of mariners,' I said.
She dived; and quit of dragon, Fiend and her
I turned my gaze to the encounter of
The later genius, who of my pride and fear
And love
No monster made but me.

FRAGMENT OF A LOST POEM*

O the clear moment, when from the mouth
A word flies, current immediately
Among friends; or when a loving gift astounds
As the identical wish nearest the heart;
Or when a stone, volleyed in sudden danger,
Strikes the rabid beast full on the snout!

Moments in never. . . .

GALATEA AND PYGMALION*

Galatea, whom his furious chisel
From Parian stone had by greed enchanted,
Fulfilled, so they say, Pygmalion's longings:
   Stepped from the pedestal on which she stood,
Bare in his bed laid her down, lubricious,
With low responses to his drunken raptures,
   Enroyalled his body with her demon blood.

Alas, Pygmalion had so well plotted
The articulation of his woman monster
That schools of eager connoisseurs beset
   Her single person with perennial suit;
Whom she (a judgement on the jealous artist)
Admitted rankly to a comprehension
   Of themes that crowned her own, not his repute.

THE DEVIL'S ADVICE TO STORY-TELLERS

Lest men suspect your tale to be untrue,
Keep probability – some say – in view.
But my advice to story-tellers is:
Weigh out no gross of probabilities,
Nor yet make diligent transcriptions of

Known instances of virtue, crime or love.
To forge a picture that will pass for true,
Do conscientiously what liars do –
Born liars, not the lesser sort that raid
The mouths of others for their stock-in-trade:
Assemble, first, all casual bits and scraps
That may shake down into a world perhaps;
People this world, by chance created so,
With random persons whom you do not know –
The teashop sort, or travellers in a train
Seen once, guessed idly at, not seen again;
Let the erratic course they steer surprise
Their own and your own and your readers' eyes;
Sigh then, or frown, but leave (as in despair)
Motive and end and moral in the air;
Nice contradiction between fact and fact
Will make the whole read human and exact.

LUNCH-HOUR BLUES*

His ears discount the ragged noise,
  His nose, the tangled smell;
His eyes when prodigies go past
  Look up, but never dwell.

His tongue not even registers
  The juices of his plate,
His hands (some other eater's hands?)
  Will not communicate.

He's thrown the senses from their seat,
  As Indian heroes do –
An act more notable were not
  The mind unseated too.

O yogey-bogey lunching man,
  Lunch on, against the bill –
Your service to the ascetic rule
  And to the chiming till.

HOTEL BED AT LUGANO*

Even in hotel beds the hair tousles.
But this is observation, not complaint –
'Complaints should please be dropped in the complaint-box' –
'Which courteously we beg you to vacate
In that clean state as you should wish to find it.'

And the day after Carnival, today,
I found, in the square, a crimson cardboard heart:
'Anna Maria', it read. Otherwise, friends,
No foreign news – unless that here they drink
Red wine from china bowls; here anis-roots
Are stewed like turnips; here funiculars
Light up at dusk, two crooked constellations;
And if bells peal a victory or great birth,
That will be cows careering towards the pail.

'It is not yet the season,' pleads the Porter,
'That comes in April, when the rain most rains.'
Trilingual Switzer fish in Switzer lakes
Pining for rain and bread-crumbs of the season,
In thin reed-beds you pine!

A-bed drowsing,
(While the hair slowly tousles) uncomplaining . . .
Anna Maria's heart under my pillow
Provokes no furious dream. Who is this Anna?
A Switzer maiden among Switzer maidens,
Child of the children of that fox who never
Ate the sour grapes: her teeth not set on edge.

PROGRESSIVE HOUSING

At history's compulsion
A welcome greeted once
All gross or trivial objects
That reached, by grand endurance,
Their bicentenary year.

But not two thousand years
Could sanctify this building
With bat-and-ivy ruin,
Or justify these furnishings
As woe-begone antiques.

No doubt it is good news
That the spell of age is lifted,
The museums' greed rebuked:
Yet might this not have come about
Less nastily perhaps?

LEDA*

Heart, with what lonely fears you ached,
  How lecherously mused upon
That horror with which Leda quaked
  Under the spread wings of the swan.

Then soon your mad religious smile
  Made taut the belly, arched the breast,
And there beneath your god awhile
  You strained and gulped your beastliest.

Pregnant you are, as Leda was,
  Of bawdry, murder and deceit;
Perpetuating night because
  The after-languors hang so sweet.

THE FLORIST ROSE*

This wax-mannequin nude, the florist rose,
She of the long stem and too glossy leaf,
Is dead to honest greenfly and leaf-cutter:
Behind plate-glass watches the yellow fogs.

Claims kin with the robust male aeroplane
Whom eagles hate and phantoms of the air,
Who has no legend, as she breaks from legend –
From fellowship with sword and sail and crown.

Experiment's flower, scentless (he its bird);
Is dewed by the spray-gun; is tender-thorned;
Pouts, false-virginal, between bud and bloom;
Bought as a love-gift, droops within the day.

BEING TALL

Long poems written by tall men
Wear a monstrous look; but then
Would these do better to write short
Like poets of the midget sort?

Here is no plea for medium height
In poets or what poets write:
Only a trifle to recall
The days when I had grown too tall,

When jealous dwarfs leered up at me
From somewhere between shoe and knee.
I grinned them my contempt and fear,
Stooping till our heads came near.

Then all I wrote, until in rage
I whipped them off the path and page,
Bent like a hook this way and that –
And who could guess what I was at?

But rage was not enough to teach
My natural height and breadth and reach:
It wanted love with kindly phlegm
To shrink my bones and straighten them.

AT FIRST SIGHT*

'Love at first sight,' some say, misnaming
Discovery of twinned helplessness
Against the huge tug of procreation.

But friendship at first sight? This also
Catches fiercely at the surprised heart
So that the cheek blanches and then blushes.

RECALLING WAR*

Entrance and exit wounds are silvered clean,
The track aches only when the rain reminds.
The one-legged man forgets his leg of wood,
The one-armed man his jointed wooden arm.
The blinded man sees with his ears and hands
As much or more than once with both his eyes.
Their war was fought these twenty years ago
And now assumes the nature-look of time,
As when the morning traveller turns and views
His wild night-stumbling carved into a hill.

What, then, was war? No mere discord of flags
But an infection of the common sky
That sagged ominously upon the earth
Even when the season was the airiest May.
Down pressed the sky, and we, oppressed, thrust out
Boastful tongue, clenched fist and valiant yard.
Natural infirmities were out of mode,
For Death was young again: patron alone
Of healthy dying, premature fate-spasm.

Fear made fine bed-fellows. Sick with delight
At life's discovered transitoriness,
Our youth became all-flesh and waived the mind.
Never was such antiqueness of romance,
Such tasty honey oozing from the heart.
And old importances came swimming back –
Wine, meat, log-fires, a roof over the head,
A weapon at the thigh, surgeons at call.
Even there was a use again for God –
A word of rage in lack of meat, wine, fire,
In ache of wounds beyond all surgeoning.

War was return of earth to ugly earth,
War was foundering of sublimities,
Extinction of each happy art and faith
By which the world had still kept head in air,
Protesting logic or protesting love,
Until the unendurable moment struck –
The inward scream, the duty to run mad.

And we recall the merry ways of guns –
Nibbling the walls of factory and church
Like a child, piecrust; felling groves of trees
Like a child, dandelions with a switch.
Machine-guns rattle toy-like from a hill,
Down in a row the brave tin-soldiers fall:
A sight to be recalled in elder days
When learnedly the future we devote
To yet more boastful visions of despair.

X

Detective, criminal or corpse –
Who is the I of the story?
Agreed, the first stage of a narrative
Permits mystification – the I
Rainbowing clues and fancies.
That is the time of drawing-room charades:
Each mask resembles every other mask,

And every beard is false.
But now the story hardens and grows adult:
By the beginning of the final chapter
Holmes and Moriarty are distinct,
The corpse at least not either's –
I joins merrily in the man-hunt
With a key to the code.

The great K.C. is briefed at last,
The Judge is trying on his sternest wig,
The public queueing up with camp-stools.
Do you dare to tell us, I, at this late hour,
That who you are still waits decision?
Malice Aforethought or Unfit to Plead?

PARENT TO CHILDREN*

When you grow up, are no more children,
Nor am I then your parent:
The day of settlement falls.

'Parent', mortality's reminder,
In each son's mouth or daughter's
A word of shame and rage!

I, who begot you, ask no pardon of you;
Nor may the soldier ask
Pardon of the strewn dead.

The procreative act was blind:
It was not you I sired then –
For who sires friends, as you are mine now?

In fear begotten, I begot in fear.
Would you have had me cast fear out
So that you should not be?

TO CHALLENGE DELIGHT*

Living is delight –
Lovers, even, confess it;
And what could compare
With the pain these suffer?
Delight is all repeating –
Doves coo, cats purr, men sing.

'Challenge delight, of purpose,
And you pull Nature's nose
In self-spite, you slap her face
In the portico of her palace,
Exchange her sportive sun
For a black perfection.'

Thus hardly anybody
Will make delight his study.
Its meaning to know
Would be emptier than sorrow,
That Sunday morning respite
From a hard week of delight.

TO WALK ON HILLS*

To walk on hills is to employ legs
As porters of the head and heart
Jointly adventuring towards
Perhaps true equanimity.

To walk on hills is to see sights
And hear sounds unfamiliar.
When in wind the pine-tree roars,
When crags with bleatings echo,
When water foams below the fall,
Heart records that journey
As memorable indeed;
Head reserves opinion,
Confused by the wind.

A view of three shires and the sea!
Seldom so much at once appears
Of the coloured world, says heart.
Head is glum, says nothing.

Legs become weary, halting
To sprawl in a rock's shelter,
While the sun drowsily blinks
On head at last brought low –
This giddied passenger of legs
That has no word to utter.

Heart does double duty,
As heart, and as head,
With portentous trifling.
A castle, on its crag perched,
Across the miles between is viewed
With awe as across years.

Now a daisy pleases,
Pleases and astounds, even,
That on a garden lawn could blow
All summer long with no esteem.

And the buzzard's cruel poise,
And the plover's misery,
And the important beetle's
Blue-green-shiny back. . . .

To walk on hills is to employ legs
To march away and lose the day.
Tell us, have you known shepherds?
And are they not a witless race,
Prone to quaint visions?
Not thus from solitude
(Solitude sobers only)
But from long hilltop striding.

TO BRING THE DEAD TO LIFE*

To bring the dead to life
Is no great magic.
Few are wholly dead:
Blow on a dead man's embers
And a live flame will start.

Let his forgotten griefs be now,
And now his withered hopes;
Subdue your pen to his handwriting
Until it prove as natural
To sign his name as yours.

Limp as he limped,
Swear by the oaths he swore;
If he wore black, affect the same;
If he had gouty fingers,
Be yours gouty too.

Assemble tokens intimate of him –
A seal, a cloak, a pen:
Around these elements then build
A home familiar to
The greedy revenant.

So grant him life, but reckon
That the grave which housed him
May not be empty now:
You in his spotted garments
Shall yourself lie wrapped.

TO EVOKE POSTERITY*

To evoke posterity
Is to weep on your own grave,
Ventriloquizing for the unborn:
'Would you were present in flesh, hero!
What wreaths and junketings!'

And the punishment is fixed:
To be found fully ancestral,
To be cast in bronze for a city square,
To dribble green in times of rain
And stain the pedestal.

Spiders in the spread beard;
A life proverbial
On clergy lips a-cackle;
Eponymous institutes,
Their luckless architecture.

Two more dates of life and birth
For the hour of special study
From which all boys and girls of mettle
Twice a week play truant
And worn excuses try.

Alive, you have abhorred
The crowds on holiday
Jostling and whistling – yet would you air
Your death-mask, smoothly lidded,
Along the promenade?

ANY HONEST HOUSEWIFE*

Any honest housewife could sort them out,
Having a nose for fish, an eye for apples.
Is it any mystery who are the sound,
And who the rotten? Never, by her lights.

Any honest housewife who, by ill-fortune,
Ever engaged a slut to scrub for her
Could instantly distinguish from the workers
The lazy, the liars, and the petty thieves.

Does this denote a sixth peculiar sense
Gifted to housewives for their vestal needs?
Or is it failure of the usual five
In all unthrifty writers on this head?

DEFEAT OF THE REBELS*

The enemy forces are in wild flight.
Poor souls (you say), they were intoxicated
With rhetoric and banners, thought it enough
To believe and to blow trumpets, to wear
That menacing lie in their shakos.

Enough: it falls on us to shoot them down,
The incorrigibles and cowards,
Where they shiver behind rocks, or in ditches
Seek graves that have no headstones to them –
Such prisoners were unprofitable.

Now as our vanguard, pressing on,
Dislodges them from village and town,
Who yelling abandon packs and cloaks,
Their arms and even the day's rations,
We are not abashed by victory,

We raise no pitying monument
To check the counter-stroke of fortune.
These are not spoils: we recognize
Our own strewn gear, that never had been robbed
But for our sloth and hesitancy.

THE GRUDGE

Judging the gift, his eye of greed
Weighed resentment against need.
Resentment won, for to receive
Is not so blessèd as to give:
To give is to undo a lack.
Nor could the gift be deeded back
But with vile ingratitude –
And gifts, like embassies, he viewed
As if enclaves of foreign ground.
Nor could a compromise be found

Between the giver's thoughtfulness
And his own more-than-thanklessness.
The gift held neither bribe nor blame
But with cruel aptness came,
Disproving self-sufficiency –
That cloaked-in-silence misery
Which had, itself, no gifts to make,
Grudged to bend, and would not break.

NEVER SUCH LOVE*

Twined together and, as is customary,
For words of rapture groping, they
'Never such love,' swore, 'ever before was!'
Contrast with all loves that had failed or staled
Registered their own as love indeed.

And was this not to blab idly
The heart's fated inconstancy?
Better in love to seal the love-sure lips,
For truly love was before words were,
And no word given, no word broken.

When the name 'love' is uttered
(Love, the near-honourable malady
With which in greed and haste they
Each other do infect and curse)
Or, worse, is written down. . . .

Wise after the event, by love withered,
A 'never more!' most frantically
Sorrow and shame would proclaim
Such as, they'd swear, never before were:
True lovers even in this.

THE HALFPENNY*

His lucky halfpenny after years of solace
Mixed with the copper crowd, was gone.
He grieved all day, a comic grief
But by next morning sadly verified:
His face was not his own!

A man as like his neighbours, you would say,
As halfpenny like halfpence, yet
Marked from among them by the luck
This halfpenny of halfpence brought him,
Disfigured by its loss.

Made by luck, by lack of luck unmade –
A bankrupt sameness was his doom:
To have had luck and now to have none,
To have no face but what he borrowed
From neighbours' charity.

Begging at the kerb-side, he won it back,
The very coin – fit for a fob
If such he had, but all was rags now.
'To be my ill-luck token,' he rejoiced,
'My ill luck now my own!'

Pride of differentiated face:
'And what are rags and broken shoes
When I can boast myself to strangers,
Leaping face-forward from their high roofs,
My ill luck in my hand?'

THE FALLEN SIGNPOST*

The signpost of four arms is down,
But one names your departure-town:
With this for guide you may replant
Your post and choose which road you want –

Logic that only seems obscure
To those deliberately not sure
Whether a journey should begin
With cross-roads or with origin.

The square post, and the socket square –
Now which way round to set it there?
Thus from the problem coaxing out
Four further elements of doubt,

They make the simple cross-roads be
A crux of pure dubiety
Demanding how much more concern
Than to have taken the wrong turn!

THE CHINA PLATE

From a crowded barrow in a street-market
The plate was ransomed for a few coppers,
Was brought gleefully home, given a place
On a commanding shelf.

'Quite a museum-piece,' an expert cries
(Eyeing it through the ready pocket-lens) –
As though a glass case would be less sepulchral
Than the barrow-hearse!

For weeks this plate retells the history
Whenever an eye runs in that direction:
'Near perdition I was, in a street-market
With rags and old shoes.'

'A few coppers' – here once again
The purchaser's proud hand lifts down
The bargain, displays the pot-bank sign
Scrawled raggedly underneath.

Enough, permit the treasure to forget
The emotion of that providential purchase,
Becoming a good citizen of the house
Like its fellow-crockery.

Let it dispense sandwiches at a party
And not be noticed in the drunken buzz,
Or little cakes at afternoon tea
When cakes are in demand.

Let it regain a lost habit of life,
Foreseeing death in honourable breakage
Somewhere between the kitchen and the shelf –
To be sincerely mourned.

IDLE HANDS

To-day, all day, for once he did nothing –
A proud report from one whose hands,
Of Satan warned when young, engross him
Always with over-busyness. Nothing –
Pleasure unposted in the journal.

This is for eyes that ask no illustration,
Not for those poor adepts at less than nothing
Who would enquire: Was it town-idleness,
Or did he drink the sun by the calm sea
Until the sunset washed upon his daze,
Then home to supper, and the bedside lamp?

He did nothing; tells you plainly so.

Where he did nothing is no part of this:
Whether by the wild sea or the calm sea
Or where the pavement-coloured dog befouls
The pavement-kerb. It is enough that
He did nothing, neither less nor more,
Leaving the day, for a remembrance,
A clear bubble in Time's chalky glass.

THE LAUREATE*

Like a lizard in the sun, though not scuttling
When men approach, this wretch, this thing of rage,
Scowls and sits rhyming in his horny age.

His time and truth he has not bridged to ours,
But shrivelled by long heliotropic idling
He croaks at us his out-of-date humours.

Once long ago here was a poet; who died.
See how remorse twitching his mouth proclaims
It was no natural death, but suicide.

Arrogant, lean, unvenerable, he
Still turns for comfort to the western flames
That glitter a cold span above the sea.

A JEALOUS MAN*

To be homeless is a pride
To the jealous man prowling
Hungry down the night lanes,

Who has no steel at his side,
No drink hot in his mouth,
But a mind dream-enlarged,

Who witnesses warfare,
Man with woman, hugely
Raging from hedge to hedge:

The raw knotted oak-club
Clenched in the raw fist,
The ivy-noose well flung,

The thronged din of battle,
Gaspings of the throat-snared,
Snores of the battered dying,

Tall corpses, braced together,
Fallen in clammy furrows,
Male and female,

Or, among haulms of nettle
Humped, in noisome heaps,
Male and female.

He glowers in the choked roadway
Between twin churchyards,
Like a turnip ghost.

(Here, the rain-worn headstone,
There, the Celtic cross
In rank white marble.)

This jealous man is smitten,
His fear-jerked forehead
Sweats a fine musk;

A score of bats bewitched
By the ruttish odour
Swoop singing at his head;

Nuns bricked up alive
Within the neighbouring wall
Wail in cat-like longing.

Crow, cocks, crow loud,
Reprieve the doomed devil –
Has he not died enough?

Now, out of careless sleep,
She wakes and greets him coldly,
The woman at home,

She, with a private wonder
At shoes bemired and bloody –
His war was not hers.

THE CLOAK*

Into exile with only a few shirts,
Some gold coin and the necessary papers.
But winds are contrary: the Channel packet
Time after time returns the sea-sick peer
To Sandwich, Deal or Rye. He does not land,
But keeps his cabin; so at last we find him
In humble lodgings maybe at Dieppe,
His shirts unpacked, his night-cap on a peg,
Passing the day at cards and swordsmanship
Or merry passages with chambermaids,
By night at his old work. And all is well –
The country wine wholesome although so sharp,
And French his second tongue; a faithful valet
Brushes his hat and brings him newspapers.
This nobleman is at home anywhere,
His castle being, the valet says, his title.
The cares of an estate would incommode
Such tasks as now his Lordship has in hand.
His Lordship, says the valet, contemplates
A profitable absence of some years.
Has he no friend at Court to intercede?
He wants none: exile's but another name
For an old habit of non-residence
In all but the recesses of his cloak.
It was this angered a great personage.

THE HALLS OF BEDLAM*

Forewarned of madness:
In three days' time at dusk
The fit masters him.

How to endure those days?
(Forewarned is foremad)
' – Normally, normally.'

He will gossip with children,
Argue with elders,
Check the cash account.

'I shall go mad that day –'
The gossip, the argument,
The neat marginal entry.

His case is not uncommon,
The doctors pronounce;
But prescribe no cure.

To be mad is not easy,
Will earn him no more
Than a niche in the news.

Then to-morrow, children,
To-morrow or the next day
He resigns from the firm.

His boyhood's ambition
Was to become an artist –
Like any City man's.

To the walls and halls of Bedlam
The artist is welcome –
Bold brush and full palette.

Through the cell's grating
He will watch his children
To and from school.

'Suffer the little children
To come unto me
With their Florentine hair!'

A very special story
For their very special friends –
They burst in the telling:

Of an evil thing, armed,
Tap-tapping on the door,
Tap-tapping on the floor,
'On the third day at dusk.'

Father in his shirt-sleeves
Flourishing a hatchet –
Run, children, run!

No one could stop him,
No one understood;
And in the evening papers. . . .

(Imminent genius,
Troubles at the office,
Normally, normally,
As if already mad.)

OR TO PERISH BEFORE DAY

The pupils of the eye expand
And from near-nothings build up sight;
The pupil of the heart, the ghost,
Swelling parades the dewy land:

With cowardice and with self-esteem
Makes terror in the track that through
The fragrant spotted pasture runs;
And a bird wails across the dream.

Now, if no heavenly window shines
Nor angel-voices cheer the way,
The ghost will overbear the man
And mark his head with fever-signs.

The flowers of dusk that he has pulled
To wonder at when morning's here
Are snail-shells upon straws of grass –
So easily the eye is gulled.

The sounding words that his mouth fill
Upon to-morrow's lip shall droop;
The legs that slide with skating ease
Be stiff to the awakened will.

Or, should he perish before day,
He leaves his lofty ghost behind
Perpetuating uncontrolled
This hour of glory and dismay.

A COUNTRY MANSION*

This ancient house so notable
For its gables and great staircase,
Its mulberry-trees and alleys of clipped yew,
Humbles the show of every near demesne.

At the beginning it acknowledged owners –
Father, son, grandson –
But then, surviving the last heirs of the line,
Became a place for life-tenancy only.

At the beginning, no hint of fate,
No rats and no hauntings;
In the garden, then, the fruit-trees grew
Slender and similar in long rows.

A bedroom with a low ceiling
Caused little fret at first;
But gradual generations of discomfort
Have bred an anger there to stifle sleep.

And the venerable dining-room,
Where port in Limerick glasses
Glows twice as red reflected
In the memory-mirror of the waxed table –

For a time with paint and flowered paper
A mistress tamed its walls,
But pious antiquarian hands, groping,
Rediscovered the grey panels beneath.

Children love the old house tearfully,
And the parterres, how fertile!
Married couples under the testers hugging
Enjoy carnality's bliss as nowhere else.

A smell of mould from loft to cellar,
Yet sap still brisk in the oak
Of the great beams: if ever they use a saw
It will stain, as cutting a branch from a green tree.

. . . Old Parr had lived one hundred years and five
(So to King Charles he bragged)
When he did open penance, in a sheet,
For fornication with posterity.

Old Parr died; not so the mansion
Whose inhabitants, bewitched,
Pour their fresh blood through its historic veins
And, if a tile blow from the roof, tremble.

The last-born of this race of sacristans
Broke the long spell, departed;
They lay his knife and fork at every meal
And every evening warm his bed;

Yet cannot draw him back from the far roads
For trifling by the lily-pool
Or wine at the hushed table where they meet,
The guests of genealogy.

It was his childhood's pleasure-ground
And still may claim his corpse,
Yet foster-cradle or foster-grave
He will not count as home.

This rebel does not hate the house,
Nor its dusty joys impugn:
No place less reverend could provoke
So proud an absence from it.

He has that new malaise of time:
Gratitude choking with vexation
That he should opulently inherit
The goods and titles of the extinct.

THE EREMITES*

We may well wonder at those bearded hermits
Who like the scorpion and the basilisk
Couched in the desert sands, to undo
Their scurfy flesh with tortures.

They drank from pools fouled by the ass and camel,
Chewed uncooked millet pounded between stones,
Wore but a shame-rag, dusk or dawn,
And rolled in thorny places.

In the wilderness there are no women;
Yet hermits harbour in their shrunken loins
A penitential paradise,
A leaping-house of glory.

Solomons of a thousand lusty love-chants,
These goatish men, burned Aethiopian black,
Kept vigil till the angelic whores
Should lift the latch of pleasure.

And what Atellan orgies of the soul
Were celebrated then among the rocks
They testify themselves in books
That rouse Atellan laughter.

Haled back at last to wear the ring and mitre,
They clipped their beards and, for their stomachs' sake,
Drank now and then a little wine,
And tasted cakes and honey.

Observe then how they disciplined the daughters
Of noble widows, who must fast and thirst,
Abjure down-pillows, rouge and curls,
Deform their delicate bodies:

Whose dreams were curiously beset by visions
Of stinking hermits in a wilderness
Pressing unnatural lusts on them
Until they wakened screaming.

Such was the virtue of our pious fathers:
To refine pleasure in the hungry dream.
Pity for them, but pity too for us –
Our beds by their leave lain in.

ADVOCATES*

Fugitive firs and larches for a moment
Caught, past midnight, by our headlight beam
On that mad journey through unlasting lands
I cannot put a name to, years ago,
(And my companions drowsy-drunk) – those trees
Resume again their sharp appearance, perfect
Of spur and tassel, claiming memory,
Claiming affection: 'Will we be included
In the catalogue? Yes, yes?' they plead.

Green things, you are already there enrolled.
And should a new resentment gnaw in me
Against my dear companions of that journey
(Strangers already then, in thought and deed)
You shall be advocates, charged to deny
That all the good I lived with them is lost.

SELF-PRAISE*

No, self-praise does not recommend.
  What shall I do with mine
When so few Englishmen pretend
  Not to be dogs or swine,

That to assume the peacock's part,
  To scream and spread the tail,
Is held a doom-defying art
  And witnesses turn pale?

But praise from fellow-creatures is
  (All Englishmen agree)
The sweetest of experiences
  And confers modesty,

And justifies the silent boast
  Of a bemedalled line:
The most dog-true of dogs, the most
  Egregious swine of swine.

O, let me suffer in self-praise,
  Unfit to occupy
The kennel, for my headstrong ways,
  Too squeamish for the sty.

THE CHALLENGE*

In ancient days a glory swelled my thighs,
And sat like fear between my shoulder-blades,
And made the young hair bristle on my poll.

Sun was my crown, green grassflesh my estate,
The wind a courtier, fanning at my cheek,
And plunged I in the stream, its waters hissed.

Queens I had to try my glory on,
And glory-princes my queens bore to me.
Royally I swept off all caitiff crowns.

Were the queens whores? the princes parricides?
Or were the tumbled crowns again worn high?
No, I was king then, if kings ever were.

O cousin princes, glory is hard put by,
And green grassflesh is lovely to a king.
My hawks were lightning darted from my fist.

Time was my chronicler, my deeds age-new,
And death no peril, nor decay of powers.
Glory sat firmly in my body's thrones.

Only, at midnight, rose another crown
That drained the wholesome colour from my realm,
That stilled the wind and froze the headlong stream.

I said: A challenge not to be endured,
A shadow clouding the sweet drunken hour
When with my queens in love I company.

I left the palace sleeping, I rode out,
I flew my hawk at that thin, mocking crown,
I emptied my full quiver at the sky.

Where went my hawk? He came not home again.
What ailed my horse? He cast me like a sack.
The crown moved ghostly off against the dawn.

And from that hour, though the sun burned as fierce,
Though the wind brought me frequency of spice,
Glory was gone, and numb was all my flesh.

Whose weakling is the vanquished of the Moon?
His own heart's weakling: thievishly he longs
To diadem his head with stolen light.

The Moon's the crown of no high-walled domain
Conquerable by angry reach of pride:
Her icy lands welcome no soldiery.

Thus I was shamed, I wandered in the fields,
I let my nails grow long and my hair long,
Neglecting all the business of my day.

No lovely queen nor wisest minister
Could medicine me out of my wretchedness:
The palace fell in ruins, the land smoked.

In my lost realm, if grass or flower yet grew,
It sprouted from the shade of broken walls.
I threw the walls flat, crushing flower and grass.

At length in my distemper's latest hour
I rose up shuddering, reckless to live
An idiot pawn of that inhuman power.

Over the mountain peak I watched her glide
And stood dumbfoundered by her reasoned look.
With answering reason my sick heart renewed.

So peace fell sudden, and in proof of peace
There sat my flown hawk, hooded on my fist,
And with my knees I gripped my truant horse.

Toward that most clear, unscorching light I spurred.
Whiter and closer shone the increasing disc,
Until it filled the sky, scattering my gaze.

When I might see once more, the day had come
And I was riding through gold harvest-fields,
Toward a rebuilded city, and my home.

Here then in majesty I rule again,
And grassflesh pays me tribute as of old;
In wind and sun and stream my joys I take,
Bounded by white horizons beyond touch.

TO THE SOVEREIGN MUSE*

Debating here one night we reckoned that
Between us we knew all the poets
Who bore that sacred name: none bore it clear,
Not one. Some we commended
For being all they might be in a day
To which poetry was a shrouded emblem,
And some we frowned upon for lawyers' clerks
Drafting conveyances on moral sheepskin,
Or for pantomimists making parody
Of a magnificence they feared to acclaim.

This was to praise you, Sovereign muse,
And to your love our pride devote,
Who pluck the speech-thread from a jargon-tangled
Fleece of a thousand tongues, wills, voices,
To be a single speech, twisted fine;
Snapping it short like Fate then –
'Thus much, no more –'

Thereafter, in acknowledgement of you
We might no longer feign and stutter
As poets of the passionate chance,
Nor claim the indulgence of the hour.
Our tongues must prompter be than those
That wagged with modish lamentation –
Or lost men, otherwise, and renegades
To our confession, maudlin-sane must die
Suicides on the stair of yesterday.

THE AGES OF OATH*

To find a garden-tulip growing
Among wild primroses of a wild field,
Or a cuckoo's egg in a blackbird's nest,
Or a giant mushroom, a whole basketful –
The memorable feats of childhood!
Once, by the earthworks, scratching in the soil,
My stick turned up a Roman amber bead. . . .

The lost, the freakish, the unspelt
Drew me: for simple sights I had no eye.
And did I swear allegiance then
To wildness, not (as I thought) to truth –
Become a virtuoso, and this also,
Later, of simple sights, when tiring
Of unicorn and upas?

Did I forget how to greet plainly
The especial sight, how to know deeply
The pleasure shared by upright hearts?
And is this to begin afresh, with oaths
On the true book, in the true name,
Now stammering out my praise of you,
Like a boy owning his first love?

LIKE SNOW*

She, then, like snow in a dark night,
Fell secretly. And the world waked
With dazzling of the drowsy eye,
So that some muttered 'Too much light',
And drew the curtains close.
Like snow, warmer than fingers feared,
And to soil friendly;
Holding the histories of the night
In yet unmelted tracks.

THE CLIMATE OF THOUGHT*

The climate of thought has seldom been described.
It is no terror of Caucasian frost,
Nor yet that brooding Hindu heat
For which a loin-rag and a dish of rice
Suffice until the pestilent monsoon.
But, without winter, blood would run too thin;
Or, without summer, fires would burn too long.
In thought the seasons run concurrently.

Thought has a sea to gaze, not voyage, on;
And hills, to rough the edge of the bland sky,
Not to be climbed in search of blander prospect;
Few birds, sufficient for such caterpillars
As are not fated to turn butterflies;
Few butterflies, sufficient for such flowers
As are the luxury of a full orchard;
Wind, sometimes, in the evening chimneys; rain
On the early morning roof, on sleepy sight;
Snow streaked upon the hilltop, feeding
The fond brook at the valley-head
That greens the valley and that parts the lips;
The sun, simple, like a country neighbour;
The moon, grand, not fanciful with clouds.

END OF PLAY*

We have reached the end of pastime, for always,
Ourselves and everyone, though few confess it
Or see the sky other than, as of old,
A foolish smiling Mary-mantle blue;

Though life may still seem to dawdle golden
In some June landscape among giant flowers,
The grass to shine as cruelly green as ever,
Faith to descend in a chariot from the sky –

May seem only: a mirror and an echo
Mediate henceforth with vision and sound.
The cry of faith, no longer mettlesome,
Sounds as a blind man's pitiful plea of 'blind'.

We have at last ceased idling, which to regret
Were as shallow as to ask our milk-teeth back;
As many forthwith do, and on their knees
Call lugubriously upon chaste Christ.

We tell no lies now, at last cannot be
The rogues we were – so evilly linked in sense
With what we scrutinized that lion or tiger
Could leap from every copse, strike and devour us.

No more shall love in hypocritic pomp
Conduct its innocents through a dance of shame,
From timid touching of gloved fingers
To frantic laceration of naked breasts.

Yet love survives, the word carved on a sill
Under antique dread of the headsman's axe;
It is the echoing mind, as in the mirror
We stare on our dazed trunks at the block kneeling.

THE FALLEN TOWER OF SILOAM*

Should the building totter, run for an archway!
We were there already – already the collapse
Powdered the air with chalk, and shrieking
Of old men crushed under the fallen beams
Dwindled to comic yelps. How unterrible
When the event outran the alarm
And suddenly we were free –

Free to forget how grim it stood,
That tower, and what wide fissures ran
Up the west wall, how rotten the under-pinning
At the south-eastern angle. Satire
Had curled a gentle wind around it,
As if to buttress the worn masonry;
Yet we, waiting, had abstained from satire.

It behoved us, indeed, as poets
To be silent in Siloam, to foretell
No visible calamity. Though kings
Were crowned and gold coin minted still and horses
Still munched at nose-bags in the public streets,
All such sad emblems were to be condoned:
An old wives' tale, not ours.

THE GREAT-GRANDMOTHER

That aged woman with the bass voice
And yellowing white hair: believe her.
Though to your grandfather, her son, she lied
And to your father disingenuously
Told half the tale as the whole,
Yet she was honest with herself,
Knew disclosure was not yet due,
Knows it is due now.

She will conceal nothing of consequence
From you, her great-grandchildren
(So distant the relationship,
So near her term),
Will tell you frankly, she has waited
Only for your sincere indifference
To exorcize that filial regard
Which has estranged her, seventy years,
From the folk of her house.

Confessions of old distaste
For music, sighs and roses –
Their false-innocence assaulting her,
Breaching her hard heart;
Of the pleasures of a full purse,
Of clean brass and clean linen,
Of being alone at last;
Disgust with the ailing poor
To whom she was bountiful;
How the prattle of young children
Vexed more than if they whined;
How she preferred cats.

She will say, yes, she acted well,
Took such pride in the art
That none of them suspected, even,
Her wrathful irony
In doing what they asked
Better than they could ask it. . . .
But, ah, how grudgingly her will returned
After the severance of each navel-cord,

And fled how far again,
When again she was kind!

She has outlasted all man-uses,
As was her first resolve:
Happy and idle like a port
After the sea's recession,
She does not misconceive the nature
Of shipmen or of ships.
Hear her, therefore, as the latest voice;
The intervening generations (drifting
On tides of fancy still), ignore.

NO MORE GHOSTS*

The patriarchal bed with four posts
Which was a harbourage of ghosts
Is hauled out from the attic glooms
And cut to wholesome furniture for wholesome rooms;

Where they (the ghosts) confused, abused, thinned,
Forgetful how they sighed and sinned,
Cannot disturb our ordered ease
Except as summer dust tickles the nose to sneeze.

We are restored to simple days, are free
From cramps of dark necessity,
And one another recognize
By an immediate love that signals at our eyes.

No new ghosts can appear. Their poor cause
Was that time freezes, and time thaws;
But here only such loves can last
As do not ride upon the weathers of the past.

LEAVING THE REST UNSAID*

Finis, apparent on an earlier page,
With fallen obelisk for colophon,
Must this be here repeated?

Death has been ruefully announced
And to die once is death enough,
Be sure, for any life-time.

Must the book end, as you would end it,
With testamentary appendices
And graveyard indices?

But no, I will not lay me down
To let your tearful music mar
The decent mystery of my progress.

So now, my solemn ones, leaving the rest unsaid,
Rising in air as on a gander's wing
At a careless comma,

From NO MORE GHOSTS

(1940)

THE GLUTTON*

Beyond the Atlas roams a glutton
Lusty and sleek, a shameless robber,
Sacred to Aethiopian Aphrodite;
The aborigines harry it with darts,
And its flesh is esteemed, though of a fishy tang
Tainting the eater's mouth and lips.

Ourselves once, wandering in mid-wilderness
And by despair drawn to this diet,
Before the meal was over sat apart
Loathing each other's carrion company.

A LOVE STORY*

The full moon easterly rising, furious,
Against a winter sky ragged with red;
The hedges high in snow, and owls raving –
Solemnities not easy to withstand:
A shiver wakes the spine.

In boyhood, having encountered the scene,
I suffered horror: I fetched the moon home,
With owls and snow, to nurse in my head
Throughout the trials of a new Spring,
Famine unassuaged.

But fell in love, and made a lodgement
Of love on those chill ramparts.
Her image was my ensign: snows melted,
Hedges sprouted, the moon tenderly shone,
The owls trilled with tongues of nightingale.

These were all lies, though they matched the time,
And brought me less than luck: her image
Warped in the weather, turned beldamish.
Then back came winter on me at a bound,
The pallid sky heaved with a moon-quake.

Dangerous it had been with love-notes
To serenade Queen Famine.
In tears I recomposed the former scene,
Let the snow lie, watched the moon rise, suffered the owls,
Paid homage to them of unevent.

THE THIEVES*

Lovers in the act dispense
With such meum-tuum sense
As might warningly reveal
What they must not pick or steal,
And their nostrum is to say:
'I and you are both away.'

After, when they disentwine
You from me and yours from mine,
Neither can be certain who
Was that I whose mine was you.
To the act again they go
More completely not to know.

Theft is theft and raid is raid
Though reciprocally made.
Lovers, the conclusion is
Doubled sighs and jealousies
In a single heart that grieves
For lost honour among thieves.

TO SLEEP*

The mind's eye sees as the heart mirrors:
Loving in part, I did not see you whole,
Grew flesh-enraged that I could not conjure
A whole you to attend my fever-fit
In the doubtful hour between a night and day
And be Sleep that had kept so long away.

Of you sometimes a hand, a brooch, a shoe
Wavered beside me, unarticulated –
As the vexed insomniac dream-forges;
And the words I chose for your voice to speak
Echoed my own voice with its dry creak.

Now that I love you, now that I recall
All scattered elements of will that swooped
By night as jealous dreams through windows
To circle above the beds like bats,
Or as dawn-birds flew blindly at the panes
In curiosity rattling out their brains –

Now that I love you, as not before,
Now you can be and say, as not before:
The mind clears and the heart true-mirrors you
Where at my side an early watch you keep
And all self-bruising heads loll into sleep.

From WORK IN HAND

(1942)

DAWN BOMBARDMENT*

Guns from the sea open against us:
The smoke rocks bodily in the casemate
And a yell of doom goes up.
We count and bless each new, heavy concussion –
Captives awaiting rescue.

Visiting angel of the wild-fire hair
Who in dream reassured us nightly
Where we lay fettered,
Laugh at us, as we wake – our faces
So tense with hope the tears run down.

THE WORMS OF HISTORY*

On the eighth day God died; his bearded mouth
That had been shut so long flew open.
So Adam's too in a dismay like death –
But the world still rolled on around him,
Instinct with all those lesser powers of life
That God had groaned against but not annulled.

'All-Excellent', Adam had titled God,
And in his mourning now demeaned himself
As if all excellence, not God, had died;
Chose to be governed by those lesser powers,
More than inferior to excellence –
The worms astir in God's corrupt flesh.

God died, not excellence his name:
Excellence lived, but only was not God.
As for those lesser powers who played at God,
Bloated with Adam's deferential sighs
In mourning for expired divinity,
They reigned as royal monsters upon earth.

Adam grew lean, and wore perpetual black;
He made no reaching after excellence.
Eve gave him sorry comfort for his grief
With birth of sons, and mourning still he died.
Adam was buried in one grave with God
And the worms ranged and ravaged in between.

Into their white maws fell abundance
Of all things rotten. They were greedy-nosed
To smell the taint out and go scavenging,
Yet over excellence held no domain.
Excellence lives; they are already dead –
The ages of a putrefying corpse.

A WITHERING HERB*

Ambition in the herb denied his root.
In dreams of the dark he whispered:
'O to be all flower, and to star the sky –
True brother to the moon, that stemless flower
Who long has cherished me!'

Disdained the happy sun of morning,
Held it gross rival to the sovereign moon –
Thus for ambition cast his cloak of leaves
Yet could not snap the stem, to float upward
And from his roots be free:
So withered staunchly.

THE SHOT*

The curious heart plays with its fears:
To hurl a shot through the ship's planks,
Being assured that the green angry flood
Is charmed and dares not dance into the hold –
Nor first to sweep a lingering glance around
For land or shoal or cask adrift.
'So miracles are done; but madmen drown.'

O weary luxury of hypothesis –
For human nature, honest human nature
(Which the fear-pampered heart denies)
Knows its own miracle: not to go mad.
Will pitch the shot in fancy, hint the fact,
Will bore perhaps a meagre auger hole
But stanch the spurting with a tarred rag,
And will not drown, nor even ride the cask.

DREAM OF A CLIMBER*

Watch how this climber raises his own ladder
From earth to heaven, and not in a night
Nor from the secret, stony pillow.
(World patents pending; tested in the shops.)

Here's quality timber, nosings of pure brass,
The perfect phallo-spiritual tilt,
A fuzzy puff of cloud on top –
Excellent lure for angels and archangels!

Come, climber, with your scientific hat
And beady gambler's eye, ascend!
He pauses, poses for his camera-man:
'Well-known Climber About to Ascend.'

But in the published print, we may be sure,
He will appear, not on the lowest rung
But nearly out of view, almost in the cloud,
Leaning aside for an angel to pass,
His muscular broad hands a-glint in the sun,
And crampons on his feet.

LOLLOCKS*

By sloth on sorrow fathered,
These dusty-featured Lollocks
Have their nativity in all disordered
Backs of cupboard drawers.

They play hide and seek
Among collars and novels
And empty medicine bottles,
And letters from abroad
That never will be answered.

Every sultry night
They plague little children,
Gurgling from the cistern,
Humming from the air,
Skewing up the bed-clothes,
Twitching the blind.

When the imbecile agèd
Are over-long in dying
And the nurse drowses,
Lollocks come skipping
Up the tattered stairs
And are nasty together
In the bed's shadow.

The signs of their presence
Are boils on the neck,
Dreams of vexation suddenly recalled
In the middle of the morning,
Languor after food.

Men cannot see them,
Men cannot hear them,
Do not believe in them –
But suffer the more
Both in neck and belly.

Women can see them –
O those naughty wives
Who sit by the fireside
Munching bread and honey,
Watching them in mischief
From corners of their eyes,
Slily allowing them to lick
Honey-sticky fingers.

Sovereign against Lollocks
Are hard broom and soft broom,
To well comb the hair,
To well brush the shoe,
And to pay every debt
As it falls due.

DESPITE AND STILL

Have you not read
The words in my head,
And I made part
Of your own heart?
We have been such as draw
The losing straw –
You of your gentleness,
I of my rashness,
Both of despair –

Yet still might share
This happy will:
To love despite and still.
Never let us deny
The thing's necessity,
But, O, refuse
To choose
Where chance may seem to give
Loves in alternative.

THE SUICIDE IN THE COPSE

The suicide, far from content,
Stared down at his own shattered skull:
Was this what he meant?

Had not his purpose been
To liberate himself from duns and dolts
By a change of scene?

From somewhere came a roll of laughter:
He had looked so on his wedding-day,
And the day after.

There was nowhere at all to go,
And no diversion now but to peruse
What literature the winds might blow

Into the copse where his body lay:
A year-old sheet of sporting news,
A crumpled schoolboy essay.

FRIGHTENED MEN*

We were not ever of their feline race,
Never had hidden claws so sharp as theirs
In any half-remembered incarnation;
Have only the least knowledge of their minds
Through a grace on their part in thinking aloud;
And we remain mouse-quiet when they begin
Suddenly in their unpredictable way
To weave an allegory of their lives,
Making each point by walking round it –
Then off again, as interest is warmed.
What have they said? Or unsaid? What?
We understood the general drift only.

They are punctilious as implacable,
Most neighbourly to those who love them least.
A shout will scare them. When they spring, they seize.
The worst is when they hide from us and change
To something altogether other:
We meet them at the door, as who returns
After a one-hour-seeming century
To a house not his own.

A STRANGER AT THE PARTY

For annoyance, not shame,
   Under their covert stares
She would not give her name
   Nor demand theirs.

Soon everyone at the party,
   Who knew everyone,
Eyed her with plain envy
   For knowing none –

Such neighbourly mistrust
   Breathed across the floor,
Such familiar disgust
   With what they were and wore –

Until, as she was leaving,
   Her time out-stayed,
They tried to say they loved her;
   But pride forbade.

THE OATH*

The doubt and the passion
Falling away from them,
   In that instant both
Take timely courage
From the sky's clearness
   To confirm an oath.

Her loves are his loves,
His trust is her trust;
   Else all were grief
And they, lost ciphers
On a yellowing page,
   Death overleaf.

Rumour of old battle
Growls across the air;
   Then let it growl
With no more terror
Than the creaking stair
   Or the calling owl.

She knows, as he knows,
Of a faithful-always
   And an always-dear
By early emblems
Prognosticated,
   Fulfilled here.

LANGUAGE OF THE SEASONS*

Living among orchards, we are ruled
By the four seasons necessarily:
This from unseasonable frosts we learn
Or from usurping suns and haggard flowers –
Legitimist our disapproval.

Weather we knew, not seasons, in the city
Where, seasonless, orange and orchid shone,
Knew it by heavy overcoat or light,
Framed love in later terminologies
Than here, where we report how weight of snow,
Or weight of fruit, tears branches from the tree.

MID-WINTER WAKING

Stirring suddenly from long hibernation,
I knew myself once more a poet
Guarded by timeless principalities
Against the worm of death, this hillside haunting;
And presently dared open both my eyes.

O gracious, lofty, shone against from under,
Back-of-the-mind-far clouds like towers;
And you, sudden warm airs that blow
Before the expected season of new blossom,
While sheep still gnaw at roots and lambless go –

Be witness that on waking, this mid-winter,
I found her hand in mine laid closely
Who shall watch out the Spring with me.
We stared in silence all around us
But found no winter anywhere to see.

THE ROCK AT THE CORNER*

The quarrymen left ragged
A rock at the corner;
But over it move now
The comforting fingers
Of ivy and briar.

Nor will it need assurance
Of nature's compassion
When presently it weathers
To a noble landmark
Of such countenance

That travellers in winter
Will see it as a creature
On guard at the corner
Where deep snows ingratiate
The comforts of death.

From POEMS 1938-1945

(1945)

THE BEACH

Louder than gulls the little children scream
Whom fathers haul into the jovial foam;
But others fearlessly rush in, breast high,
Laughing the salty water from their mouths –
Heroes of the nursery.

The horny boatman, who has seen whales
And flying fishes, who has sailed as far
As Demerara and the Ivory Coast,
Will warn them, when they crowd to hear his tales,
That every ocean smells alike of tar.

THE VILLAGERS AND DEATH

The Rector's pallid neighbour at The Firs,
Death, did not flurry the parishioners.
Yet from a weight of superstitious fears
Each tried to lengthen his own term of years.
He was congratulated who combined
Toughness of flesh and weakness of the mind
In consequential rosiness of face.
This dull and not ill-mannered populace
Pulled off their caps to Death, as they slouched by,
But rumoured him both atheist and spy.
All vowed to outlast him (though none ever did)
And hear the earth drum on his coffin-lid.
Their groans and whispers down the village street
Soon soured his nature, which was never sweet.

THE DOOR*

When she came suddenly in
It seemed the door could never close again,
Nor even did she close it – she, she –
The room lay open to a visiting sea
Which no door could restrain.

Yet when at last she smiled, tilting her head
To take her leave of me,
Where she had smiled, instead
There was a dark door closing endlessly,
The waves receded.

UNDER THE POT

Sulkily the sticks burn, and though they crackle
  With scorn under the bubbling pot, or spout
Magnanimous jets of flame against the smoke,
  At each heel end a dirty sap breaks out.

Confess, creatures, how sulkily ourselves
  We hiss with doom, fuel of a sodden age –
Not rapt up roaring to the chimney stack
  On incandescent clouds of spirit or rage.

THROUGH NIGHTMARE

Never be disenchanted of
That place you sometimes dream yourself into,
Lying at large remove beyond all dream,
Or those you find there, though but seldom
In their company seated –

The untameable, the live, the gentle.
Have you not known them? Whom? They carry
Time looped so river-wise about their house
There's no way in by history's road
To name or number them.

In your sleepy eyes I read the journey
Of which disjointedly you tell; which stirs
My loving admiration, that you should travel
Through nightmare to a lost and moated land,
Who are timorous by nature.

TO LUCIA AT BIRTH*

Though the moon beaming matronly and bland
   Greets you, among the crowd of the new-born,
With 'welcome to the world' yet understand
   That still her pale, lascivious unicorn
And bloody lion are loose on either hand:
   With din of bones and tantarará of horn
Their fanciful cortège parades the land –
   Pest on the high road, wild-fire in the corn.

Outrageous company to be born into,
   Lunatics of a royal age long dead.
Then reckon time by what you are or do,
   Not by the epochs of the war they spread.
   Hark how they roar; but never turn your head.
Nothing will change them, let them not change you.

DEATH BY DRUMS*

If I cried out in anger against music,
  It was not that I cried
Against the wholesome bitter arsenic
  Necessary for suicide:
For suicide in the drums' racking riot
  Where horned moriscoes wailing to their bride
Scare every Lydian songster from the spot.

SHE TELLS HER LOVE WHILE HALF ASLEEP*

She tells her love while half asleep,
  In the dark hours,
    With half-words whispered low:
As Earth stirs in her winter sleep
  And puts out grass and flowers
    Despite the snow,
    Despite the falling snow.

INSTRUCTIONS TO THE ORPHIC ADEPT*

[In part translated from the *Timpone Grande* and *Campagno* Orphic tablets.]

So soon as ever your mazed spirit descends
From daylight into darkness, Man, remember
What you have suffered here in Samothrace,
What you have suffered.

After your passage through Hell's seven floods,
Whose fumes of sulphur will have parched your throat,
The Halls of Judgement shall loom up before you,
A miracle of jasper and of onyx.
To the left hand there bubbles a black spring
Overshadowed with a great white cypress.
Avoid this spring, which is Forgetfulness;
Though all the common rout rush down to drink,
Avoid this spring!

To the right hand there lies a secret pool
Alive with speckled trout and fish of gold;
A hazel overshadows it. Ophion,
Primaeval serpent straggling in the branches,
Darts out his tongue. This holy pool is fed
By dripping water; guardians stand before it.
Run to this pool, the pool of Memory,
Run to this pool!

Then will the guardians scrutinize you, saying:
'Who are you, who? What have you to remember?
Do you not fear Ophion's flickering tongue?
Go rather to the spring beneath the cypress,
Flee from this pool!'

Then you shall answer: 'I am parched with thirst.
Give me to drink. I am a child of Earth,
But of Sky also, come from Samothrace.
Witness the glint of amber on my brow.
Out of the Pure I come, as you may see.
I also am of your thrice-blessèd kin,
Child of the three-fold Queen of Samothrace;
Have made full quittance for my deeds of blood,
Have been by her invested in sea-purple,
And like a kid have fallen into milk.
Give me to drink, now I am parched with thirst,
Give me to drink!'

But they will ask you yet: 'What of your feet?'
You shall reply: 'My feet have borne me here
Out of the weary wheel, the circling years,
To that still, spokeless wheel: – Persephone.
Give me to drink!'

Then they will welcome you with fruit and flowers,
And lead you toward the ancient dripping hazel,
Crying: 'Brother of our immortal blood,
Drink and remember glorious Samothrace!'
Then you shall drink.

You shall drink deep of that refreshing draught,
To become lords of the uninitiated
Twittering ghosts, Hell's countless populace –
To become heroes, knights upon swift horses,
Pronouncing oracles from tall white tombs
By the nymphs tended. They with honey water
Shall pour libations to your serpent shapes,
That you may drink.

THESEUS AND ARIADNE*

High on his figured couch beyond the waves
He dreams, in dream recalling her set walk
Down paths of oyster-shell bordered with flowers,
Across the shadowy turf below the vines.
He sighs: 'Deep sunk in my erroneous past
She haunts the ruins and the ravaged lawns.'

Yet still unharmed it stands, the regal house
Crooked with age and overtopped by pines
Where first he wearied of her constancy.
And with a surer foot she goes than when
Dread of his hate was thunder in the air,
When the pines agonized with flaws of wind
And flowers glared up at her with frantic eyes.
Of him, now all is done, she never dreams
But calls a living blessing down upon
What he supposes rubble and rank grass;
Playing the queen to nobler company.

LAMENT FOR PASIPHAË*

Dying sun, shine warm a little longer!
My eye, dazzled with tears, shall dazzle yours,
Conjuring you to shine and not to move.
You, sun, and I all afternoon have laboured
Beneath a dewless and oppressive cloud –
A fleece now gilded with our common grief
That this must be a night without a moon.
Dying sun, shine warm a little longer!

Faithless she was not: she was very woman,
Smiling with dire impartiality,
Sovereign, with heart unmatched, adored of men,
Until Spring's cuckoo with bedraggled plumes
Tempted her pity and her truth betrayed.
Then she who shone for all resigned her being,
And this must be a night without a moon.
Dying sun, shine warm a little longer!

THE TWELVE DAYS OF CHRISTMAS*

The impassioned child who stole the axe of power,
Debauched his virgin mother
And vowed in rage he would be God the Father,

Who, grown to strength, strangled her lion twins
And from a cloud, in chains,
Hung her with anvils at her ankle bones,

Who whipped her daughters with a bull's pizzle,
Forced them to take the veil
And heard their loveless prayers with a lewd smile –

Senile at last the way of all flesh goes:
Into the kitchen where roast goose,
Plum-pudding and mince-pies his red robes grease.

She from the tree-top, true to her deserts,
With wand and silver skirts
Presides unravished over all pure hearts.

COLD WEATHER PROVERB*

Fearless approach and puffed feather
In birds, famine bespeak;
In man, belly filled full.

TO JUAN AT THE WINTER SOLSTICE*

There is one story and one story only
That will prove worth your telling,
Whether as learned bard or gifted child;
To it all lines or lesser gauds belong
That startle with their shining
Such common stories as they stray into.

Is it of trees you tell, their months and virtues,
Or strange beasts that beset you,
Of birds that croak at you the Triple will?
Or of the Zodiac and how slow it turns
Below the Boreal Crown,
Prison of all true kings that ever reigned?

Water to water, ark again to ark,
From woman back to woman:
So each new victim treads unfalteringly
The never altered circuit of his fate,
Bringing twelve peers as witness
Both to his starry rise and starry fall.

Or is it of the Virgin's silver beauty,
All fish below the thighs?
She in her left hand bears a leafy quince;
When with her right she crooks a finger, smiling,
How may the King hold back?
Royally then he barters life for love.

Or of the undying snake from chaos hatched,
Whose coils contain the ocean,
Into whose chops with naked sword he springs,
Then in black water, tangled by the reeds,
Battles three days and nights,
To be spewed up beside her scalloped shore?

Much snow is falling, winds roar hollowly,
The owl hoots from the elder,
Fear in your heart cries to the loving-cup:
Sorrow to sorrow as the sparks fly upward.
The log groans and confesses:
There is one story and one story only.

Dwell on her graciousness, dwell on her smiling,
Do not forget what flowers
The great boar trampled down in ivy time.
Her brow was creamy as the crested wave,
Her sea-grey eyes were wild
But nothing promised that is not performed.

SATIRES AND GROTESQUES

THE PERSIAN VERSION

Truth-loving Persians do not dwell upon
The trivial skirmish fought near Marathon.
As for the Greek theatrical tradition
Which represents that summer's expedition
Not as a mere reconnaissance in force

By three brigades of foot and one of horse
(Their left flank covered by some obsolete
Light craft detached from the main Persian fleet)
But as a grandiose, ill-starred attempt
To conquer Greece – they treat it with contempt;
And only incidentally refute
Major Greek claims, by stressing what repute
The Persian monarch and the Persian nation
Won by this salutary demonstration:
Despite a strong defence and adverse weather
All arms combined magnificently together.

THE WEATHER OF OLYMPUS*

Zeus was once overheard to shout at Hera:
  'You hate it, do you? Well, I hate it worse –
East wind in May, sirocco all the Summer.
  Hell take this whole impossible Universe!'

A scholiast explains his warm rejoinder,
  Which sounds too man-like for Olympic use,
By noting that the snake-tailed Chthonian winds
  Were answerable to Fate alone, not Zeus.

APOLLO OF THE PHYSIOLOGISTS

Despite this learned cult's official
And seemingly sincere denial
That they either reject or postulate
God, or God's scientific surrogate,
Prints of a deity occur *passim*
Throughout their extant literature. They make him
A dumb, dead-pan Apollo with a profile
Drawn in Victorian-Hellenistic style –
The pallid, bald, partitioned head suggesting
Wholly abstract cerebral functioning;
Or nude and at full length, this deity

Displays digestive, venous, respiratory
And nervous systems painted in bold colour
On his immaculate exterior.
Sometimes, *in verso*, a bald, naked Muse,
His consort, flaunts her arteries and sinews,
While, upside-down, crouched in her chaste abdomen,
Adored by men and wondered at by women,
Hangs a Victorian-Hellenistic foetus –
Fruit of her academic god's afflatus.

THE OLDEST SOLDIER

The sun shines warm on seven old soldiers
   Paraded in a row,
Perched like starlings on the railings –
   Give them plug-tobacco!

They'll croon you the Oldest-Soldier Song:
   Of Harry who took a holiday
From the sweat of ever thinking for himself
   Or going his own bloody way.

It was arms-drill, guard and kit-inspection,
   Like dreams of a long train-journey,
And the barrack-bed that Harry dossed on
   Went rockabye, rockabye, rockabye.

Harry kept his rifle and brasses clean,
   But Jesus Christ, what a liar!
He won the Military Medal
   For his coolness under fire.

He was never the last on parade
   Nor the first to volunteer,
And when Harry rose to be storeman
   He seldom had to pay for his beer.

Twenty-one years, and out Harry came
   To be odd-job man, or janitor,
Or commissionaire at a picture-house,
   Or, some say, bully to a whore.

But his King and Country calling Harry,
   He reported again at the Depôt,
To perch on this railing like a starling,
   The oldest soldier of the row.

GROTESQUES*

I

My Chinese uncle, gouty, deaf, half-blinded,
And more than a trifle absent-minded,
Astonished all St James's Square one day
By giving long and unexceptionably exact directions
To a little coolie girl, who'd lost her way.

II

The Lion-faced Boy at the Fair
And the Heir Apparent
Were equally slow at remembering people's faces.
But whenever they met, incognito, in the Brazilian
Pavilion, the Row and such-like places,
They exchanged, it is said, their sternest nods –
Like gods of dissimilar races.

III

Dr Newman with the crooked pince-nez
Had studied in Vienna and Chicago.
Chess was his only relaxation.
And Dr Newman remained unperturbed
By every nastier manifestation
Of pluto-democratic civilization:
All that was cranky, corny, ill-behaved,

Unnecessary, askew or orgiastic
Would creep unbidden to his side-door (hidden
Behind a poster in the Tube Station,
Nearly half-way up the moving stairs),
Push its way in, to squat there undisturbed
Among box-files and tubular steel-chairs.

He was once seen at the Philharmonic Hall
Noting the reactions of two patients,
With pronounced paranoiac tendencies,
To old Dutch music. He appeared to recall
A tin of lozenges in his breast-pocket,
Put his hand confidently in –
And drew out a black imp, or sooterkin,
Six inches long, with one ear upside-down,
Licking at a vanilla ice-cream cornet –
Then put it back again with a slight frown.

IV

A Royal Duke, with no campaigning medals
To dignify his Orders, he would speak
Nostalgically at times of Mozambique
Where once the ship he cruised in ran aground:
How he drank cocoa, from a sailor's mug,
Poured from the common jug,
While loyal toasts went round.

V

Sir John addressed the Snake-god in his temple,
Which was full of bats, not as a votary
But with the somewhat cynical courtesy,
Just short of condescension,
He might have paid the Governor-General
Of a small, hot, backward colony.
He was well versed in primitive religion,
But found this an embarrassing occasion:
The God was immense, noisy and affable,
Began to tickle him with a nervous chuckle,
Unfobbed a great gold clock for him to listen,
Hissed like a snake, and swallowed him at one mouthful.

VI

All horses on the racecourse of Tralee
Have four more legs in gallop than in trot –
Two pairs fully extended, two pairs not;
And yet no thoroughbred with either three
Or five legs but is mercilessly shot.
I watched a filly gnaw her fifth leg free,
Warned by a speaking mare since turned silentiary.

THE EUGENIST*

Come, human dogs, interfertilitate –
Blackfellow and white lord, brown, yellow and red!
Accept the challenge of the lately bred
Newfoundland terrier with the dachshund gait.[1]

Breed me gigantic pygmies, meek-eyed Scots,
Phlegmatic Irish, perfume-hating Poles,
Poker-faced, toothy, pigtailed Hottentots,
And Germans with no envy in their souls.

[1] *See:* Charles R. Stockard and collaborators: *The genetic and endocrinic basis for differences in form and behaviour, as elucidated by studies of contrasted pure-line dogbreeds and their hybrids.* (Philadelphia, 1941.)

1805*

At Viscount Nelson's lavish funeral,
While the mob milled and yelled about St Paul's,
A General chatted with an Admiral:

'One of your Colleagues, Sir, remarked today
That Nelson's *exit*, though to be lamented,
Falls not inopportunely, in its way.'

'He was a thorn in our flesh,' came the reply –
'The most bird-witted, unaccountable,
Odd little runt that ever I did spy.

'One arm, one peeper, vain as Pretty Poll,
  A meddler, too, in foreign politics
And gave his heart in pawn to a plain moll.

'He would dare lecture us Sea Lords, and then
  Would treat his ratings as though men of honour
And play at leap-frog with his midshipmen!

'We tried to box him down, but up he popped,
  And when he'd banged Napoleon at the Nile
Became too much the hero to be dropped.

'You've heard that Copenhagen "blind eye" story?
  We'd tied him to Nurse Parker's apron-strings –
By G–d, he snipped them through and snatched the glory!'

'Yet,' cried the General, 'six-and-twenty sail
  Captured or sunk by him off Tráfalgár –
That writes a handsome *finis* to the tale.'

'Handsome enough. The seas are England's now.
  That fellow's foibles need no longer plague us.
He died most creditably, I'll allow.'

'And, Sir, the secret of his victories?'
  'By his unServicelike, familiar ways, Sir,
He made the whole Fleet love him, damn his eyes!'

AT THE SAVOY CHAPEL

[From *World's Press News*, 22 February, 1945. 'Alexander Clifford, the war correspondent, is today marrying Flight Officer Jenny Nicholson, daughter of Robert Graves. They met in the front line.']

Up to the wedding, formal with heirloom lace,
Press-cameras, carnations out of season,
Well-mellowed priest and well-trained choristers,

The relatives come marching, such as meet
Only at weddings and at funerals,
The elder generation with the eldest.

Family features for years undecided
What look to wear against a loveless world
Fix, as the wind veers, in the same grimace.

Each eyes the others with a furtive pity:
'Heavens, how she has aged – and he,
Grey hair and sunken cheeks, what a changed man!'

They stare wistfully at the bride (released
From brass buttons and the absurd salute)
In long white gown, bouquet and woman's pride.

'How suitable!' they whisper, and the whisper
'How suitable!' rustles from pew to pew;
To which I nod suitably grave assent.

Now for you, loving ones, who kneel at the altar
And preside afterwards at table –
The trophy sword that shears the cake recalling

What god you entertained last year together,
His bull neck looped with guts,
Trampling corpse-carpet through the villages –

Here is my private blessing: so to remain
As today you are, with features
Resolute and unchangeably your own.

From COLLECTED POEMS (1914-1947)

(1948)

TO POETS UNDER PISCES*

Until the passing years establish
Aquarius who with fruitful spate
All dried pools will at last replenish,
Resign yourselves to celebrate,
Poets, with grief or hate,
These gasping rainbowed flurries of the Fish.

JUNE*

June, the jolly season of most bloodshed:
Soldiers with roses in their rifle barrels
And children, cherries bobbing at their ears,
Who roar them on like furious adjutants
Where the broad oak its feathered bonnet rears.

THE LAST DAY OF LEAVE*

(1916)

We five looked out over the moor
At rough hills blurred with haze, and a still sea:
Our tragic day, bountiful from the first.

We would spend it by the lily lake
(High in a fold beyond the farthest ridge),
Following the cart-track till it faded out.

The time of berries and bell-heather;
Yet all that morning nobody went by
But shepherds and one old man carting turfs.

We were in love: he with her, she with him,
And I, the youngest one, the odd man out,
As deep in love with a yet nameless muse.

No cloud; larks and heath-butterflies,
And herons undisturbed fishing the streams;
A slow cool breeze that hardly stirred the grass.

When we hurried down the rocky slope,
A flock of ewes galloping off in terror,
There shone the waterlilies, yellow and white.

Deep water and a shelving bank.
Off went our clothes and in we went, all five,
Diving like trout between the lily groves.

The basket had been nobly filled:
Wine and fresh rolls, chicken and pineapple –
Our braggadocio under threat of war.

The fire on which we boiled our kettle
We fed with ling and rotten blackthorn root;
And the coffee tasted memorably of peat.

Two of us might stray off together
But never less than three kept by the fire,
Focus of our uncertain destinies.

We spoke little, our minds in tune –
A sigh or laugh would settle any theme;
The sun so hot it made the rocks quiver.

But when it rolled down level with us,
Four pairs of eyes sought mine as if appealing
For a blind-fate-aversive afterword: –

'Do you remember the lily lake?
We were all there, all five of us in love,
Not one yet killed, widowed or broken-hearted.'

TO BE CALLED A BEAR*

Bears gash the forest trees
  To mark the bounds
  Of their own hunting grounds;
They follow the wild bees
  Point by point home
  For love of honeycomb;
They browse on blueberries.

Then should I stare
If I am called a bear,
And it is not the truth?
Unkempt and surly with a sweet tooth
I tilt my muzzle toward the starry hub
Where Queen Callisto guards her cub;

But envy those that here
  All winter breathing slow
  Sleep warm under the snow,
That yawn awake when the skies clear,
  And lank with longing grow
No more than one brief month a year.

A CIVIL SERVANT*

While in this cavernous place employed
  Not once was I aware
Of my officious other-self
  Poised high above me there,

My self reversed, my rage-less part,
  A slimy yellowish cone –
Drip, drip; drip, drip – so down the years
  I stalagmized in stone.

Now pilgrims to the cave, who come
  To chip off what they can,
Prod me with child-like merriment:
  'Look, look! It's like a man!'

GULLS AND MEN*

The naturalists of the Bass Rock
  On this vexatious point agree:
That sea-birds of all sorts that flock
  About the Bass, repeatedly
    Collide in mid-flight,

And neither by design, in play,
  Nor by design, in shrewd assault,
But (as these patient watchers say,
  Eyes that are seldom proved at fault)
    By lack of foresight.

Stupidity, which poor and rich
  Hold the recognizance of man,
Precious stupidity, of which
  Let him denude himself who can
    And stand at God's height –

Stupidity that brings to birth
  More, always more, than to the grave,
The burden of all songs on earth,
  And by which men are brave
    And women contrite –

This jewel bandied from a cliff
  By gulls and razor-bills and such!
Where is man's vindication if
  Perfectibility's as much
    Bird-right as man-right?

MAGICAL POEMS

THE ALLANSFORD PURSUIT*

[As danced by North-country witches at their Sabbaths. A restoration of the fragmentary seventeenth-century text.]

Cunning and art he did not lack
But aye her whistle would fetch him back.

O, I shall go into a hare
With sorrow and sighing and mickle care,
And I shall go in the Devil's name
Aye, till I be fetchèd hame.
    – Hare, take heed of a bitch greyhound
    Will harry thee all these fells around,
    For here come I in Our Lady's name
    All but for to fetch thee hame.

Cunning and art, etc.

Yet I shall go into a trout
With sorrow and sighing and mickle doubt,
And show thee many a crooked game
Ere that I be fetchèd hame.
    – Trout, take heed of an otter lank
    Will harry thee close from bank to bank,
    For here come I in Our Lady's name
    All but for to fetch thee hame.

Cunning and art, etc.

Yet I shall go into a bee
With mickle horror and dread of thee,
And flit to hive in the Devil's name
Ere that I be fetchèd hame.
    – Bee, take heed of a swallow hen
    Will harry thee close, both butt and ben,
    For here come I in Our Lady's name
    All but for to fetch thee hame.

Cunning and art, etc.

Yet I shall go into a mouse
And haste me unto the miller's house,
There in his corn to have good game
Ere that I be fetchèd hame.
  – Mouse, take heed of a white tib-cat
  That never was baulked of mouse or rat,
  For I'll crack thy bones in Our Lady's name:
  Thus shalt thou be fetchèd hame.

Cunning and art, etc.

AMERGIN'S CHARM*

[The text restored from mediaeval Irish and Welsh variants.]

I am a stag: *of seven tines,*
I am a flood: *across a plain,*
I am a wind: *on a deep lake,*
I am a tear: *the Sun lets fall,*
I am a hawk: *above the cliff,*
I am a thorn: *beneath the nail,*
I am a wonder: *among flowers,*
I am a wizard: *who but I*
Sets the cool head aflame with smoke?

I am a spear: *that roars for blood,*
I am a salmon: *in a pool,*
I am a lure: *from paradise,*
I am a hill: *where poets walk,*
I am a boar: *renowned and red,*
I am a breaker: *threatening doom,*
I am a tide: *that drags to death,*
I am an infant: *who but I*
Peeps from the unhewn dolmen arch?

I am the womb: *of every holt,*
I am the blaze: *on every hill,*
I am the queen: *of every hive,*
I am the shield: *for every head,*
I am the grave: *of every hope.*

THE SIRENS' WELCOME TO CRONOS*

Cronos the Ruddy, steer your boat
Toward Silver Island whence we sing;
Here you shall pass your days.

Through a thick-growing alder-wood
We clearly see, but are not seen,
Hid in a golden haze.

Our hair the hue of barley sheaf,
Our eyes the hue of blackbird's egg,
Our cheeks like asphodel.

Here the wild apple blossoms yet;
Wrens in the silver branches play
And prophesy you well.

Here nothing ill or harsh is found.
Cronos the Ruddy, steer your boat
Across these placid straits,

With each of us in turn to lie
Taking your pleasure on young grass
That for your coming waits.

No grief nor gloom, sickness nor death,
Disturbs our long tranquillity;
No treachery, no greed.

Compared with this, what are the plains
Of Elis, where you ruled as king?
A wilderness indeed.

A starry crown awaits your head,
A hero feast is spread for you:
Swineflesh, milk and mead.

DICHETAL DO CHENNAIB*

'Today it is by the finger ends that the poet effects the *Dichetal do chennaib*, and this is the way he does it. When he sees the required person or object before him he at once makes a poem with his finger tips, or in his mind without reflexion, composing and repeating simultaneously.'

(Mediaeval Irish scholiast on the *Senchus Mor*.)

Tree powers, finger tips,
First pentad of the four,
Discover all your poet asks
Drumming on his brow.

Birch-peg, throbbing thumb,
By power of divination,
Birch, bring him news of love;
Loud knocks the heart.

Rowan-rod, forefinger,
By power of divination,
Unriddle him a riddle;
The key's cast away.

Ash, middle finger,
By power of divination
Weather-wise, fool otherwise,
Mete him out the winds.

Alder, physic finger,
By power of divination
Diagnose all maladies
Of a doubtful mind.

Willow-wand, earfinger,
By power of divination
Force confessions from the mouth
Of a mouldering corpse.

Finger-ends, five twigs,
Trees, true-divining trees,
Discover all your poet asks
Drumming on his brow.

THE BATTLE OF THE TREES*

[Text reassembled and restored from the deliberately confused mediaeval Welsh poem-medley, *Câd Goddeu*, in the *Red Book of Hergest*, hitherto regarded as nonsensical.]

The tops of the beech tree
Have sprouted of late,
Are changed and renewed
From their withered state.

When the beech prospers,
Though spells and litanies
The oak tops entangle,
There is hope for trees.

I have plundered the fern,
Through all secrets I spy,
Old Math ap Mathonwy
Knew no more than I.

With nine sorts of faculty
God has gifted me:
I am fruit of fruits gathered
From nine sorts of tree –

Plum, quince, whortle, mulberry,
Raspberry, pear,
Black cherry and white
With the sorb in me share.

From my seat at Fefynedd,
A city that is strong,
I watched the trees and green things
Hastening along.

Retreating from happiness
They would fain be set
In forms of the chief letters
Of the alphabet.

Wayfarers wondered,
  Warriors were dismayed
At renewal of conflicts
  Such as Gwydion made,

Under the tongue root
  A fight most dread,
And another raging
  Behind, in the head.

The alders in the front line
  Began the affray.
Willow and rowan-tree
  Were tardy in array.

The holly, dark green,
  Made a resolute stand;
He is armed with many spear points
  Wounding the hand.

With foot-beat of the swift oak
  Heaven and earth rung;
'Stout Guardian of the Door',
  His name in every tongue.

Great was the gorse in battle,
  And the ivy at his prime;
The hazel was arbiter
  At this charmed time.

Uncouth and savage was the fir,
  Cruel the ash-tree –
Turns not aside a foot-breadth,
  Straight at the heart runs he.

The birch, though very noble,
  Armed himself but late:
A sign not of cowardice
  But of high estate.

The heath gave consolation
  To the toil-spent folk,
The long-enduring poplars
  In battle much broke.

Some of them were cast away
  On the field of fight
Because of holes torn in them
  By the enemy's might.

Very wrathful was the vine
  Whose henchmen are the elms;
I exalt him mightily
  To rulers of realms.

Strong chieftains were the blackthorn
  With his ill fruit,
The unbeloved whitethorn
  Who wears the same suit,

The swift-pursuing reed,
  The broom with his brood,
And the furze but ill-behaved
  Until he is subdued.

The dower-scattering yew
  Stood glum at the fight's fringe,
With the elder slow to burn
  Amid fires that singe,

And the blessed wild apple
  Laughing in pride
From the *Gorchan* of Maelderw
  By the rock side.

In shelter linger
  Privet and woodbine,
Inexperienced in warfare,
  And the courtly pine.

But I, although slighted
   Because I was not big,
Fought, trees, in your array
   On the field of Goddeu Brig.

THE SONG OF BLODEUWEDD*

[Text reassembled and restored from the same poem-medley as the foregoing.]

Not of father nor of mother
Was my blood, was my body.
I was spellbound by Gwydion,
Prime enchanter of the Britons,
When he formed me from nine blossoms,
   Nine buds of various kind:
From primrose of the mountain,
Broom, meadow-sweet and cockle,
   Together intertwined,
From the bean in its shade bearing
A white spectral army
   Of earth, of earthy kind,
From blossoms of the nettle,
Oak, thorn and bashful chestnut –
Nine powers of nine flowers,
   Nine powers in me combined,
      Nine buds of plant and tree.
Long and white are my fingers
      As the ninth wave of the sea.

INTERCESSION IN LATE OCTOBER*

How hard the year dies: no frost yet.
On drifts of yellow sand Midas reclines,
Fearless of moaning reed or sullen wave.
Firm and fragrant still the brambleberries.
On ivy-bloom butterflies wag.

Spare him a little longer, Crone,
For his clean hands and love-submissive heart.

THE TETRAGRAMMATON*

[A magical gloss on Numbers vi, 23-27.]

Light was his first day of Creation,
Peace after labour was his seventh day,
Life and the Glory are his day of days.

He carved his law on tables of sapphirus,
Jerusalem shines with his pyrope gates,
Four cherubs fetch him amber from the north.

Acacia yields her timber for his ark,
Pomegranate sanctifies his priestly hem,
His hyssop sprinkles blood at every door.

Holy, Holy, Holy, is his name.

NUNS AND FISH*

Circling the circlings of their fish
  Nuns walk in white and pray;
  For he is chaste as they,
  Who was dark-faced and hot in Silvia's day,
And in his pool drowns each unspoken wish.

THE DESTROYER*

Swordsman of the narrow lips,
Narrow hips and murderous mind
Fenced with chariots and ships,
By your joculators hailed
The mailed wonder of mankind,
Far to westward you have sailed.

You it was dared seize the throne
Of a blown and amorous prince
Destined to the Moon alone,
A lame, golden-heeled decoy,
Joy of hens that gape and wince
Inarticulately coy.

You who, capped with lunar gold
Like an old and savage dunce,
Let the central hearth go cold,
Grinned, and left us here your sword
Warden of sick fields that once
Sprouted of their own accord.

Gusts of laughter the Moon stir
That her Bassarids now bed
With the ignoble usurer
While an ignorant pale priest
Rides the beast with a man's head
To her long-omitted feast.

RETURN OF THE GODDESS*

Under your Milky Way
   And slow-revolving Bear
Frogs from the alder thicket pray
In terror of your judgement day,
   Loud with repentance there.

The log they crowned as king
  Grew sodden, lurched and sank;
An owl floats by on silent wing,
Dark water bubbles from the spring;
  They invoke you from each bank.

At dawn you shall appear,
  A gaunt red-leggèd crane,
You whom they know too well for fear,
Lunging your beak down like a spear
  To fetch them home again.

Sufficiunt
Tecum,
Caryatis,
Domnia
Quina.

From POEMS AND SATIRES 1951

(1951)

THE WHITE GODDESS*

All saints revile her, and all sober men
Ruled by the God Apollo's golden mean –
In scorn of which we sailed to find her
In distant regions likeliest to hold her
Whom we desired above all things to know,
Sister of the mirage and echo.

It was a virtue not to stay,
To go our headstrong and heroic way
Seeking her out at the volcano's head,
Among pack ice, or where the track had faded
Beyond the cavern of the seven sleepers:
Whose broad high brow was white as any leper's,
Whose eyes were blue, with rowan-berry lips,
With hair curled honey-coloured to white hips.

Green sap of Spring in the young wood a-stir
Will celebrate the Mountain Mother,
And every song-bird shout awhile for her;
But we are gifted, even in November
Rawest of seasons, with so huge a sense
Of her nakedly worn magnificence
We forget cruelty and past betrayal,
Heedless of where the next bright bolt may fall.

THE CHINK*

A sunbeam on the well-waxed oak,
  In shape resembling not at all
The ragged chink by which it broke
  Into this darkened hall,
Swims round and golden over me,
The sun's plenipotentiary.

So may my round love a chink find:
  With such address to break
Into your grief-occluded mind
  As you shall not mistake
  But, rising, open to me for truth's sake.

COUNTING THE BEATS

You, love, and I,
(He whispers) you and I,
And if no more than only you and I
What care you or I?

Counting the beats,
Counting the slow heart beats,
The bleeding to death of time in slow heart beats,
Wakeful they lie.

Cloudless day,
Night, and a cloudless day,
Yet the huge storm will burst upon their heads one day
From a bitter sky.

Where shall we be,
(She whispers) where shall we be,
When death strikes home, O where then shall we be
Who were you and I?

Not there but here,
(He whispers) only here,
As we are, here, together, now and here,
Always you and I.

Counting the beats,
Counting the slow heart beats,
The bleeding to death of time in slow heart beats,
Wakeful they lie.

THE JACKALS' ADDRESS TO ISIS*

Grant Anup's children this:
To howl with you, Queen Isis,
Over the scattered limbs of wronged Osiris.
What harder fate than to be woman?
She makes and she unmakes her man.
In Jackal-land it is no secret
Who tempted red-haired, ass-eared Set
To such bloody extreme; who most
Must therefore mourn and fret
To pacify the unquiet ghost.
And when Horus your son
Avenges this divulsion,
Sceptre in fist, sandals on feet,
We shall return across the sand
From loyal Jackal-land
To gorge five nights and days on ass's meat.

THE DEATH ROOM*

Look forward, truant, to your second childhood.
The crystal sphere discloses
Wall-paper roses mazily repeated
In pink and bronze, their bunches harbouring
Elusive faces, under an inconclusive
Circling, spidery, ceiling craquelure,
And, by the window-frame, the well-loathed, lame,
Damp-patch, cross-patch, sleepless L-for-Lemur
Who, puffed to giant size,
Waits jealously till children close their eyes.

THE YOUNG CORDWAINER*

She: Love, why have you led me here
To this lampless hall,
A place of despair and fear
Where blind things crawl?

He: Not I, but your complaint
Heard by the riverside
That primrose scent grew faint
And desire died.

She: Kisses had lost virtue
As yourself must know;
I declared what, alas, was true
And still shall do so.

He: Mount, sweetheart, this main stair
Where bandogs at the foot
Their crooked gilt teeth bare
Between jaws of soot.

She: I loathe them, how they stand
Like prick-eared spies.
Hold me fast by the left hand;
I walk with closed eyes.

He: Primrose has periwinkle
As her mortal fellow:
Five leaves, blue and baleful,
Five of true yellow.

She: Overhead, what's overhead?
Where would you take me?
My feet stumble for dread,
My wits forsake me.

He: Flight on flight, floor above floor,
In suspense of doom
To a locked secret door
And a white-walled room.

She: Love, have you the pass-word,
  Or have you the key,
With a sharp naked sword
  And wine to revive me?

He: Enter: here is starlight,
  Here the state bed
Where your man lies all night
  With blue flowers garlanded.

She: Ah, the cool open window
  Of this confessional!
With wine at my elbow,
And sword beneath the pillow,
  I shall perfect all.

YOUR PRIVATE WAY*

Whether it was your way of walking
Or of laughing moved me,
At sight of you a song wavered
Ghostly on my lips; I could not voice it,
Uncertain what the notes or key.

Be thankful I am no musician,
Sweet Anonymity, to madden you
With your own private walking-laughing way
Imitated on a beggar's fiddle
Or blared across the square on All Fools' Day.

MY NAME AND I*

The impartial Law enrolled a name
  For my especial use:
My rights in it would rest the same
Whether I puffed it into fame
  Or sank it in abuse.

Robert was what my parents guessed
   When first they peered at me,
And *Graves* an honourable bequest
With Georgian silver and the rest
   From my male ancestry.

They taught me: 'You are *Robert Graves*
   (Which you must learn to spell),
But see that *Robert Graves* behaves,
Whether with honest men or knaves,
   Exemplarily well.'

Then though my I was always I,
   Illegal and unknown,
With nothing to arrest it by –
As will be obvious when I die
   And *Robert Graves* lives on –

I cannot well repudiate
   This noun, this natal star,
This gentlemanly self, this mate
So kindly forced on me by fate,
   Time and the registrar;

And therefore hurry him ahead
   As an ambassador
To fetch me home my beer and bread
Or commandeer the best green bed,
   As he has done before.

Yet, understand, I am not he
   Either in mind or limb;
My name will take less thought for me,
In worlds of men I cannot see,
   Than ever I for him.

CONVERSATION PIECE

By moonlight
At midnight,
Under the vines,
A hotel chair
Settles down moodily before the headlines
Of a still-folded evening newspaper.

The other chair
Of the pair
Lies on its back,
Stiff as in pain,
Having been overturned with an angry crack;
And there till morning, alas, it must remain.

On the terrace
No blood-trace,
No sorry glitter
Of a knife, nothing:
Not even the fine-torn fragments of a letter
Or the dull gleam of a flung-off wedding-ring.

Still stable
On the table
Two long-stemmed glasses,
One full of drink,
Watch how the rat among the vines passes
And how the moon trembles on the crag's brink.

THE GHOST AND THE CLOCK

About midnight my heart began
        To trip again and knock.
The tattered ghost of a tall man
Looked fierce at me as in he ran,
        But fiercer at the clock.

It was, he swore, a long, long while
Until he'd had the luck
To die and make his domicile
On some ungeographic isle
Where no hour ever struck.

'But now, you worst of clocks,' said he,
'Delayer of all love,
In vengeance I've recrossed the sea
To jerk at your machinery
And give your hands a shove.'

So impotently he groped and peered
That his whole body shook!
I could not laugh at him; I feared
This was no ghost but my own weird,
And closer dared not look.

ADVICE ON MAY DAY

Never sing the same song twice
Lest she disbelieve it.
Though reproved as over-nice,
Never sing the same song twice –
Unobjectionable advice,
Would you but receive it:
Never sing the same song twice
Lest she disbelieve it.

Never sing a song clean through,
You might disenchant her;
Venture on a verse or two
(Indisposed to sing it through),
Let that seem as much as you
Care, or dare, to grant her;
Never sing your song clean through,
You might disenchant her.

Make no sermon on your song
  Lest she turn and rend you.
Fools alone deliver long
Sermons on a May-day song;
Even a smile may put you wrong,
  Half a word may end you:
Make no sermon on your song
  Lest she turn and rend you.

FOR THE RAIN IT RAINETH EVERY DAY

Arabs complain – or so I have been told –
  Interminably of heat, as Lapps complain
Even of seasonable Christmas cold;
  Nor are the English yet inured to rain
Which still, my angry William, as of old
  Streaks without pause your birthday window pane.
    But you are English too;
    How can I comfort you?

Suppose I said: 'Those gales that eastward ride
  (Their wrath portended by a sinking glass)
With good St George of England are allied'?
  Suppose I said: 'They freshen the Spring grass,
Arab or Lapp would envy a fireside
  Where such green-fingered elementals pass'?
    No, you are English too;
    How could that comfort you?

QUESTIONS IN A WOOD

The parson to his pallid spouse,
  The hangman to his whore,
Do both not mumble the same vows,
  Both knock at the same door?

And when the fury of their knocks
  Has waned, and that was that,
What answer comes, unless the pox
  Or one more parson's brat?

Tell me, my love, my flower of flowers,
  True woman to this man,
What have their deeds to do with ours
  Or any we might plan?

Your startled gaze, your restless hand,
  Your hair like Thames in flood,
And choked voice, battling to command
  The insurgence of your blood:

How can they spell the dark word said
  Ten thousand times a night
By women as corrupt and dead
  As you are proud and bright?

And how can I, in the same breath,
  Though warned against the cheat,
Vilely deliver love to death
  Wrapped in a rumpled sheet?

Yet, if from delicacy of pride
  We choose to hold apart,
Will no blue hag appear, to ride
  Hell's wager in each heart?

THE PORTRAIT*

She speaks always in her own voice
Even to strangers; but those other women
Exercise their borrowed, or false, voices
Even on sons and daughters.

She can walk invisibly at noon
Along the high road; but those other women
Gleam phosphorescent – broad hips and gross fingers –
Down every lampless alley.

She is wild and innocent, pledged to love
Through all disaster; but those other women
Decry her for a witch or a common drab
And glare back when she greets them.

Here is her portrait, gazing sidelong at me,
The hair in disarray, the young eyes pleading:
'And you, love? As unlike those other men
As I those other women?'

DARIEN*

It is a poet's privilege and fate
To fall enamoured of the one Muse
Who variously haunts this island earth.

She was your mother, Darien,
And presaged by the darting halcyon bird
Would run green-sleeved along her ridges,
Treading the asphodels and heather-trees
With white feet bare.

Often at moonrise I had watched her go,
And a cold shudder shook me
To see the curved blaze of her Cretan axe.
Averted her set face, her business
Not yet with me, long-striding,
She would ascend the peak and pass from sight.
But once at full moon, by the sea's verge,
I came upon her without warning.

Unrayed she stood, with long hair streaming,
A cockle-shell cupped in her warm hands,
Her axe propped idly on a stone.

No awe possessed me, only a great grief;
Wanly she smiled, but would not lift her eyes
(As a young girl will greet the stranger).
I stood upright, a head taller than she.
'See who has come,' said I.

She answered: 'If I lift my eyes to yours
And our eyes marry, man, what then?
Will they engender my son Darien?
Swifter than wind, with straight and nut-brown hair,
Tall, slender-shanked, grey-eyed, untameable;
Never was born, nor ever will be born
A child to equal my son Darien,
Guardian of the hid treasures of your world.'

I knew then by the trembling of her hands
For whom that flawless blade would sweep:
My own oracular head, swung by its hair.

'Mistress,' I cried, 'the times are evil
And you have charged me with their remedy.
O, where my head is now, let nothing be
But a clay counterfeit with nacre blink:
Only look up, so Darien may be born!

'He is the northern star, the spell of knowledge,
Pride of all hunters and all fishermen,
Your deathless fawn, an eaglet of your eyrie,
The topmost branch of your unfellable tree,
A tear streaking the summer night,
The new green of my hope.'
                                        Lifting her eyes,
She held mine for a lost eternity.
'Sweetheart,' said I, 'strike now, for Darien's sake!'

THE SURVIVOR*

To die with a forlorn hope, but soon to be raised
By hags, the spoilers of the field, to elude their claws
And stand once more on a well-swept parade-ground,
Scarred and bemedalled, sword upright in fist
At head of a new undaunted company:

Is this joy? – to be doubtless alive again,
And the others dead? Will your nostrils gladly savour
The fragrance, always new, of a first hedge-rose?
Will your ears be charmed by the thrush's melody
Sung as though he had himself devised it?

And is this joy: after the double suicide
(Heart against heart) to be restored entire,
To smooth your hair and wash away the life-blood,
And presently seek a young and innocent bride,
Whispering in the dark: 'for ever and ever'?

PROMETHEUS

Close bound in a familiar bed
All night I tossed, rolling my head;
Now dawn returns in vain, for still
The vulture squats on her warm hill.

I am in love as giants are
That dote upon the evening star,
And this lank bird is come to prove
The intractability of love.

Yet still, with greedy eye half shut,
Rend the raw liver from its gut:
Feed, jealousy, do not fly away –
If she who fetched you also stay.

SATIRES

QUEEN-MOTHER TO NEW QUEEN

Although only a fool would mock
The secondary joys of wedlock
(Which need no recapitulation),
The primary's the purer gold,
Even in our exalted station,
For all but saint or hoary cuckold.

Therefore, if ever the King's eyes
Turn at odd hours to your sleek thighs,
Make no delay or circumvention
But do as you should do, though strict
To guide back his bemused attention
Towards privy purse or royal edict,

And stricter yet to leave no stain
On the proud memory of his reign –
You'll act the wronged wife, if you love us.
Let them not whisper, even in sport:
'His Majesty's turned parsimonious
And keeps no whore now but his Consort.'

SECESSION OF THE DRONES

These drones, seceding from the hive,
    In self-felicitation
That henceforth they will throng and thrive
    Far from the honeyed nation,

Domesticate an old cess-pit,
    Their hairy bellies warming
With buzz of psychologic wit
    And homosexual swarming.

Engrossed in pure coprophily,
Which makes them mighty clever,
They fabricate a huge King Bee
To rule all hives for ever.

DAMOCLES

Death never troubled Damocles,
Nor did the incertitude
When the sword, swung by a light breeze,
Cast shadows on his food –
'A thread is spun
For every son,'
Said he, 'of Pyrrha's brood.'

But great Zeus cursed him, none the less,
With foresight to deplore
The end of that day's childishness,
And he could eat no more:
His fame would float
Through anecdote
Into dead metaphor.

Then orators from every land,
Caught by the same disease,
With thump of fist or saw of hand
Or sinking to their knees,
Would madly boom
Of the world's doom
And swords of Damocles.

HOMAGE TO TEXAS

It's hardly wise to generalize
   About a state or city;
But Texan girls are decent girls
   And bold as they are pretty.

Who dared the outrageous unicorn
   Through lonely woods a-leaping?
Who made him halt and lower his horn
   And couch beside her, weeping?

Not Helen (wonder of her sex)
   Nor Artemis, nor Pallas;
No, sir: a girl from Houston, Tex.,
   Though some claim it was Dallas.

He told her: 'Ma'am, your Lone Star State,
   Though maybe short on schooling,
Outshines the whole bright forty-eight' –
   And so it did, no fooling.

THE DILEMMA*

When Time, though granting scope enough
   For any conversationalist,
Gives the sworn poet a rebuff,
   Should he indeed desist?

Should he to timeless bogs retreat,
   His pace slowed to an old man's pace,
Where antique histories interlace
   Around a hearth of peat?

Or, rather, take revenge on Time,
   Stalking into those flood-lit stews:
Drown conversation with a crime,
   Pause, yell and blow the fuse?

Sadist and masochist in me,
  Each boasting himself more than half,
Press the dilemma feverishly
  And raise hell if I laugh.

GENERAL BLOODSTOCK'S LAMENT FOR ENGLAND

'This image (seemingly animated) walks with them in the fields in broad Day-light; and if they are employed in delving, harrowing, Seed-sowing or any other Occupation, they are at the same time mimicked by the ghostly Visitant. Men of the Second Sight . . . call this reflex-man a Co-walker, every way like the Man, as his Twin-brother and Companion, haunting as his Shadow.'

Kirk's *Secret Commonwealth*, 1691.

Alas, England, my own generous mother,
One gift I have from you I hate,
The second sight: I see your weird co-walker,
Silver-zoned Albion, stepping in your track,
Mimicking your sad and doubtful gait,
Your clasped hands, your head-shakings, your bent back.

The white hem of a winding sheet
Draws slowly upward from her feet;
Soon it will mount knee-high, then to the thigh.
It crackles like the parchment of the treaties,
Bonds, contracts and conveyances,
With which, beggared and faint and like to die,
You signed away your island sovereignty
To rogues who learned their primer at your knees.

'¡WELLCOME, TO THE CAVES OF ARTÁ!'*

'They are hollowed out in the see coast at the muncipal terminal of Capdepera, at nine kilometer from the town of Artá in the Island of Mallorca, with a suporizing infinity of graceful colums of 21 meter and by downward, wich prives the spectator of all animacion and plunges in dumbness. The way going is very picturesque, serpentine between style mountains, til the arrival at the esplanade of the vallee called "The Spider". There are good enlacements of the railroad with autobuses of excursion, many days of the week, today actually Wednesday and Satturday. Since many centuries renown foreing visitors have explored them and wrote thier eulogy about, included Nort-American geoglogues.'

From a Tourist leaflet.

Such subtile filigranity and nobless of construccion
  Here fraternise in harmony, that respiracion stops.
While all admit thier impotence (though autors most formidable)
  To sing in words the excellence of Nature's underprops,
Yet stalactite and stalagmite together with dumb language
  Make hymnes to God wich celebrate the stregnth of water
    drops.

¿You, also, are you capable to make precise in idiom
  Consideracions magic of ilusions very wide?
Alraedy in the Vestibule of these Grand Caves of Artá
  The spirit of the human verb is darked and stupefyed;
So humildy you trespass trough the forest of the colums
  And listen to the grandess explicated by the guide.

From darkness into darkness, but at measure, now descending
  You remark with what esxactitude he designates each bent;
'The Saloon of Thousand Banners', or 'The Tumba of Napoleon',
  'The Grotto of the Rosary', 'The Club', 'The Camping Tent'.
And at 'Cavern of the Organ' there are knocking streange
    formacions
  Wich give a nois particular pervoking wonderment.

¡Too far do not adventure, sir! For, further as you wander,
  The every of the stalactites will make you stop and stay.
Grand peril amenaces now, your nostrills aprehending
  An odour least delicious of lamentable decay.
It is some poor touristers, in the depth of obscure cristal,
  Wich deceased of thier emocion on a past excursion day.

TO A POET IN TROUBLE*

Cold wife and angry mistress
And debts: all three?
Though they combine to kill you
Be grateful to the Goddess,
(Our cruel patroness),
For this felicity:
Your poems now ring true.

From POEMS 1953

(1953)

TO CALLIOPE*

Permit me here a simple brief aside,
  Calliope,
You who have shown such patience with my pride
  And obstinacy:

Am I not loyal to you? I say no less
  Than is to say;
If more, only from angry-heartedness,
  Not for display.

But you know, I know, and you know I know
  My principal curse:
Shame at the mounting dues I have come to owe
  A devil of verse,

Who caught me young, ingenuous and uncouth,
  Prompting me how
To evade the patent clumsiness of truth –
  Which I do now.

No: nothing reads so fresh as I first thought,
  Or as you could wish –
Yet must I, when far worse is eagerly bought,
  Cry stinking fish?

THE STRAW

Peace, the wild valley streaked with torrents,
A hoopoe perched on his warm rock. Then why
This tremor of the straw between my fingers?

What should I fear? Have I not testimony
In her own hand, signed with her own name
That my love fell as lightning on her heart?

These questions, bird, are not rhetorical.
Watch how the straw twitches and leaps
As though the earth quaked at a distance.

Requited love; but better unrequited
If this chance instrument gives warning
Of cataclysmic anguish far away.

Were she at ease, warmed by the thought of me,
Would not my hand stay steady as this rock?
Have I undone her by my vehemence?

THE FOREBODING*

Looking by chance in at the open window
  I saw my own self seated in his chair
With gaze abstracted, furrowed forehead,
  Unkempt hair.

I thought that I had suddenly come to die,
  That to a cold corpse this was my farewell,
Until the pen moved slowly upon paper
  And tears fell.

He had written a name, yours, in printed letters:
  One word on which bemusedly to pore –
No protest, no desire, your naked name,
  Nothing more.

Would it be tomorrow, would it be next year?
  But the vision was not false, this much I knew;
And I turned angrily from the open window
  Aghast at you.

Why never a warning, either by speech or look,
  That the love you cruelly gave me could not last?
Already it was too late: the bait swallowed,
  The hook fast.

CRY FAUGH!*

Caria and Philistia considered
Only pre-marital adventures wise;
The bourgeois French argue contrariwise.

Socrates and Plato burked the issue
(Namely, how man-and-woman love should be)
With homosexual ideology.

Apocalyptic Israelites, foretelling
The Imminent End, called only for a chaste
Sodality: all dead below the waist.

Curious, various, amoral, moral –
Tell me, what elegant square or lumpish hamlet
Lives free from nymphological disquiet?

'Yet males and females of the lower species
Contrive to eliminate the sexual problem,'
Scientists ponder: 'Why not learn from them?'

Cry faugh! on science, ethics, metaphysics,
On antonyms of sacred and profane –
Come walk with me, love, in a golden rain

Past toppling colonnades of glory,
The moon alive on each uptilted face:
Proud remnants of a visionary race.

HERCULES AT NEMEA*

Muse, you have bitten through my fool's-finger.
Fierce as a lioness you seized it
In your white teeth most amorously;
And I stared back, dauntless and fiery-eyed,
Challenging you to maim me for my pride.

See me a fulvous hero of nine fingers –
Sufficient grasp for bow and arrow.
My beard bristles in exultation:
Let all Nemea look and understand
Why you have set your mark on this right hand.

DIALOGUE ON THE HEADLAND

She: You'll not forget these rocks and what I told you?
He: How could I? Never: whatever happens.
She: What do you think might happen?
Might you fall out of love? – did you mean that?
He: Never, never! 'Whatever' was a sop
For jealous listeners in the shadows.
She: You haven't answered me. I asked:
'What do you think might happen?'
He: Whatever happens: though the skies should fall
Raining their larks and vultures in our laps –
She: 'Though the seas turn to slime' – say that –
'Though water-snakes be hatched with six heads.'
He: Though the seas turn to slime, or tower
In an arching wave above us, three miles high –
She: 'Though she should break with you' – dare you say that?
'Though she deny her words on oath.'
He: I had that in my mind to say, or nearly;
It hurt so much I choked it back.
She: How many other days can't you forget?
How many other loves and landscapes?
He: You are jealous?
She: Damnably.
He: The past is past.
She: And this?
He: Whatever happens, this goes on.
She: Without a future? Sweetheart, tell me now:
What do you want of me? I must know that.
He: Nothing that isn't freely mine already.
She: Say what is freely yours and you shall have it.
He: Nothing that, loving you, I could dare take.
She: O, for an answer with no 'nothing' in it!

He: Then give me everything that's left.
She: Left after what?
He: After whatever happens:
Skies have already fallen, seas are slime,
Watersnakes poke and peer six-headedly –
She: And I lie snugly in the Devil's arms.
He: I said: 'Whatever happens.' Are you crying?
She: You'll not forget me – ever, ever, ever?

LOVERS IN WINTER*

The posture of the tree
  Shows the prevailing wind;
And ours, long misery
  When you are long unkind.

But forward, look, we lean –
  Not backward as in doubt –
And still with branches green
  Ride our ill weather out.

ESAU AND JUDITH*

Robbed of his birthright and his blessing
Esau sought refuge in the wilderness,
An outlaw girding at the world's deceit.
He took to wife Judith, daughter of Heth,
Tall and grey-eyed, a priestess of her grove.
The curse lay heavy on their marriage-couch.

She was that sea which God had held corrupt;
Her tides he praised and her curvetting fish,
Though with no comprehension of their ways;
As a man blind from birth fondly adores
Fantasies of imagined gold and blue –
The curse lay heavy on their marriage-couch.

For how might Esau strive against his blood?
Had Isaac and Rebekah not commanded:
'Take thee a daughter from thy father's house!' –
Isaac who played the pander with Rebekah,
Even as Abraham had done with Sarah?
The curse lay heavy on their marriage-couch.

THE MARK

If, doubtful of your fate,
You seek to obliterate
And to forget
The counter-mark I set
In the warm blue-veined nook
Of your elbow crook,
How can you not repent
The experiment?

No knife nor fang went in
To lacerate the skin;
Nor may the eye
Tetter or wen descry:
The place which my lips pressed
Is coloured like the rest
And fed by the same blood
Of womanhood.

Acid, pumice-stone,
Lancings to the bone,
Would be in vain.
Here must the mark remain
As witness to such love
As nothing can remove
Or blur, or hide,
Save suicide.

WITH THE GIFT OF A RING*

If one of thy two loves be wroth
And cry: 'Thou shalt not love us both,
Take one or 'tother!', O then choose
Him that can nothing thee refuse!
Only a rogue would tear a part,
How small soever, from thy heart;
As Adam sought to plunder Eve's
(What time they clad themselves in leaves),
Conjuring her to make an end
Of dalliance with her cursèd friend –
Too late, now she had learned to tell
False love from true, and ill from well.

LIADAN AND CURITHIR*

Even in childhood
Liadan never would
   Accept love simply,
But stifled longing
And went away to sing
   In strange company.

Alas, for Liadan!
To fear perfection
   Was her ill custom:
Choosing a scruple
That might seem honourable,
   For retreat therefrom.

Herself she enticed
To be nunned for Christ,
   Though in marriage sought
By a master-poet
On whom her heart was set –
   Curithir of Connaught;

And raised a wall
As it were of crystal
   Her grief around.
He might not guess
The cause of her fickleness
   Nor catch one sound.

She was walled soon after
Behind stones and mortar,
   From whence too late
He heard her keening,
Sighing and complaining
   Of her dire self-hate.

THE SEA HORSE*

Since now in every public place
Lurk phantoms who assume your walk and face,
You cannot yet have utterly abjured me
Nor stifled the insistent roar of sea.

Do as I do: confide your unquiet love
(For one who never owed you less than love)
To this indomitable hippocamp,
Child of your element, coiled a-ramp,
Having ridden out worse tempests than you know of;
Under his horny ribs a blood-red stain
Portends renewal of our pain.
Sweetheart, make much of him and shed
Tears on his taciturn dry head.

THE DEVIL AT BERRY POMEROY*

Snow and fog unseasonable,
The cold remarkable,
Children sickly;
Green fruit lay thickly
Under the crab-tree
And the wild cherry.
I heard witches call
Their imps to the Hall:
'Hey, Ilemauzar,
Sack-and-Sugar,
Peck-in-the-Crown,
Come down, come down!'
I heard bells toll
For a monster's soul
That was born, half dead,
With a double head;
I saw ghosts leap
From the ruined keep;
I saw blows thwack
On the raw back
Of a dying ass.
Blight was on the grass,
Poison in the cup
(Lover, drink up!),
With envy, slander,
Weasels a-wander,
Incest done
Between mother and son,
Murder of hags
For their money-bags,
Wrath, rape,
And the shadowy ape
Which a lady, weeping,
Leads by a string
From first twilight
Until past midnight
Through the Castle yard –
'Blow winds, blow hard!'
So the Devil snaps his chain
And renews his reign

To the little joy
Of Berry Pomeroy.

REPROACH TO JULIA

Julia: how Irishly you sacrifice
Love to pity, pity to ill-humour,
Yourself to love, still haggling at the price.

DETHRONEMENT*

With pain pressing so close about your heart,
Stand (it behoves you), head uncovered,
To watch how she enacts her transformations –
Bitch, vixen, sow – the laughing, naked queen
Who has now dethroned you.

Hymns to her beauty or to her mercy
Would be ill-conceived. Your true anguish
Is all that she requires. You, turned to stone,
May not speak nor groan, shall stare dumbly,
Grinning dismay.

But as the play ends, or in its after-hush,
O then, deluded, flee! Her red-eared hounds
Scramble upon your track; past either cheek
Swan-feathered arrows whistle, or cruelly comb
Long furrows in your scalp.

Run, though you hope for nothing: to stay your foot
Would be ingratitude, a sour denial
That the life she bestowed was sweet.
Therefore be fleet, run gasping, draw the chase
Up the grand defile.

They will rend you to rags assuredly
With half a hundred love-bites –
Your hot blood an acceptable libation
Poured to Persephone, in whose domain
You shall again find peace.

CAT-GODDESSES*

A perverse habit of cat-goddesses –
Even the blackest of them, black as coals
Save for a new moon blazing on each breast,
With coral tongues and beryl eyes like lamps,
Long-leggèd, pacing three by three in nines –
This obstinate habit is to yield themselves,
In verisimilar love-ecstasies,
To tatter-eared and slinking alley-toms
No less below the common run of cats
Than they above it; which they do for spite,
To provoke jealousy – not the least abashed
By such gross-headed, rabbit-coloured litters
As soon they shall be happy to desert.

THE BLUE-FLY

Five summer days, five summer nights,
The ignorant, loutish, giddy blue-fly
Hung without motion on the cling peach,
Humming occasionally: 'O my love, my fair one!'
        As in the *Canticles*.

Magnified one thousand times, the insect
Looks farcically human; laugh if you will!
Bald head, stage-fairy wings, blear eyes,
A caved-in chest, hairy black mandibles,
        Long spindly thighs.

The crime was detected on the sixth day.
What then could be said or done? By anyone?
It would have been vindictive, mean and what-not
To swat that fly for being a blue-fly,
    For debauch of a peach.

Is it fair, either, to bring a microscope
To bear on the case, even in search of truth?
Nature, doubtless, has some compelling cause
To glut the carriers of her epidemics –
    Nor did the peach complain.

RHEA*

On her shut lids the lightning flickers,
Thunder explodes above her bed,
An inch from her lax arm the rain hisses;
Discrete she lies,

Not dead but entranced, dreamlessly
With slow breathing, her lips curved
In a half-smile archaic, her breast bare,
Hair astream.

The house rocks, a flood suddenly rising
Bears away bridges: oak and ash
Are shivered to the roots – royal green timber.
She nothing cares.

(Divine Augustus, trembling at the storm,
Wrapped sealskin on his thumb; divine Gaius
Made haste to hide himself in a deep cellar,
Distraught by fear.)

Rain, thunder, lightning: pretty children.
'Let them play,' her mother-mind repeats;
'They do no harm, unless from high spirits
Or by mishap.'

THE HERO*

This prince's immortality was confirmed
With envious rites paid him by such poor souls
As, dying, were condemned to flit like bats
In endless caverns of oblivion:
For he alone, amid excessive keening,
Might voyage to that island paradise,
In the red West,
Where bees come thronging to the apple flow
And thrice three damsels in a tall house
Tend the mead-vat of inspiration.

They feel no envy now, those poor souls.
Did not some bald Cilician sell them
Mansions in Heaven, and at a paltry price:
Offering crowns of gold for scabbed heads,
Robes of state for vitiliginous backs?
No blood is poured now at the hero's tomb,
No prayers intoned,
The island paradise is unfrequented,
And neither Finn, nor Ogier, nor Arthur,
Returns to prophesy our common doom.

MARGINAL WARNING

Prejudice, as the Latin shows,
Means that you follow your own nose
Like an untutored spaniel; hence,
A nose being no good evidence
That Farmer Luke hangs from a limb
With cart-rope tightly trussing him,
Till twelve unblinking pairs of eyes
Can view the corpse and authorize
A coroner to shake his head
For: 'Gentlemen, this man is dead',
Your blind prognostication is
Roundly condemned as prejudice;
And should you further speculate,

Snuffing once more, upon what date
His cowman strung him to the tree:
The case being now *sub judice*,
Contempt of court will be the cry
To challenge and arrest you by –
What will your children think of you,
Docked of your nose and your ears too?

THE ENCOUNTER*

Soon after dawn in hottest June (it may
For all I know, have been Midsummer's Day)
An hour at which boulevardiers are few,
From either end of the grand avenue
Flanked with basilicas and palaces
And shaded by long rows of ancient trees,
A man drew near, his lips in rage compressed,
Marching alone, magnificently dressed –
This, rose on green; that, mulberry on gold –
Two tall unyielding men of the same mould
Who wore identical helmets, cloaks and shoes
And long straight swords they had well learned to use,
Both being luckless fellows, paired by fate
In bonds of irremediable hate.

Closer they steered: although the walk was wide,
A scant inch served as margin to their pride.
The encounter surely could but end in blows;
Yet neither thought to tweak his enemy's nose,
Or jostle him, or groan, or incur guilt
By a provocative grasp at the sword hilt,
Each setting such reliance on mischance
He sauntered by without a sidelong glance.

I'M THROUGH WITH YOU FOR EVER*

The oddest, surely, of odd tales
   Recorded by the French
Concerns a sneak thief of Marseilles
   Tried by a callous Bench.

His youth, his innocency, his tears –
   No, nothing could abate
Their sentence of 'One hundred years
   In galleys of the State.'

Nevertheless, old wives affirm
   And annalists agree,
He sweated out the whole damned term,
   Bowed stiffly, and went free.

Then come, my angry love, review
   Your sentence of today.
'For ever' was unjust of you,
   The end too far away.

Give me four hundred years, or five –
   Can rage be so intense? –
And I will sweat them out alive
   To prove my impenitence.

WITH HER LIPS ONLY*

This honest wife, challenged at dusk
At the garden gate, under a moon perhaps,
In scent of honeysuckle, dared to deny
Love to an urgent lover: with her lips only,
Not with her heart. It was no assignation;
Taken aback, what could she say else?
For the children's sake, the lie was venial;
'For the children's sake', she argued with her conscience.

Yet a mortal lie must follow before dawn:
Challenged as usual in her own bed,
She protests love to an urgent husband,
Not with her heart but with her lips only;
'For the children's sake', she argues with her conscience,
'For the children' – turning suddenly cold towards them.

THE BLOTTED COPY-BOOK*

He broke school bounds, he dared defy
The Master's atrabilious eye,
Diced, swigged raw brandy, used foul oaths,
Wore shamelessly Corinthian clothes,
And taught St Dominic's to mock
At gown and hood and whipping-block.

The boy's a nabob now, retired
With wealth enough to be admired
Even by the School Governors
(Benignly sycophantic bores)
Who call on him to give away
Prize-medals on Foundation Day.

Will he at last, or will he not,
His yellowing copy-book unblot:
Accede, and seriously confess
A former want of seriousness,
Or into a wild fury burst
With: 'Let me see you in Hell first!'?

THE SACRED MISSION*

The ungainsayable, huge, cooing message
Hurtles suddenly down the dawn streets:
Twenty loudspeakers, twenty lovesick voices
Each zealous to enlarge his own range
And dominate the echoing border-zones.

Now the distressed whimper of little children,
The groans of sick men cheated in their hope
Of snatching a light sleep from the jaws of pain,
The curses, even, of the unregenerate –
All are submerged in the rising sea of noise
Which floods each room and laps round every pillow,
Roaring the mercy of Christ's limitless love.

FROM THE EMBASSY

I, an ambassador of Otherwhere
To the unfederated states of Here and There
Enjoy (as the phrase is)
Extra-territorial privileges.
With heres and theres I seldom come to blows
Or need, as once, to sandbag all my windows.
And though the Otherwhereish currency
Cannot be quoted yet officially,
I meet less hindrance now with the exchange
Nor is my garb, even, considered strange;
And shy enquiries for literature
Come in by every post, and the side door.

SIROCCO AT DEYÁ*

How most unnatural-seeming, yet how proper;
The sea like a cat with fur rubbed the wrong way,
As the sirocco with its furnace flavour
Dashes at full tilt around the village
['From every-which-a-way, hot as a two-buck pistol']
Stripping green olives from the blown-back boughs,
Scorching the roses, blinding the eyes with sand;
While slanderous tongues in the small cafés
And in the tightly-shuttered limestone houses
Clack defamation, incite and invite
Knives to consummate their near-murders . . . .
Look up, a great grey cloud broods nonchalant
On the mountain-top nine hundred feet above us,
Motionless and turgid, blotting out the sun,
And from it sneers a supercilious Devil:
'Mere local wind: no messenger of mine!'

From COLLECTED POEMS 1955

(1955)

PENTHESILEIA*

Penthesileia, dead of profuse wounds,
Was despoiled of her arms by Prince Achilles
Who, for love of that fierce white naked corpse,
Necrophily on her committed
In the public view.

Some gasped, some groaned, some bawled their indignation,
Achilles nothing cared, distraught by grief,
But suddenly caught Thersites' obscene snigger
And with one vengeful buffet to the jaw
Dashed out his life.

This was a fury few might understand,
Yet Penthesileia, hailed by Prince Achilles
On the Elysian plain, pauses to thank him
For avenging her insulted womanhood
With sacrifice.

POETS' CORNER*

De ambobus mundis ille
Convoravit diligens . . .

The Best of Both Worlds being Got
Between th'Evangel and the Pot,
He, though Exorbitantly Vice'd,
Had Re-discover'd Thirst for Christ
And Fell a Victim (Young as This)
To Ale, God's Love and Syphilis.

Here then in Triumph See Him Stand,
Laurels for Halo, Scroll in Hand,
Whyle Ganymeds and Cherubim
And Squabby Nymphs Rejoyce with Him:
Aye, Scroll Shall Fall and Laurels Fade
Long, Long before his Debts are Pay'd.

CORONATION ADDRESS*

I remember, Ma'am, a frosty morning
When I was five years old and brought ill news,
Marching solemnly upstairs with the paper
Like an angel of doom; knocked gently.
'Father, the *Times* has a black border. Look!
The Queen is dead.'
                                        Then I grew scared
When big tears started, ran down both his cheeks
To hang glistening in the red-grey beard –
A sight I had never seen before.

My mother thought to comfort him, leaned closer,
Whispering softly: 'It was a ripe old age. . . .
She saw her century out.' The tears still flowed,
He could not find his voice. My mother ventured:
'We have a King once more, a real King.
"God Save the King" is in the Holy Bible.
Our Queen was, after all, only a woman.'

At that my father's grief burst hoarsely out.
'Only a woman! You say it to my face?
Queen Victoria only a woman! What?
Was the orb nothing? Was the sceptre nothing?
To cry "God Save the King" is honourable,
But to serve a Queen is lovely. Listen now:
Could I have one wish for this son of mine . . . '

A wish fulfilled at last after long years.

Think well, Ma'am, of your great-great-grandmother
Who earned love, who bequeathed love to her sons,
Yet left one crown in trust for you alone.

BEAUTY IN TROUBLE*

Beauty in trouble flees to the good angel
  On whom she can rely
To pay her cab-fare, run a steaming bath,
  Poultice her bruised eye;

Will not at first, whether for shame or caution,
  Her difficulty disclose;
Until he draws a cheque book from his plumage,
  Asking how much she owes.

(Breakfast in bed: coffee and marmalade,
  Toast, eggs, orange-juice,
After a long, sound sleep – the first since when? –
  And no word of abuse.)

Loves him less only than her saint-like mother,
  Promises to repay
His loans and most seraphic thoughtfulness
  A million-fold one day.

Beauty grows plump, renews her broken courage
  And, borrowing ink and pen,
Writes a news-letter to the evil angel
  (Her first gay act since when?):

The fiend who beats, betrays and sponges on her,
  Persuades her white is black,
Flaunts vespertilian wing and cloven hoof;
  And soon will fetch her back.

Virtue, good angel, is its own reward:
  Your guineas were well spent.
But would you to the marriage of true minds
  Admit impediment?

A LOST JEWEL

Who on your breast pillows his head now,
Jubilant to have won
The heart beneath on fire for him alone,

At dawn will hear you, plagued by nightmare,
Mumble and weep
About some blue jewel you were sworn to keep.

Wake, blink, laugh out in reassurance,
Yet your tears will say:
'It was not mine to lose or give away.

'For love it shone – never for the madness
Of a strange bed –
Light on my finger, fortune in my head.'

Roused by your naked grief and beauty,
For lust he will burn:
'Turn to me, sweetheart! Why do you not turn?'

THE WINDOW SILL*

Presage and caveat not only seem
To come in dream,
But do so come in dream.

When the cock crew and phantoms floated by,
This dreamer I
Out of the house went I,

Down long unsteady streets to a queer square;
And who was there,
Or whom did I know there?

Julia, leaning on her window sill.
'I love you still,'
She said, 'O love me still!'

I answered: 'Julia, do you love me best?'
'What of this breast,'
She mourned, 'this flowery breast?'

Then a wild sobbing spread from door to door,
And every floor
Cried shame on every floor,

As she unlaced her bosom to disclose
Each breast a rose,
A white and cankered rose.

SPOILS*

When all is over and you march for home,
The spoils of war are easily disposed of:
Standards, weapons of combat, helmets, drums
May decorate a staircase or a study,
While lesser gleanings of the battlefield –
Coins, watches, wedding-rings, gold teeth and such –
Are sold anonymously for solid cash.

The spoils of love present a different case,
When all is over and you march for home:
That lock of hair, these letters and the portrait
May not be publicly displayed; nor sold;
Nor burned; nor returned (the heart being obstinate) –
Yet never dare entrust them to a safe
For fear they burn a hole through two-foot steel.

From THE CROWNING PRIVILEGE

(1955)

THE CLEARING

Above this bramble-overarched long lane
Where an autochthonous owl flits to and fro
  In silence,
Above these tangled trees – their roots encumbered
By strawberries, mushrooms, pignuts, flowers' and weeds'
  Exuberance –
The planetary powers gravely observe
  With what dumb patience
You stand at twilight in despair of love,
Though the twigs crackling under a light foot
  Declare her immanence.

THE THREE PEBBLES*

(*In thirty of these burials, the black deposit of fragmentized pots contained a small white quartz pebble associated with two pieces of alien ware, one red porphyry, the other a greenish stone, probably porphyry also. Their presence was clearly intentional.* – Proceedings of the Cumberland and Westmorland Archaeological Society, New Series, vol. xiv.)

Is red the ghost of green? and green, of red?
And white, the impartial light upon them shed?
And I, my own twin warring against me?

Then, woman, take two jewels of porphyry,
Well matched in weight, one green, one angry red:
To light them with yourself, a pure moon-crystal,
And lay them on my bier when I am dead.

POSSIBLY*

Possibly is not a monosyllable;
    Then answer me
At once if possible
    Monosyllabically,
No will be good, *Yes* even better
Though longer by one letter.

Possibly is not a monosyllable,
    And my heart flies shut
At the warning rumble
    Of a suspended *But* . . .
O love, be brief and exact
In confession of simple fact.

END OF THE WORLD

When, at a sign, the Heavenly vault entire
Founders and your accustomed world of men
Drops through the fundament – too vast a crash
To register as sound – and you plunge with it,
Trundling, head over heels, in dark confusion
Of trees, churches, elephants, railway trains,
And the cascading seven seas:

It cannot signify how deep you fall
From everything to nothing. Nothingness
Cushions disaster, and this much is sure:
A buoyant couch will bear you up at last,
Aloof, alone – but for the succuba.

TO A PEBBLE IN MY SHOE*

I cannot pity you,
Poor pebble in my shoe,
  Now that the heel is sore;
You planned to be a rock
And a stumbling block,
  Or was it perhaps more?

But now be grateful if
You vault over the cliff,
  Shaken from my shoe;
Where lapidary tides
May scour your little sides
  And even polish you.

THE TENANTS*

Pictures and books went off ahead this morning:
  The furniture is sold (and tells you so);
Both trunks are packed, and seven suit-cases;
  A cat glides petulantly to and fro,
    Afraid to leave us.

Now massive walls and stairs, for so long certain,
  Retreat and fade like a mirage at sea;
Your room and mine lose their established meanings –
  By dawn tomorrow let them cease to be
    Or to concern us!

We faced a scowl from window, door and fireplace,
  Even in the kitchen, when we first were here;
It cost us years of kindness to placate them.
  But now each scowl resolves into a leer
    With which to speed us.

How dared we struggle with a house of phantoms,
  Soaked in ill luck? And when we go away,
Confess, can you and I be certain whether
  The ghost of our unhappiness will stay
    Or follow with us?

MY MORAL FORCES

My moral forces, always dissipated
  If I condone the least
Fault that I should have hated
  In (say)
Politician, prostitute, or priest,

Appear fanatical to a degree
  If ever I dispute
Claims of integrity
  Advanced (say)
By politician, priest, or prostitute.

But though your prostitute, priest, or politician
  Be good or bad
As such, I waive the ambition
  To curl (say)
Chameleon-like on a Scots tartan plaid.

INTERVIEW

Sixty bound books, an entire bookcase full,
All honest prose, without one duplicate.

Why written? *Answer:* for my self-support –
I was too weak to dig, too proud to beg.

Worth reading? *Answer:* this array of titles
Argues a faithful public following.

Will I not add to the above statement,
Touching (however lightly) on my verse?

Answer: this question makes me look a fool,
As who breeds dogs because he loves a cat.

From 5 PENS IN HAND

(1958)

THE FACE IN THE MIRROR

Grey haunted eyes, absent-mindedly glaring
From wide, uneven orbits; one brow drooping
Somewhat over the eye
Because of a missile fragment still inhering,
Skin deep, as a foolish record of old-world fighting.

Crookedly broken nose – low tackling caused it;
Cheeks, furrowed; coarse grey hair, flying frenetic;
Forehead, wrinkled and high;
Jowls, prominent; ears, large; jaw, pugilistic;
Teeth, few; lips, full and ruddy; mouth, ascetic.

I pause with razor poised, scowling derision
At the mirrored man whose beard needs my attention,
And once more ask him why
He still stands ready, with a boy's presumption,
To court the queen in her high silk pavilion.

FORBIDDEN WORDS*

There are some words carry a curse with them:
Smooth-trodden, abstract, slippery vocables.
They beckon like a path of stepping stones;
But lift them up and watch what writhes or scurries!

Concepts barred from the close language of love –
Darling, you use no single word of the list,
Unless ironically in truth's defence
To volley it back against the abstractionist.

Which is among your several holds on my heart;
For you are no uninstructed child of Nature,
But passed in schools and attained the laurel wreath:
Only to trample it on Apollo's floor.

SONG FOR NEW YEAR'S EVE

Chill moonlight flooding from chill sky
   Has drowned the embers' glow.
Your pale hands glitter; you and I
   Out in the fields must go,

Where cat-ice glazes every rut
   And firs with snow are laced,
Where wealth of bramble, crab and nut
   Lies tumbled into waste.

The owlets raise a lovely din,
   The fox has his desire,
And we shall welcome New Year in
   With frost instead of fire.

ALEXANDER AND QUEEN JANET*

On Janet come so late
To their banquet of state
   The angels nobly smile;
But Alexander thrusts away his plate.

'Janet, where have you been?
Janet, what have you seen?
   Your lover is abashed:
For want of you we have sat down thirteen.'

'I have nowhere been,
And nothing have I seen.
   Were it not for Alexander
You had no reason to sit down thirteen.'

Sweet wine for Janet now,
Fresh costards from the bough
   Of Paradise, white bread
Which they must force between her lips somehow.

'I could not wish,' says she,
'For prettier company,
  Angels of light, than yours,
Yet crystal cups and dishes are not for me.

'Though Alexander dine
On Heaven's own bread and wine,
  And Paradisal fruit,
Such delicacies are not for me or mine.

'Do you approve the grace
Of my form or my face?
  It springs from earth,' says Janet,
'And must be welcomed in a greener place.'

At this the angels hide
Their proud heads, mortified;
  Being deep in love with Janet
And jealous, too, for Alexander's pride.

Queen Janet softly goes
Treading on her tip toes
  To the bright table head;
She lays before her man a damask rose.

'Is it still your desire
To shiver at my fire?
  Then come now, Alexander,
Or stay and be a monk, or else a friar.'

'My lambkin, my sweet,
I have dined on angels' meat,
  And in you I had trusted
To attend their call and make my joy complete.'

'Do you come? Do you stay?
Alexander, say!
  For if you will not come
This gift rose I must surely snatch away.'

'Janet, how can I come?
Eat only a crumb
   Of bread, essay this wine!
In God's name sit beside me; or be dumb.'

Her back Janet turns,
Dumbly she spurns
   The red rose with her shoe;
But in each cheek another red rose burns.

The twelve angels, alas,
Are brought to a sad pass:
   Their lucent plumage pales,
Their glittering sapphire eyes go dull as glass.

Now Alexander's soul
Flies up from the brain hole,
   To circle like a bat
Above his body threshing past control.

It was Queen Janet's power
Turned the sweet wine sour,
   Shrivelled the apples' bloom,
And the bread crumbled into dusty flour.

THE CORAL POOL

It was a hippocamp addressed her darling,
   Perched on the coral branches of a pool
Where light reflected back from violet moss
   And fishes veered above in a tight school:

'Daughter, no sea is deep enough for drowning;
   Therefore let none seem broad enough for you,
My foal, my fledgeling bird, my dragon-imp,
   Or understand a tithe of what you do.

'To wanton fish never divulge your secret,
  But only to our mistress of the tides
Whose handy-men are octopus and crab,
  At whose white heel the amorous turtle glides.'

GRATITUDE FOR A NIGHTMARE

His appearances are incalculable,
His strength terrible,
I do not know his name.

Huddling pensive for weeks on end, he
Gives only random hints of life, such as
Strokes of uncomfortable coincidence.

To eat heartily, dress warmly, lie snugly
And earn respect as a leading citizen
Granted long credit at all shops and inns –

How dangerous! I had feared this shag demon
Would not conform with my conformity
And in some leaner belly make his lair.

But now in dream he suddenly bestrides me. . . .
'All's well,' I groan, and fumble for a light,
Brow bathed in sweat, heart pounding.

FRIDAY NIGHT*

Love, the sole Goddess fit for swearing by,
Concedes us graciously the little lie:
The white lie, the half-lie, the lie corrective
Without which love's exchange might prove defective,
Confirming hazardous relationships
By kindly *maquillage* of Truth's pale lips.

This little lie was first told, so they say,
On the sixth day (Love's planetary day)
When, meeting her full-bosomed and half dressed,
Jove roared out suddenly: 'Hell take the rest!
Six hard days of Creation are enough' –
And clasped her to him, meeting no rebuff.

Next day he rested, and she rested too.
The busy little lie between them flew:
'If this be not perfection,' Love would sigh,
'Perfection is a great, black, thumping lie. . . . '
Endearments, kisses, grunts, and whispered oaths;
But were her thoughts on breakfast, or on clothes?

THE NAKED AND THE NUDE*

For me, the naked and the nude
(By lexicographers construed
As synonyms that should express
The same deficiency of dress
Or shelter) stand as wide apart
As love from lies, or truth from art.

Lovers without reproach will gaze
On bodies naked and ablaze;
The Hippocratic eye will see
In nakedness, anatomy;
And naked shines the Goddess when
She mounts her lion among men.

The nude are bold, the nude are sly
To hold each treasonable eye.
While draping by a showman's trick
Their dishabille in rhetoric,
They grin a mock-religious grin
Of scorn at those of naked skin.

The naked, therefore, who compete
Against the nude may know defeat;
Yet when they both together tread
The briary pastures of the dead,
By Gorgons with long whips pursued,
How naked go the sometime nude!

WOMAN AND TREE

To love one woman, or to sit
   Always beneath the same tall tree,
Argues a certain lack of wit
   Two steps from imbecility.

A poet, therefore, sworn to feed
   On every food the senses know,
Will claim the inexorable need
   To be Don Juan Tenorio.

Yet if, miraculously enough,
   (And why set miracles apart?)
Woman and tree prove of a stuff
   Wholly to glamour his wild heart?

And if such visions from the void
   As shone in fever there, or there,
Assemble, hold and are enjoyed
   On climbing one familiar stair . . . ?

To change and chance he took a vow,
   As he thought fitting. None the less,
What of a phoenix on the bough,
   Or a sole woman's fatefulness?

DESTRUCTION OF EVIDENCE

You neigh and flaunt your coat of sorrel-red,
O long-winged Pegasus sprung from my head,
Walking the lawn so lively and complete
That, like a wolf, my after-birth I eat –
Must he be told, the astonished passer-by,
I did not draw you down from a clear sky?

THE SECOND-FATED*

My stutter, my cough, my unfinished sentences,
Denote an inveterate physical reluctance
To use the metaphysical idiom.
Forgive me: what I am saying is, perhaps this: –

Your accepted universe, by Jove's naked hand
Or Esmun's, or Odomankoma's, or Marduk's –
Choose which name jibes – formed scientifically
From whatever there was before Time was,
And begging the question of perfect consequence,
May satisfy the general run of men
(If 'run' be an apt term for patent paralytics)
That blueprints destine all they suffer here,
But does not satisfy certain few else.

Fortune enrolled me among the second-fated
Who have read their own obituaries in *The Times*,
Have heard 'Where, death, thy sting? Where, grave, thy victory?'
Intoned with unction over their still clay,
Have seen two parallel red-ink lines drawn
Under their manic-depressive bank accounts,
And are therefore strictly forbidden to walk in grave-yards
Lest they scandalize the sexton and his bride.

We, to be plain with you, taking advantage
Of a brief demise, visited first the Pit,
A library of shades, completed characters;
And next the silver-bright Hyperborean Queendom,
Basking under the sceptre of Guess Whom?
Where pure souls matrilineally foregather.
We were then shot through by merciful lunar shafts
Until hearts tingled, heads sang, and praises flowed;
And learned to scorn your factitious universe
Ruled by the death which we had flouted;
Acknowledging only that from the Dove's egg hatched
Before aught was, but wind – unpredictable
As our second birth would be, or our second love:
A moon-warmed world of discontinuance.

A SLICE OF WEDDING CAKE*

Why have such scores of lovely, gifted girls
   Married impossible men?
Simple self-sacrifice may be ruled out,
   And missionary endeavour, nine times out of ten.

Repeat 'impossible men': not merely rustic,
   Foul-tempered or depraved
(Dramatic foils chosen to show the world
   How well women behave, and always have behaved).

Impossible men: idle, illiterate,
   Self-pitying, dirty, sly,
For whose appearance even in City parks
   Excuses must be made to casual passers-by.

Has God's supply of tolerable husbands
   Fallen, in fact, so low?
Or do I always over-value woman
   At the expense of man?
                                        Do I?
                                                It might be so.

A PLEA TO BOYS AND GIRLS

You learned Lear's *Nonsense Rhymes* by heart, not rote;
You learned Pope's *Iliad* by rote, not heart;
These terms should be distinguished if you quote
My verses, children – keep them poles apart –
And call the man a liar who says I wrote
All that I wrote in love, for love of art.

A BOUQUET FROM A FELLOW ROSEMAN*

Oh, what does the roseman answer
On receiving a gift bouquet
Of raddled and blowsy roses
From the garden across the way,
From a fellow roseman?

If the roseman is a roseman is a roseman,
And nothing other at all,
He flings that bouquet of roses
Clear over his garden wall
Like a proper roseman.

But, if only a week-end roseman,
He does what he has to do:
'What beautiful blooms,' he answers,
'How exceedingly kind of you!'
To the flattered roseman;

And never escapes the insistent
Arrival of new bouquets,
All equally damned and dismal,
All hankering for his praise
As a fellow roseman.

YES

The Romans had no word for YES,
  So mean they were, and stiff;
With SI the Spaniards make you guess
  (Their YES conceals an IF);
OUI means no more than 'so I hear';
  JA sounds a little coarse;
Then, child, say YES, polite and clear –
  Not UH-HUH, like a horse.

THE OUTSIDER

Glandular change provokes a vague content,
  St Martin's summer blossoms warm and sweet.
Frail, balding, toothless, yet benevolent
  The outsider has attained the inside seat
Which once he scorned; all angry passion spent,
  And twelve disciples prostrate at his feet.

Now that his once outrageous heresies
  Stand firmly in the schools' curriculum,
Should he be vexed if young fools think him wise
  Whom their grandfathers prayed to be struck dumb?
And should he disavow old truth as lies,
  Which on obsequious lips it has become?

From STEPS

(1958)

THE ENLISTED MAN*

Yelled Corporal Punishment at Private Reasons:
  'Rebels like you have no right to enlist –
  Or to exist!'
Major Considerations leered approval,
  Clenching his fist,
  And gave his fierce moustache a fiercer twist.
So no appeal, even to General Conscience,
  Kept Private Reasons' name off the defaulter-list.

MIKE AND MANDY*

Mandy: O, I'd like to be a Rug
Basking by the fireside
In a farm-house parlour.

Mike: If you were the Rug,
I'd like to be a Hard Broom
And scratch you all over.

Mandy: If you were the Hard Broom,
I'd like to be a Kitchen Maid
And toss you in a corner.

Mike: If you were a Kitchen Maid,
I'd like to be the Farmer
And show you who was master.

Mandy: If you were the Farmer,
I'd like to be his Wife
And strike you with a poker.

Mike: If you were his Wife,
I'd like to be the Constable
And grab you by the shoulder.

Mandy: If you were the Constable,
I'd like to be a Rug,
Lying by the fireside
In that farm-house parlour –
To slide and trip you up
And make you bang your head
On the corner of the firegrate
And kill you stone dead.

NOTHING

NOTHING is circular,
Like the empty centre
Of a smoke-ring's shadow:
That colourless zero
Marked on a bare wall –
Nothing at all
And reflected in a mirror.

Then need you wonder
If the trained philosopher
Who seeks to define NOTHING
As absence of anything,
A world more logistically
Than, above, I
(Though my terms are cosier),

And claims he has found
That NOTHING is not round
Or hardly ever,
Will run a brain-fever
To the precise degree
Of one hundred and three
On Fahrenheit's thermometer?

CALL IT A GOOD MARRIAGE*

Call it a good marriage –
For no one ever questioned
Her warmth, his masculinity,
Their interlocking views;
Except one stray graphologist
Who frowned in speculation
At her h's and her s's,
His p's and w's.

Though few would still subscribe
To the monogamic axiom
That strife below the hip-bones
Need not estrange the heart,
Call it a good marriage:
More drew those two together,
Despite a lack of children,
Than pulled them apart.

Call it a good marriage:
They never fought in public,
They acted circumspectly
And faced the world with pride;
Thus the hazards of their love-bed
Were none of our damned business –
Till as jurymen we sat upon
Two deaths by suicide.

READ ME, PLEASE!*

If, as well may happen,
   On an autumn day
When white clouds go scudding
   And winds are gay,

Some earth-bound spirit,
   A man lately dead,
(Your fellow-clerk) should take it
   Into his crazed head

To adopt a more venturesome
  Shape than a dead leaf
And wish you a 'good morning'
  Abrupt and brief,

He will come disguised
  As a sheet of newspaper
Charging across the square
  With a clumsy caper,

To flatten himself out
  Across your shins and knees
In a suppliant posture:
  'Read me, please!'

Then scanning every column
  On both sides, with care,
You will find that clerk's name
  Printed somewhere –

Unless, perhaps, in warning
  The sheet comes blown
And the name which you stumble on
  Is, alas, your own.

THE TWIN OF SLEEP*

Death is the twin of Sleep, they say:
  For I shall rise renewed,
Free from the cramps of yesterday,
  Clear-eyed and supple-thewed.

But though this bland analogy
  Helps other folk to face
Decrepitude, senility,
  Madness, disease, disgrace,

I do not like Death's greedy looks:
  Give me his twin instead –
Sleep never auctions off my books,
  My boots, my shirts, my bed.

AROUND THE MOUNTAIN*

Some of you may know, others perhaps can guess
  How it is to walk all night through summer rain
(Thin rain that shrouds a beneficent full moon),
  To circle a mountain, and then limp home again.

The experience varies with a traveller's age
  And bodily strength, and strength of the love affair
That harries him out of doors in steady drizzle,
  With neither jacket nor hat, and holds him there.

Still, let us concede some common elements:
  Wild-fire that, until midnight, burns his feet;
And surging rankly up, strong on the palate,
  Scents of July, imprisoned by long heat.

Add: the sub-human, black tree-silhouettes
  Against a featureless pale pall of sky;
Unseen, gurgling water; the bulk and menace
  Of entranced houses; a wraith wandering by.

Milestones, each one witness of a new mood –
  Anger, desperation, grief, regret;
Her too-familiar face that whirls and totters
  In memory, never willing to stay set.

Whoever makes the desired turning-point,
  Which means another fifteen miles to go,
Learns more from dawn than love, so far, has taught him:
  Especially the false dawn, when cocks first crow.

Those last few miles are easy: being assured
    Of the truth, why should he fabricate fresh lies?
His house looms up; the eaves drip drowsily;
    The windows blaze to a resolute sunrise.

BIBLIOGRAPHICAL AND TEXTUAL NOTES

Listed below are abbreviations for the books by Robert Graves in which the poems in this volume appear, and for other works and manuscript collections cited in the notes.

These are followed by an alphabetical list giving publication details for each poem; and notes on the poems.

ABBREVIATIONS

Robert Graves: Poetry and Prose

For books in which poems in this volume were first published, the month as well as the year of publication is given; these dates are based on Higginson (see 'Bibliography', below).

5PH — *5 Pens in Hand* (New York: Doubleday, March 1958).
10PM — *Ten Poems More* (Paris: Hours Press (limited edition), June 1930).
AHH — *Ann at Highwood Hall: Poems for Children*, illustrated by Edward Ardizzone (London: Cassell, 1964; New York: Doubleday, 1964).
BG — *Beyond Giving* (Hatfield: Stellar Press (privately printed), 1969).
CP38 — *Collected Poems* (London: Cassell, Nov. 1938; New York: Random House, March 1939).
CP14-47 — *Collected Poems (1914-1947)* (London: Cassell, April 1948).
CP55 — *Collected Poems 1955* (New York: Doubleday, June 1955).
CP59 — *Collected Poems 1959* (London: Cassell, 1959).
CP61 — *Collected Poems* (New York: Doubleday, 1961).
CP65 — *Collected Poems 1965* (London: Cassell, 1965).
CP75 — *Collected Poems 1975* (London: Cassell, 1975); *New Collected Poems* (New York: Doubleday, 1977).
CrP — *The Crowning Privilege* (London: Cassell, Sept. 1955).
CS — *Country Sentiment* (London: Secker, 1920; New York: Knopf, 1920).
CWP — *Collected Writings on Poetry*, edited by Paul O'Prey (Manchester: Carcanet, 1995).
FC — *Food for Centaurs* (New York: Doubleday, 1960).
FF — *Fairies and Fusiliers* (London: Heinemann, 1917; New York: Knopf, 1918).
GD — *Goliath and David* (London: Chiswick Press (privately printed), 1916).
GF — *The Golden Fleece* (London: Cassell, Oct. 1944); *Hercules, My Shipmate* (New York: Creative Age Press, Sept. 1945).
GM — *The Greek Myths* (Harmondsworth: Penguin, 1955; second edition, 1960). References are to the second edition.
GTAT29 — *Good-bye to All That: An Autobiography* (London: Cape, 1929).

MBH	*Mock Beggar Hall* (London: Hogarth Press, 1924).
MDC	*The More Deserving Cases: Eighteen Old Poems for Reconsideration* (Marlborough: Marlborough College Press, 1962).
NMG	*No More Ghosts: Selected Poems* (London: Faber, Sept. 1940).
NP62	*New Poems 1962* (London: Cassell, 1962; New York: Doubleday, 1963).
OB	*Over the Brazier* (London: Poetry Bookshop, 1916).
P14-26	*Poems (1914-26)* (London: Heinemann, 1927; New York: Doubleday, Doran, 1929).
P14-27	*Poems (1914-27)* (London: Heinemann (limited edition), June 1927).
P29	*Poems 1929* (London: Seizin Press (limited edition), Dec. 1929).
P26-30	*Poems 1926-1930* (London: Heinemann, Feb. 1931).
P30-33	*Poems 1930-1933* (London: Barker, May 1933).
P38-45	*Poems 1938-1945* (London: Cassell, Nov. 1945; New York: Creative Age Press, June 1946).
P53	*Poems 1953* (London: Cassell, Sept. 1953).
P68-70	*Poems 1968-1970* (London: Cassell, 1970; New York: Doubleday, 1971).
P70-72	*Poems 1970-1972* (London: Cassell, 1972; New York: Doubleday, 1973).
PAL	*Poems About Love* (New York: Doubleday, 1969; London: Cassell, 1969).
PBFS	*The Poor Boy Who Followed His Star* (London: Cassell, 1968).
PF	*The Penny Fiddle: Poems for Children*, illustrated by Edward Ardizzone (London: Cassell, 1960; New York: Doubleday, 1961).
P-G	*The Pier-Glass* (London: Secker, 1921; New York: Knopf, 1921).
PS51	*Poems and Satires 1951* (London: Cassell, Nov. 1951).
RG25	*Robert Graves*, Augustan Books of Modern Poetry (London: Benn, 1925).
RG43	*Robert Graves*, Augustan Poets, 2 (London: Eyre and Spottiswoode, 1943).
S	*Steps* (London: Cassell, Nov. 1958).
SL 1	*In Broken Images: Selected Letters of Robert Graves 1914-1946*, edited by Paul O'Prey (London: Hutchinson, 1982).
SL 2	*Between Moon and Moon: Selected Letters of Robert Graves 1946-1972*, edited by Paul O'Prey (London: Hutchinson, 1984).
SP57	*Poems Selected by Himself* (Harmondsworth: Penguin, 1957).
SP58	*The Poems of Robert Graves: Chosen by Himself* (New York: Doubleday Anchor, 1958).
SPP	*Selected Poetry and Prose of Robert Graves*, chosen, introduced and annotated by James Reeves (London: Hutchinson, 1961).
TB	*Treasure Box* (London: Chiswick Press (privately printed), 1919).

TWE	*To Whom Else?* (Deyá: Seizin Press (limited edition), July 1931).
W	*Whipperginny* (London: Heinemann, 1923; New York: Knopf, 1923).
WG	*The White Goddess* (editions below)
WG48	*The White Goddess: A Historical Grammar of Poetic Myth* (London: Faber, 1948; New York: Creative Age Press, 1948).
WG52	*The White Goddess: A Historical Grammar of Poetic Myth*, second edition (London: Faber, 1952; New York: Vintage, 1958).
WG61	*The White Goddess: A Historical Grammar of Poetic Myth*, third edition (London: Faber, 1961); revised edition, edited by Grevel Lindop (Manchester: Carcanet, 1997).
WH	*Welchman's Hose* (London: The Fleuron (limited edition), 1925).
WIH	*Work in Hand* (London: Hogarth Press, March 1942).

Bibliography

Higginson — Fred H. Higginson, *A Bibliography of the Writings of Robert Graves*, second edition, revised by William Proctor Williams (Winchester: St. Paul's Bibliographies, 1987).

Biography

RPG 1	Richard Perceval Graves, *Robert Graves: The Assault Heroic 1895-1926* (London: Weidenfeld and Nicolson, 1986).
RPG 2	Richard Perceval Graves, *Robert Graves: The Years with Laura 1926-1940* (London: Weidenfeld and Nicolson, 1990).
RPG 3	Richard Perceval Graves, *Robert Graves and the White Goddess 1940-1985* (London: Weidenfeld and Nicolson, 1995).

Manuscripts

All manuscript (*ms.*), typescript (*ts.*) and draft materials referred to in the notes are at Buffalo (see below), unless otherwise specified.

Buffalo	The Robert Graves Collection in the Poetry/Rare Books Collection, University Libraries, State University of New York at Buffalo.
Canelluñ	The collection at Robert Graves's house, Canelluñ, in Deyá, Mallorca.
Carbondale	The Morris Library, Southern Illinois University at Carbondale.
Diary	Robert Graves's diary, February 1935-May 1939, at the University of Victoria, British Columbia, Canada.
Texas	The Harry Ransom Humanities Research Center, the University of Texas at Austin.

THE POEMS: PUBLICATION DETAILS

This list summarizes the publication history of the poems in this volume. After each title, the data is given as follows: where first publication was in a periodical or anthology, the month and year (followed by (*E*) if *Epilogue*); the book by Graves in which the poem first appeared; and other books by him in which it was reprinted, if any. For abbreviations and dates of first book publication, see above. (The reader is referred to Higginson – on which the list is based – for other publication details.)

1805, Oct. 1942, *P38-45, CP14-47, CP55, SP57, SP58, CP59, SPP, CP61, CP65, CP75*

Act V, Scene 5, *10PM, P26-30, CP38, CP14-47, CP55, SP58, CP59, SPP, CP61*

Advice on May Day, Sept. 1950, *PS51*

Advocates (The Advocates), *CP38, NMG, CP14-47, CP55, SP57, SP58, CP59, CP61, CP65, CP75*

Against Kind, *P29, P26-30*

Ages of Oath, The, *CP38, CP14-47, CP55, SP57, SP58, CP59, CP61, CP65, CP75*

Alexander and Queen Janet (A Ballad of Alexander and Queen Janet), Dec. 1956, *5PH, S, CP59, CP61*

Allansford Pursuit, The, *CP14-47, WG, CP55, SP58*

Amergin's Charm (The Alphabet Calendar of Amergin), *CP14-47, WG, CP55, SP58, CP59, CP61*

Anagrammagic (The Tow-Path), *P29, P26-30*

Any Honest Housewife (The Poets), *CP38, NMG, CP14-47, CP55, SP57, SP58, CP59, SPP, CP61, CP65, CP75*

Apollo of the Physiologists, Summer 1943, *P38-45, CP14-47, CP55, SP58, CP59, CP61, CP65, CP75*

Around the Mountain, July 1958, *S, CP59, FC, CP61, CP65, PAL, CP75*

As It Were Poems, i, ii, iii, *TWE, P30-33*

At First Sight, *CP38, CP14-47, CP55, SP57, SP58, CP59, SPP, CP61, CP65, PAL, CP75*

At the Savoy Chapel, *P38-45, CP14-47, CP55, SP58, CP59, CP61*

Back Door, *P29*

Bards, The, (Lust in Song), *P30-33, CP38, NMG, CP14-47, CP55, SP57, SP58, CP59, CP61, CP65, CP75*

Battle of the Trees, The, Dec. 1945, *CP14-47, WG, CP55, SP58, CP59, CP61*

Bay of Naples, *P26-30*

Beach, The, Summer 1943, *P38-45, CP14-47, CP55, SP57, SP58, CP59, SPP, CP61, CP65, CP75*

Beauty in Trouble, Oct. 1954, *CP55, CrP, SP57, SP58, CP59, CP61, CP65, PAL, CP75*

Being Tall, *CP38*

Blotted Copy-Book, The, *P53, MDC*
Blue-Fly, The, July 1953, *P53, CP55, SP57, SP58, CP59, CP61, CP65, PAL, CP75*
Bouquet from a Fellow Roseman, A, June 1956, *5PH, SP58*
Brother, *P26-30, PS51, CP55, SP58, CP59, SPP, CP61, CP65, CP75*

Cabbage Patch (Green Cabbage Wit), *P29, P26-30*
Call It a Good Marriage, Oct. 1958, *S, CP59, FC, CP61, CP65, PAL, CP75*
Callow Captain, *CP38, CP14-47, CP55, SP58, CP59, CP61*
Castle, The, (Castle), *P29, P26-30, CP38, NMG, CP14-47, CP55, SP57, SP58, CP59, CP61, CP65, CP75*
Cat-Goddesses, March 1953, *P53, CP55, SP57, SP58, CP59, CP61, CP65, PAL, CP75*
Certain Mercies, *CP38, NMG, CP14-47, CP55, SP57, SP58, CP59, CP61, CP65, CP75*
Challenge, The, Nov. 1935 (*E*), *CP38, CP14-47, CP55, SP58*
China Plate, The, *CP38, CP14-47, CP55, SP57, SP58, CP59, SPP, CP61*
Chink, The, June 1949, *PS51, CP55, SP57, SP58, CP59, CP61, CP65, CP75*
Christmas Robin, The, (Wanderings of Christmas), Dec. 1935, *CP38, S, CP59, FC, CP61, CP65, PAL, CP75*
Civil Servant, A, *CP14-47, CP55, SP58, CP59, CP61*
Clearing, The, April 1955, *CrP, 5PH*
Climate of Thought, The, July 1936 (*E*), *CP38, CP14-47, CP55, SP58, CP59, CP61, CP65, CP75*
Cloak, The, April 1937 (*E*), *CP38, NMG, CP14-47, CP55, SP57, SP58, CP59, SPP, CP61, CP65, CP75*
Clock Man, The, (The Clock Men), *P30-33, CP38, CP14-47*
Cold Weather Proverb, *P38-45, CP14-47, CP55, SP58, CP59, CP61*
Commons of Sleep, The, *P30-33*
Conversation Piece, Aug. 1949, *PS51, CP55, SP57, SP58, CP59, CP61*
Coral Pool, The, April 1956, *5PH, SP58, S, CP59, CP61*
Coronation Address, June 1953, *CP55, CrP, SP58*
Counting the Beats, April 1950, *PS51, CP55, SP57, SP58, CP59, CP61, CP65, PAL, CP75*
Country Mansion, A, *CP38, CP14-47, CP55, SP57, SP58, CP59, CP61, CP65, CP75*
Cry Faugh! Dec. 1951, *P53, CP55, SP58, CP59, CP61, CP65, CP75*
Cuirassiers of the Frontier, The, *CP38, NMG, CP14-47, CP55, SP57, SP58, CP59, CP61, CP65, CP75*

Damocles, *PS51*
Danegeld, *P30-33*
Darien, Summer 1951, *PS51, CP55, SP57, SP58, CP59, CP61, CP65, CP75*
Dawn Bombardment, *WIH, P38-45, CP14-47, CP55, SP57, SP58, CP59, CP61, CP65, PAL, CP75*

Death by Drums, Jan. 1944, *P38-45, CP14-47, CP55, SP58, CP59, CP61, CP65, CP75*
Death Room, The, Feb. 1950, *PS51, CP55, SP57, SP58, CP59, CP61, CP65, CP75*
Defeat of the Rebels, *CP38, NMG, CP14-47, CP55, SP57, SP58, CP59, CP61*
Despite and Still, *WIH, P38-45, CP14-47, CP55, SP57, SP58, CP59, CP61, CP65, CP75*
Destroyer, The, *CP14-47, WG, CP55, SP58, CP59, CP61*
Destruction of Evidence, Dec. 1956, *5PH*
Dethronement, Dec. 1952, *P53, CP55, SP58, CP59, CP61*
Devil at Berry Pomeroy, The, Jan. 1953, *P53, CP55, SP58*
Devil's Advice to Story-Tellers, The, *CP38, CP14-47, CP55, SP57, SP58, CP59, CP61, CP65, CP75*
Devilishly Provoked (Devilishly Disturbed), *TWE, P30-33, MDC*
Dialogue on the Headland, June 1952, *P53, CP55, SP57, SP58, CP59, CP61, CP65, PAL, CP75*
Dichetal do Chennaib, *CP14-47, WG*
Dilemma, The, *PS51*
Dismissal (A), *P29, P26-30*
Door, The, Jan. 1944, *P38-45, CP14-47, CP55, SP57, SP58, CP59, CP61, CP65, PAL, CP75*
Down, Wanton, Down! *P30-33, CP38, NMG, CP14-47, CP55, SP57, SP58, CP59, CP61, CP65, PAL, CP75*
Dragons, *P26-30*
Dream of a Climber, *WIH, P38-45, CP14-47, CP55, SP58, CP59, CP61*

Encounter, The, Aug. 1953, *P53*
End of Play, April 1937 (*E*), *CP38, NMG, CP14-47, CP55, SP57, SP58, CP59, CP61, CP65, PAL, CP75*
End of The World, *CrP, 5PH*
Enlisted Man, The, May 1958, *S, CP59*
Eremites, The, *CP38, CP14-47, CP55, SP58*
Esau and Judith, *P53*
Eugenist, The, Oct. 1942, *P38-45, CP14-47, CP55, SP58, CP59, CP61*

Face in the Mirror, The, Jan. 1957, *5PH, S, CP59, CP61, CP65, PAL, CP75*
Fallen Signpost, The, *CP38, CP14-47, CP55, SP58, CP59, CP61*
Fallen Tower of Siloam, The, *CP38, NMG, CP14-47, CP55, SP57, SP58, CP59, CP61, CP65, CP75*
Felloe'd Year, The, *TWE, P30-33*
Fiend, Dragon, Mermaid, Nov. 1935 (*E*), *CP38*
Florist Rose, The, *CP38, NMG, CP14-47, CP55, SP57, SP58, CP59, CP61, CP65, CP75*
Flying Crooked, *P26-30, CP38, NMG, CP14-47, CP55, SP57, SP58, CP59, SPP, CP61, CP65, CP75*

Foolish Senses, The, *TWE, P30-33, CP38*
For the Rain It Raineth Every Day, March 1951, *PS51*
Forbidden Words, *5PH, S, CP59, CP61, CP65, PAL, CP75*
Foreboding, The, Dec. 1951, *P53, CP55, SP57, SP58, CP59, CP61, CP65, PAL, CP75*
Former Attachment, A, (Quayside), *P29, P26-30, CP38, CP14-47, CP55, SP57, SP58, CP59, CP61, CP65, CP75*
Fragment of a Lost Poem, *CP38, CP14-47, CP55, SP57, SP58, CP59, CP61, CP65, CP75*
Friday Night, Nov. 1957, *5PH, S, CP59, CP61, CP65, CP75*
Frightened Men, *WIH, P38-45, CP14-47, CP55, SP57, SP58, CP59, CP61, CP65, CP75*
From the Embassy, April 1953, *P53, CP55, SP57, SP58, CP59, CP61, CP65, CP75*
Front Door Soliloquy (Front Door), *P29, P26-30, CP38, CP14-47, CP55, SP58, CP59, CP61, CP65, CP75*
Furious Voyage, The, (The Dead Ship; Ship Master), *P14-27, P26-30, CP38, NMG, CP14-47, CP55, SP57, SP58, CP59, CP61, CP65, CP75*

Galatea and Pygmalion, *CP38, CP14-47, CP55, SP58, CP59, CP61*
Gardener (The Awkward Gardener), *P14-27, P26-30, CP38, CP14-47, CP55, SP57, SP58, CP59, SPP, CP61, CP65, CP75*
General Bloodstock's Lament for England, *PS51, CP55, SP58, CP59, CP61*
Ghost and the Clock, The, July 1951, *PS51*
Glutton, The, (The Beast), *NMG, WIH, P38-45, CP14-47, CP55, SP58, CP59, CP61*
Goblet, The, *CP38*
Gratitude for a Nightmare, June 1956, *5PH, S, CP59, CP61, CP65, CP75*
Great-Grandmother, The, *CP38, NMG, CP14-47, CP55, SP57, SP58, CP59, SPP, CP61, CP65, CP75*
Grotesques, i, ii, iii, iv, v, Summer 1943, *P38-45, CP14-47, CP55, SP57, SP58, CP59, CP61, CP65, CP75*
Grotesques, vi, *CP55, SP57, SP58, CP59, CP61, CP65, CP75*
Grudge, The, *CP38*
Guessing Black or White, *P29, P26-30*
Gulls and Men, *CP14-47, CP55, SP58, CP59, CP61*

Halfpenny, The, April 1937 (*E*), *CP38*
Halls of Bedlam, The, *CP38, CP14-47, CP55, SP57, SP58, CP59, CP61, CP65, CP75*
Hector, *P29, P26-30*
Hell, *P14-27, P26-30, CP38, CP14-47, CP55, SP57, SP58, CP59, CP61, CP65, CP75*

Hercules at Nemea, Dec. 1951, *P53, CP55, SP58, CP59, CP61, CP65, PAL, CP75*
Hero, The, *P53*
History of the Word, *10PM, P26-30, CP38, CP14-47, CP55, SP58, CP59, CP61*
Homage to Texas, Sept. 1950, *PS51*
Hotel Bed at Lugano (Hotel Bed), *CP38, 5PH, S, CP59, CP61*

I'm Through with You For Ever, March 1952, *P53, CP55, SP57, SP58, CP59, CP61*
Idle Hands, *CP38*
In Broken Images, *P29, P26-30, CP38, CP14-47, CP55, SP57, SP58, CP59, CP61, CP65, CP75*
In No Direction, *P29, P26-30, CP38, CP14-47, CP55, SP57, SP58, CP59, SPP, CP61, CP65, CP75*
Instructions to the Orphic Adept, *GF, P38-45, CP14-47, CP55, SP57, SP58, CP59, CP61, CP65, CP75*
Intercession in Late October, Oct. 1947, *CP14-47, CP55, SP57, SP58, CP59, CP61*
Interruption, *10PM, P26-30, CP38, CP14-47, CP55, SP58, CP59, CP61, CP65, CP75*
Interview, *CrP*
It Was All Very Tidy, *P29, P26-30, CP38, CP14-47, CP55, SP57, SP58, CP59, CP61, CP65, CP75*

Jackals' Address to Isis, The, Feb. 1950, *WG52, WG61, PS51, CP55, SP58, CP59, CP61*
Jealous Man, A, April 1937 (*E*), *CP38, NMG, CP14-47, CP55, SP57, SP58, CP59, CP61, CP65, PAL, CP75*
June, *CP14-47*

Lament for Pasiphaë, *GF, P38-45, CP14-47, CP55, SP57, SP58, CP59, CP61, CP65, PAL, CP75*
Language of the Seasons, *WIH, P38-45, CP14-47, CP55, SP57, SP58, CP59, CP61, CP65, CP75*
Largesse to the Poor, *TWE, P30-33, CP38, CP14-47*
Last Day of Leave, The, Nov. 1947, *CP14-47, CP55, SP58, CP59, CP61*
Laureate, The, May 1938, *CP38, NMG, CP14-47, CP55, SP57, SP58, CP59, SPP, CP61, CP65, CP75*
Leaving the Rest Unsaid, *CP38, P53, CP55, SP57, SP58, CP59, CP61, CP65, CP75*
Leda, *CP38, CP14-47, CP55, SP58, CP59, CP61, CP65, CP75*
Legs, The, *TWE, P30-33, CP38, NMG, CP14-47, CP55, SP57, SP58, CP59, CP61, CP65, CP75*
Liadan and Curithir, Sept. 1953, *P53, CP55, SP58, CP59, CP61, CP65, CP75*

Like Snow, Nov. 1935 (*E*), *CP38, CP14-47, CP55, SP58, CP59, CP61, CP65, PAL, CP75*

Lollocks, *WIH, P38-45, CP14-47, CP55, SP57, SP58, CP59, SPP, CP61, CP65, CP75*

Lost Acres (The), *P14-27, P26-30, CP38, CP14-47, CP55, SP57, SP58, CP59, SPP, CP61, CP65, CP75*

Lost Jewel, A, Dec. 1954, *CP55, CrP, SP57, SP58, CP59, CP61, CP65, PAL, CP75*

Love Story, A, *NMG, WIH, P38-45, CP14-47, CP55, SP57, SP58, CP59, CP61, CP65, PAL, CP75*

Lovers in Winter, Jan. 1952, *P53, CP55, SP57, SP58, CP59, CP61, CP65, CP75*

Lunch-Hour Blues, April 1937 (*E*), *CP38*

Marginal Warning, *P53*

Mark, The, July 1953, *P53, CP55, SP57, SP58, CP59, CP61*

Mid-Winter Waking, *WIH, P38-45, CP14-47, CP55, SP57, SP58, CP59, CP61, CP65, PAL, CP75*

Midway, *P29, P26-30, CP38, CP14-47, CP55, SP58, CP59, CP61*

Mike and Mandy (Caroline and Charles), *S, AHH*

Music at Night, *P30-33*

My Moral Forces, *CrP*

My Name and I, Jan. 1951, *PS51, CP55, SP57, SP58, CP59, SPP, CP61, CP65, CP75*

Naked and the Nude, The, Feb. 1957, *5PH, SP58, S, CP59, CP61, CP65, CP75*

Nature's Lineaments (Landscape), *P29, P26-30, CP38, NMG, CP14-47, CP55, SP57, SP58, CP59, SPP, CP61, CP65, CP75*

Never Such Love, July 1936 (*E*), *CP38, NMG, CP14-47, CP55, SP57, SP58, CP59, CP61, CP65, PAL, CP75*

New Legends (The Age of Certainty), *10PM, P26-30, CP38, CP14-47, CP55, SP57, SP58, CP59, CP61, CP65, CP75*

Next Time, The, *P26-30, CP38, CP14-47, CP55, SP58, CP59, SPP, CP61, CP65, CP75*

No More Ghosts, *CP38, NMG, CP14-47, CP55, SP57, SP58, CP59, CP61, CP65, CP75*

Nobody, *P30-33, CP38, CP14-47, CP55, SP57, SP58, CP59, SPP, CP61, CP65, CP75*

Nothing, April 1958, *S, CP59, FC, CP61, CP65, CP75*

Nuns and Fish, Winter 1946, *CP14-47, WG*

O Jorrocks, I Have Promised, *P14-27*

Oak, Poplar, Pine, *10PM*

Oath, The, *WIH, P38-45, CP14-47, CP55, SP58, CP59, CP61, CP65, PAL, CP75*

Ogres and Pygmies, *TWE, P30-33, CP38, NMG, CP14-47, CP55, SP57, SP58, CP59, CP61, CP65, CP75*
Oldest Soldier, The, Summer 1943, *P38-45, CP14-47, CP55, SP58, CP59, CP61, CP65, CP75*
On Dwelling, *TWE, P30-33, CP38, NMG, CP14-47, CP55, SP57, SP58, CP59, SPP, CP61, CP65, CP75*
On Necessity, *TWE, P30-33*
On Portents, *TWE, P30-33, CP38, NMG, CP14-47, CP55, SP57, SP58, CP59, CP61, CP65, PAL, CP75*
On Rising Early, *TWE, P30-33, CP38, CP14-47, CP55, SP57, SP58, CP59, CP61, CP65, CP75*
Or to Perish Before Day, *CP38, CP14-47, CP55, SP58, CP59, CP61, CP65, CP75*
Outsider, The, May 1957, *5PH*

Parent to Children, April 1937 (*E*), *CP38, CP14-47, CP55, SP57, SP58*
Penthesileia, *CP55, CrP, SP58, CP59, CP61, CP65, CP75*
Persian Version, The, Summer 1943, *P38-45, CP14-47, CP55, SP57, SP58, CP59, CP61, CP65, CP75*
Philatelist-Royal, The, (Philatelist Royal), *P14-27, P26-30, MDC*
Philosopher, The, (The Cell), *P30-33, CP38, CP14-47, CP55, SP57, SP58, CP59, CP61, CP65, CP75*
Plea to Boys and Girls, A, Dec. 1956, *5PH, S, CP59, SPP, CP61, CP65, CP75*
Poets' Corner, *CP55, CrP, SP58, CP59, CP61*
Portrait, The, *PS51, CP55, SP57, SP58, CP59, CP61, CP65, PAL, CP75*
Possibly (The Question), July 1955, *CrP, 5PH, P65-68, PAL, CP75*
Progress, The, *P14-27, PS51, CP55, SP58, CP59, CP61, CP65, CP75*
Progressive Housing, *CP38*
Prometheus, Summer 1951, *PS51, CP55, SP57, SP58, CP59, CP61, CP65, CP75*

Queen-Mother to New Queen, Summer 1951, *PS51, CP55, SP58*
Questions in a Wood, Nov. 1951, *PS51, CP55, SP57, SP58, CP59, CP61, CP65, PAL, CP75*

Read Me, Please! Oct. 1958, *S, CP59, FC*
Reader Over My Shoulder, (To) The, *10PM, P26-30, CP38, CP14-47, CP55, SP57, SP58, CP59, CP61, CP65, CP75*
Reassurance to the Satyr, *P26-30*
Recalling War, *CP38, NMG, CP14-47, CP55, SP57, SP58, CP59, CP61*
Reproach to Julia, *P53, CP55, SP58, CP59, CP61*
Return Fare, *P29, P26-30*
Return of the Goddess, Oct. 1947, *CP14-47, WG, CP55, SP58, CP59, CP61, CP65, CP75*
Rhea, July 1952, *P53, CP55, SP57, SP58, CP59, CP61, CP65, PAL, CP75*
Rock at the Corner, The, *WIH, P38-45, CP14-47, CP55, SP58, CP59, CP61*

Sacred Mission, The, Oct. 1952, *P53, CP55, SP58, CP59, CP61*
Saint (The Beast), *10PM, P26-30, CP38, CP14-47, CP55, SP58, CP59*
Sea Horse, The, Aug. 1953, *P53, CP55, CrP, SP57, SP58, CP59, CP61, CP65, CP75*
Sea Side (Sandhills), *P29, P26-30, CP38, CP14-47, CP55, SP57, SP58, CP59, CP61, CP65, CP75*
Secession of the Drones, *PS51*
Second-Fated, The, Jan. 1957, *5PH, S, CP59, CP61, CP65, CP75*
Self-Praise, *CP38, CP14-47, CP55, SP58*
She Tells Her Love While Half Asleep, *GF, P38-45, CP14-47, CP55, SP57, SP58, CP59, CP61, CP65, PAL, CP75*
Sheet of Paper, A, *P29*
Shot, The, *WIH, P38-45, CP14-47, CP55, SP57, SP58, CP59, CP61, CP65, CP75*
Sick Love (Between Dark and Dark; O Love in Me), *P29, P26-30, CP38, CP14-47, CP55, SP57, SP58, CP59, CP61, CP65, PAL, CP75*
Single Fare, *P29, P26-30, CP38, CP14-47, CP55, SP58, CP59, CP61, CP65, CP75*
Sirens' Welcome to Cronos, The, Sept. 1947, *CP14-47, WG, CP55, SP58, CP59, CP61*
Sirocco at Deyá, June 1953, *P53, CP55, SP57, SP58, CP59, CP61, CP65, CP75*
Slice of Wedding Cake, A, (Bitter Thoughts on Receiving a Slice of Cordelia's Wedding Cake), July 1957, *5PH, SP58, S, CP59, CP61, CP65, PAL, CP75*
Smoky House, The, *CP38*
Song for New Year's Eve, *5PH, S*
Song of Blodeuwedd, The, Dec. 1945, *CP14-47, WG, CP55, SP57, SP58, CP59, CP61, CP65, PAL, CP75*
Song: **Lift-Boy (Lift-Boy; Tail Piece: A Song to Make You and Me Laugh),** *10PM, P26-30, CP38, CP14-47, CP55, SP57, SP58, CP59, PF, CP61, CP65, CP75*
Song: To Be Less Philosophical (To Be Less Philosophical), *P14-27, P26-30, CP38, MDC*
Spoils, May 1954, *CP55, CrP, SP57, SP58, CP59, CP61, CP65, PAL, CP75*
Stranger, The, *CP38*
Stranger at the Party, A, *WIH, P38-45, CP14-47, CP55, SP58*
Straw, The, Dec. 1951, *P53, CP55, SP57, SP58, CP59, CP61, CP65, PAL, CP75*
Succubus, The, *P30-33, CP38, CP14-47, CP55, SP57, SP58, CP59, CP61, CP65, PAL, CP75*
Suicide in the Copse, The, *WIH, P38-45, CP14-47, CP55, SP57, SP58, CP59, CP61, CP65, CP75*
Survival of Love, *10PM*
Survivor, The, May 1951, *PS51, CP55, SP57, SP58, CP59, CP61, CP65, PAL, CP75*
Synthetic Such, *P26-30, CP38, CP14-47, CP55, SP57, SP58, CP59, CP61, CP65, CP75*

Tap Room (Cracking the Nut Against the Hammer), *10PM, P26-30*
Tenants, The, Sept. 1955, *CrP*
Terraced Valley, The, *10PM, P26-30, CP38, CP14-47, CP55, SP57, SP58, CP59, CP61, CP65, PAL, CP75*
Tetragrammaton, The, *CP14-47, WG*
Theseus and Ariadne, *GF, P38-45, CP14-47, CP55, SP57, SP58, CP59, CP61, CP65, PAL, CP75*
Thief (To the Galleys), *P29, P26-30, CP38, CP14-47, CP55, SP57, SP58, CP59, CP61, CP65, CP75*
Thieves, The, *NMG, WIH, P38-45, CP14-47, CP55, SP57, SP58, CP59, CP61, CP65, PAL, CP75*
Three Pebbles, The, June 1955, *CrP*
Through Nightmare, Jan. 1944, *P38-45, CP14-47, CP55, SP57, SP58, CP59, CP61, CP65, PAL, CP75*
Time (On Time), *TWE, P30-33, CP38, CP14-47, CP55, SP57, SP58, CP59, SPP, CP61, CP65, CP75*
To a Charge of Didacticism, *P14-27*
To a Pebble in My Shoe, *CrP*
To a Poet in Trouble, *PS51*
To Be Called a Bear (To Be Named a Bear), Oct. 1947, *CP14-47, CP55, SP57, SP58, CP59, CP61, CP65, PAL, CP75*
To Bring the Dead to Life, Feb. 1936, *CP38, CP14-47, CP55, SP57, SP58, CP59, SPP, CP61, CP65, CP75*
To Calliope, *P53, CP55, SP58, CP59, CP61*
To Challenge Delight, *CP38*
To Evoke Posterity, *CP38, CP14-47, CP55, SP57, SP58, CP59, SPP, CP61, CP65, CP75*
To Juan at the Winter Solstice, *P38-45, CP14-47, CP55, SP57, SP58, CP59, CP61, CP65, PAL, CP75*
To Lucia at Birth, Jan. 1944, *P38-45, CP14-47, CP55, SP58, CP59, SPP, CP61, CP65, CP75*
To Poets Under Pisces, *CP14-47*
To Sleep, *NMG, WIH, P38-45, CP14-47, CP55, SP57, SP58, CP59, CP61, CP65, PAL, CP75*
To the Sovereign Muse, Nov. 1935 (*E*), *CP38, CP14-47*
To Walk on Hills, July 1936 (*E*), *CP38, CP14-47, CP55, SP57, SP58, CP59, CP61, CP65, CP75*
To Whom Else? *TWE, P30-33, CP38*
Trudge, Body! *P30-33, CP38, CP14-47, S, CP59, FC, CP61, CP65, CP75*
Twelve Days of Christmas, The, *P38-45, CP14-47*
Twin of Sleep, The, Sept. 1958, *S, CP59, FC, SPP, CP61, CP65, CP75*

Ulysses, *P30-33, CP38, CP14-47, CP55, SP57, SP58, CP59, CP61, CP65, CP75*
Under the Pot, Jan. 1944, *P38-45, CP14-47, CP55, SP57, SP58, CP59, SPP, CP61, CP65, CP75*

Variables of Green (Green Loving), Nov. 1935 (*E*), *CP38, CP14-47, MDC, NP62, CP65, PAL, CP75*

Villagers and Death, The, Summer 1943, *P38-45, CP14-47, CP55, SP57, SP58, CP59, CP61, CP65, CP75*

Vision in the Repair-Shop (Repair Shop), *P29, P26-30, CP38, CP14-47, CP55, SP58, CP59, CP61*

Warning to Children, April 1929, *P29, P26-30, CP38, CP14-47, CP55, SP57, SP58, CP59, PF, SPP, CP61, CP65, CP75*

Weather of Olympus, The, Summer 1943, *P38-45, CP14-47, CP55, SP57, SP58, CP59, CP61, CP65, CP75*

'¡Wellcome, to the Caves of Artá!', Dec. 1950, *PS51, CP55, SP58, CP59, CP61*

Welsh Incident (Railway Carriage), *P29, P26-30, CP38, CP14-47, CP55, SP57, SP58, CP59, CP61, CP65, CP75*

What Times Are These? *P30-33*

White Goddess, The, *WG, PS51, CP55, SP57, SP58, CP59, CP61, CP65, CP75*

Window Sill, The, Oct. 1954, *CP55, CrP, SP57, SP58, CP59, CP61, CP65, PAL, CP75*

With Her Lips Only, April 1953, *P53, CP55, SP57, SP58, CP59, CP61, CP65, PAL, CP75*

With the Gift of a Ring, Dec. 1951, *P53, CP55, SP58, CP59*

Withering Herb, A, *WIH, P38-45, CP14-47*

Without Pause, *P30-33, CP38, CP14-47*

Wm. Brazier (Pavement), *P29, P26-30, CP38, CP14-47, CP55, SP57, SP58, CP59, CP61, CP65, CP75*

Woman and Tree, June 1956, *5PH, SP58, S, CP59, CP61, CP65, CP75*

Worms of History, The, *WIH, P38-45, CP14-47, CP55, SP58, CP59, CP61*

X, *CP38*

Yes, Feb. 1957, *5PH*

Young Cordwainer, The, June 1951, *PS51, CP55, SP58, CP59, CP61, CP65, PAL, CP75*

Your Private Way, *PS51, CP55, SP57, SP58, CP59, CP61, CP65, CP75*

NOTES ON THE POEMS

The notes, like the poems, are arranged according to the first editions of Graves's books of verse, with a brief introduction to each book.

Textual notes are keyed to the text by stanza (*st.*), section (*sect.*) and line numbers (in some instances, paragraph numbers and keywords indicating sentences have also been used).

As in the text, single quotation marks have been adopted.

The data on the poems is given in this order:

i) Background information, with quotations from and/or references to other poems, letters, and prose works. When *The White Goddess* is cited, the abbreviation *WG61* is followed by the page reference to the 1961 edition, and then, after an oblique stroke, to the 1997 one.

ii) 'Text': the abbreviation for the book(s) from which the last version has been taken for the text of this edition.

iii) Previous titles (in books), and headnotes.

iv) 'Emendations': the emendation is given first, followed by a closing square bracket; the unemended text is then quoted to the right of the bracket. Where an earlier reading has been preferred, the source is indicated. *Ed.* denotes an editorial correction.

v) 'Variants': lists under this heading (or 'Other variants') are preceded and/or followed by any omitted material, together with other details about different versions. In the lists, the version in this edition is quoted on the left, followed by a closing square bracket (as with 'Emendations'); to the right of the bracket is the reading in the first edition (unless otherwise specified). When a whole line has been revised, only the line in the first edition is given. For successive quotations from the same text, the abbreviation for the book only appears after the initial quotation, to avoid undue repetition.

POEMS (1914-27) (1927)

'I have sent you a copy of my poems,' Graves wrote to Siegfried Sassoon on 5 June 1927.[1] 'Very soon I am going to give you a limited edition copy which is the same plus nine additional poems with a better paper, longer page and plain white (jap) vellum binding and plain lettering.'[2]

Poems (1914-27) was published by Heinemann in June 1927 in an edition of 115 numbered and signed copies, of which 100 were for sale; *Poems (1914-26)*, published at the beginning of the month in an edition of 1000 copies, was Graves's first *Collected Poems*.[3]

---

[1] Concerning Graves's relationship with Sassoon (1886-1967), see *Complete Poems*, Volume I, p.341, footnote 8, and 'A Letter from Wales' (*WH*) and the note on the poem (pp.66-70, 404-5); for their quarrel over *GTAT29*, see *SL 1*, pp.196-209.

[2] *SL 1*, p.175.

[3] See *Complete Poems*, Volume I, pp.413-15.

The Progress

Text: *CP75*.

Headnote in *P14-27*: '*(An early poem recast)*'.

An early ms. version entitled 'The Last March' has three five-line stanzas. The third stanza was reduced to four lines when the poem was revised and published as 'The Progress' in *P14-27*. It reappeared in its final form in *PS51* as the first of four recast poems in the concluding section, 'Revisions'.

The first two stanzas in *P14-27*:

A wilfulness to drink at every well
And hate the peace that cools
A single native spring
Marks the poor coward and the tremendous king
And many fools.

Even for the king it is a barren spell
That draws his trustless feet
To trample and depart:
It wakes in him at length a trustless heart
Ashamed before retreat.

Variants:

st. 2 l. 1 displays *CP75*] betrays *P14-27*
l. 3 Who,] That,
set] sets

Hell

Text: *CP75*.

Variants:

st. 1 l. 3 And *CP75*] So *P14-27*
st. 2 l. 1 Or] And
l. 2 sense] soul
l. 3 These the great-devil tenderly as a lover
st. 3 l. 3 steers] leads
st. 4 in *P14-27* (recast in *CP38*):

When living words and men meet, two and two
In this one-twentieth part still actual scene,
They exchange pinches at their 'How d'ye do?'
For a punctilious 'Do you mean what you mean?'

The Furious Voyage

Text: *CP75*.

Previous titles: 'The Dead Ship' (*P14-27*), 'Ship Master' (*P26-30*).

Variant:

st. 3 l. 3 its unmanageable *CP75*] an ignoble random *P14-27*

O Jorrocks, I Have Promised

See the hymn 'O Jesus, I have promised' (1869) by the English clergyman John Ernest Bode (1816-74):

> O speak to reassure me,
> To hasten or control;
> O speak, and make me listen,
> Thou Guardian of my soul.

Mr John Jorrocks, the sporting Cockney grocer, is the central character in the hunting sketches and novels by R.S. Surtees (1803-1864); cf. Graves to Sassoon, 31 Oct. 1927; *SL 1*, p.181: 'Do get on with your Jorrocks book' (i.e. *Memoirs of a Fox-Hunting Man* (London: Faber and Gwyer, 1928).

Text: *P14-27.*

Lost Acres

Text: *CP75.*

Previous title: 'The Lost Acres' (*P14-27*).

Variants:

st. 1 *l. 2* every *CP75*] each *P14-27*
st. 3 *l. 2* And] So
likely] likeliest
st. 5 *l. 1* Yet there's no scientific need
l. 2 of] in
st. 6 *l. 1* Maybe they have] They have, no doubt,
l. 3 a substance without] the substance of mere

Gardener

Text: *CP75.*

Previous title: 'The Awkward Gardener' (*P14-27*).

Variants:

st. 2 *l. 3* Said *CP75*] That *P14-27*
st. 3 *l. 3* would] could
an] the
l. 4 yard-stick] distance

The Philatelist-Royal

Text: *MDC.*

Emendations:

l. 7 wittily), *P14-27, P26-30*] wittily) *MDC*
l. 42 democratic, *P26-30*] democratic *P14-27, MDC*

When he revised the poem for *MDC* (1962), Graves evidently used the version in *P14-27*, overlooking changes in *P26-30*, where it is entitled 'Philatelist Royal' and after 'reliance' in l. 6 has 'on' in ll. 8 and 9 instead of 'in' (*P14-27, MDC*). (In the 'Contents' in *MDC* the poem is mistakenly dated 1929.)

Variants:

l. 32 mystery. *MDC*] mystery, *P14-27*
l. 44 bottle,] Bottle,

Song: To Be Less Philosophical

Text: *CP38.*

'Song:' was added to the title in *CP38.*

MDC reproduces the *P14-27* version (though dated 1931 in the 'Contents'), with two punctuation changes: the first, the omission of a comma after 'God' in st.1 l.4, has been incorporated in this edition; the second, a comma instead of a full stop after 'infinite' in st.2 l.1, is already in *CP38.*

Other variants:

st. 1 l. 3 Hearken, you *CP38*] Hearken you, *P14-27*
st. 2 l. 4 variety.] generality.
st. 3 l. 1 God, he] God *he*
l. 2 God, she] God *she*
l. 4 And likes to be correctly.

In *P14-27*, sts.4-10 have the first word in l.1 in italics.

st. 5 l. 2 From] To
l. 4 a little prize in Paris.] the Victoria Cross.
st. 6 l. 2 employed quite] used very
st. 8 l. 1 tending] coming
ll. 3-4:

To speculate more confusedly
And defy the universal.

st. 9 l. 1 Goddam] Victoria
l. 3 more personally,] confusedly
st. 10 l. 1 Paris hat] Russian count
l. 2 be divorced quite] each be served very

POEMS 1929 (1929)

Poems 1929 was printed and published in a limited edition (225 numbered, signed copies) in December 1929 by the Seizin Press, which Graves and Laura Riding set up in 1927 at their flat in Hammersmith, London.[4]

---

[4] This was the third book – 'Seizin 3' – published in London by the Seizin Press. (Seizin 1 was a collection of poems by Riding, *Love as Love, Death as Death* (1928); Seizin 2 was Gertrude Stein's *An Acquaintance with Description* (1929).) By the time *Poems 1929* appeared Graves and Riding were in Mallorca, where they arrived at the end of October 1929, and as soon as they were settled in Deyá they had the press sent over (*RPG 2*, pp.125, 129). There they published four more books,

Sick Love

Text: *CP75*.

Previous titles: 'Between Dark and Dark' (*P29*), 'O Love in Me' (*P26-30*).

Variants:

st. 1 *l. 1* Love, *CP75*] love, *P29*
l. 3 causeway,] causeway.
st. 2 *l. 3* fury:] fury,

In No Direction

Text: *CP75*.

Variants:

st. 1 *l. 4* I *CP75*] Was *P29*
st. 2 *l. 1* Either I sent] Neither to send
l. 3 might] may
sts. 3-4 in *P29*:

Nor in superstition
To approach, to edge away,
To keep a path's direction,
Nor with care to stray.

Nor to avoid the way
That was not avoided
Directionless some other day
Or that was avoided.

st. 5 *l. 1* Or called] Nor to take
l. 2 An] Some
l. 3 held] hold
l. 4 my] the
were] are

---

hand-set and hand-printed on hand-made paper, in quarto format, with covers by Len Lye (see the note on *Ten Poems More*): Graves's *To Whom Else?* (1931) (see note); Riding's *Though Gently* (1930) and *Laura and Francisca* (1931); and a selection from Len Lye's letters, *No Trouble* (1930). To Graves the word 'seizin', an archaic term for 'possession', meant (as he later recalled) 'that we were our own masters and no longer dependent on publishers who would tell us that our poems did not fit the image of poetry which they wished to present to the public'. (Quoted by James Moran, 'The Seizin Press of Laura Riding and Robert Graves', *The Black Art*, 2, no. 2 (Summer 1963), 34-9 (pp.35-6).) In 1935-7 the Seizin Press collaborated with Constable to publish nine commercially produced books of prose, including Graves's novel *Antigua, Penny, Puce* (1936), and three volumes of the periodical *Epilogue* (see the note on 'Variables of Green' (*CP38*)). Graves later used the Seizin imprint again twice to publish collections of poems by friends, Jay MacPherson's *Nineteen Poems* (1952) and Terence Hards's *As It Was* (1964). The New Seizin Press was started in Deyá by Graves's son Tomás in 1983.

In Broken Images

Text: *CP75*.

In *P29* the poem is not divided into stanzas, which first appear in *P26-30*.

Thief

Text: *CP75*.

Previous title: 'To the Galleys' (*P29*).

Variants:

l. 3 find *CP75*] have *P29*
l. 8 sour] soured
l. 11 a craft] the galley

Warning to Children

Text: *CP75*.

After thirty years a contradiction[5] was partly rectified when 'leave the string untied' (l.22 in *P29*) became, in *CP59*, 'leave the string alone!' For a further six years, however, the parcel itself remained 'untied' (l.26 in *P29*) instead of 'unopened' (l.32 in *CP65* and *CP75*; this is one of Graves's emendations in his library copy of *SPP* (1961)).

Other variants:

l. 2 All the many largeness, smallness, *P29*
l. 3 precious *CP75*] single
l. 6 Blocks] Lumps
ll. 10-11:

In the acres a brown paper
Parcel, then untie the string.

l. 15 pare] cut
l. 16 kernel] centre
l. 17 Blocks] Lumps
ll. 21-2:

In the acres a brown paper
Parcel, leave the string untied.

l. 23 For who dares] If you dare
l. 24 Finds himself at once] You will find yourself

The two lines in *P29* following l.25:

With the parcel still untied,
Just like any lump of slate,

l. 27 Finds himself] Find yourself

Lines 31-2 were added in *CP38*, where most of the other revisions appear.

---

[5] It was finally noticed by Karl Gay (Goldschmidt), Graves's assistant.

l. 33	And, if he then should] And, children, if you
l. 34	All the many largeness, smallness,
l. 35	Greatness] Fewness
	endless] single
l. 36	Precious] Endless
	he says] you say
l. 37	He lives – he] You live, you
	unties] untie

Dismissal

Text: *P26-30.*

Previous title: 'A Dismissal' (*P29*).

Guessing Black or White

Cf. 'A Journal of Curiosities (August 23rd to September 30th, 1929)' in *But It Still Goes On: An Accumulation* (London: Cape, 1930), p.141:

> Guessing Black or White. I forget who it was who once challenged me to this game. He said that he would guess right three times out of four whether I was going to say black or white. I saw that it was a question of deciding what degree I would reach of negativity, e.g. 'Not black because black the last time,' or 'black because not black because black the last time.' I defeated him by making no negative degrees, but invisibly to him tossing up a button in my pocket and choosing black or white according to which side up the button fell. He was furious when I told him how I had managed it.

Text: *P26-30.*

Against Kind

See *GTAT29*, 'Dedicatory Epilogue to Laura Riding', p.443:

> [. . .] you will be glad to find no reference at all to yourself in the body of this book. [. . .]
>
> The reason [. . .] is, of course, that by mentioning you as a character in my autobiography I would seem to be denying you in your true quality of one living invisibly, against kind, as dead, beyond event.

Cf. Riding's autograph comments on a ts. of 'Against Kind' (incorporating the *P26-30* revisions): st.3 l.2 'private': 'get more feelingful word'; st.4 l.2 'over-simple': 'not quite right'; and at the bottom of the page: 'I haven't gone on correcting this – because I don't think it's a sincere poem, especiall[y] as it goes on – a sort of duty-poem, its emotions not the same as *your* emotions.'

Text: *P26-30.*

Variants:

st. 2	*l. 4*	be *P26-30*] to *P29* (*error in ts.*)
st. 3	*l. 4*	And] So
		did not think to mourn] were not loth to lose

st. 4 *l. 1* But soon] And yet
l. 2 and] but
l. 3 Not witnessed to] Unitemized
st. 5 *l. 1* rebuttal;] omission;
st. 6 *l. 2* (now hating] (they hated
st. 7 *l. 2* Tempted] Rummaged
dulness wore] grief perplexed
st. 8 *l. 2* humouring] not humouring
st. 9 *l. 1* at last they] they therefore
st. 10 *l. 1* and] as
stay] are

The typescript with Riding's comments has 'as Gyges' for 'as a Gyges' in st.8 l.4 (and several punctuation changes not included in *P26-30*).

Midway

Text: *CP61.*

Variants:

l. 1 monstrosities *CP61*] multiples *P29*
l. 2 exiguities insufferable,] as insufferable pauciples
l. 3 own station.] convenience;
l. 5 Unless for the weather's sake or when we dance.
l. 6 no truck either] a date neither
l. 7 or] nor
l. 8 Our world] The scale
untrembling] at this point
l. 9 Old] Our
l. 11 Is quotable or is not to be quoted.
l. 13 between our buffers.] to our time-tables.
Space] space
l. 14 Amuse us merely] Once more distract us
l. 16 A necessary superstition groans
l. 17 – God's evening prayer, not ours.] and improvises God;
l. 18 read:] read
l. 19 By the unbelieving for the unremembering.

CP38 and *CP14-47* have an extra line before l.1, 'Man is the vavasour of this Creation:' (with 'his' for 'man's' in l.4).

Cabbage Patch

Text: *P26-30.*

Previous title: 'Green Cabbage Wit' (*P29*).

Emendation:

st. 3 *l. 1* green cabbage-wit *mss, ts., P29*] green-cabbage wit *P26-30*

The Castle

See the note on 'The Devil at Berry Pomeroy' (*P53*).

Text: *CP75.*

Previous title: 'Castle' (*P29, P26-30*).

Variants:

l. 7 moat – *CP75*] moats – *P29*
l. 8 *no line break in P29*
l. 10 robe] cheek
l. 19 To] And
by] in

Welsh Incident

Text: *CP75.*
Previous title: 'Railway Carriage' (*P29, P26-30*).
Variants:

l. 7 Very strange, un-Welsh, *CP75*] Various, extravagant, *P29*
l. 10 All strangest shapes, sizes and sizelessnesses, *P29*
l. 15 puce] blue
l. 16 crimson,] yellow,
purplish.] greenish.
l. 18 nor] or
l. 21 How] What
l. 36 wonder,] strangeness
l. 39 noise of scuffling?'] scuffling noise?'

The next three lines were added in *CP38*; they replaced ll.40-1 in *P29*:
'No, a loud belch, so resonant and rumbling
It robbed the hospital of five hundred pounds.'

Front Door Soliloquy

Text: *CP75.*
Previous title: 'Front Door' (*P29, P26-30*).
Variants:

l. 1 'Yet *CP75*] Since *P29*
what] that
l. 2 which] this
what] that
l. 3 which,] this,
l. 7 which] this
what,] that,
l. 11 and not wound the wood,] without wounding wood,
l. 14 what and what] that and that
which] this
l. 15 thus,] so,
l. 16 artists-of-the-world-unite,] artists of the world unite,
which,] this,
l. 17 what,] that,
l. 21 spite] love
l. 22 by] to
l. 23 you] mean,
l. 24 which] this
what] that

The last two lines in *P29* (ll.27-8):

> Keep well behind the railings, if you must watch,
> Lest they mistake you this for that you are.

Quotation marks were put around the poem when 'Soliloquy' was added to its title in *CP38*.

Anagrammagic

Just after Graves wrote this poem he received a letter from a stranger containing a series of anagrams made from the title of one of his poems, 'Attercop: The All-Wise Spider' (*MBH*); together, the anagrams recounted an 'uncomfortable' dream Graves had had two days before the letter was written.[6]

Text: *P26-30*.
Previous title: 'The Tow-Path' (*P29*).

Vision in the Repair-Shop

Text: *CP61*.
Previous title: 'Repair Shop' (*P29, P26-30*).
Variants:
The first line in *P29*, omitted in *CP38* and subsequently:
Because not nearly, therefore quite,
l. 1 Be sure the *CP61*] The
worse] more
l. 8 you saw] we see
l. 9 garage-man-in-chief,] garage-man in chief,

Nature's Lineaments

Text: *CP75*.
Previous title: 'Landscape' (*P29, P26-30*).
Emendation:
st. 5 l. 3 sheep's *P29*] sheeps' *CP59, CP65, CP75*
Variants:
st. 2 l. 3 Nor *CP75*] Or *P29*
st. 4 l. 2 That brutal-comic mind,
l. 3 Is] As

As revised for *CP38*, st.4 l.2 refers to 'Nature' as 'it'; 'she' is substituted in *CP59*.

Sea Side

Text: *CP75*.
Previous title: 'Sandhills' (*P29, P26-30*).

---

[6] See the *Star*, 22 May 1928, p.4. 'The chief scene [in the dream] was where I was being introduced to a man who came up to me at a cocktail bar and shook my hand, saying, "Perhaps you prefer not to meet me; my name is Oscar Wilde."'

sect. 1 l. 4 and *CP75*] with *P29*
sect. 2 l. 3 To] By
l. 4 see,] is
l. 5 Patterned] Disposed
l. 6 a view] the view.
ll. 7-8 (revised for *CP38*):

Rather an antique Three (beard, beard and bird,
Or three old spinning women, spinning hard)

l. 9 With] Than
The poem was divided into two sections in *P26-30*.

Wm. Brazier
Text: *CP75*.
Previous title: 'Pavement' (*P29, P26-30*).
Variants:
l. 1 Tarriers' *CP75*] Red Lion *P29*
l. 2 in Town] in the town
In *P29* and *P26-30*, l.7 has a full stop, and the closing bracket is at the end of a further line, omitted in *CP38*:
As I was saying, at the end of the Lane]
l. 16 Wasn't that pretty?] 'Isn't that pretty?'
jeered:] cried
l. 17 Dirty-face] how are you,
l. 19 were] was
l. 20 damned] dam
The closing bracket in l.20 comes at the end of the final line in *P29* and *P26-30*.

A Former Attachment
Text: *CP75*.
Previous title: 'Quayside' (*P29, P26-30*).
Variants:
l. 2 meant even less to me than *CP75*] was not nearly so good as *P29*
l. 4 slide] sliding
l. 5 become] growing
feel a calm] having real

Return Fare
Cf. *GTAT29*, 'Dedicatory Epilogue to Laura Riding', pp.444-5:

Yet I must relieve your parable of all anecdote of mine. I must tell, for instance, that in its extreme course in April last I relived the changes of many past years. That when I must suddenly hurry off to Ireland I found myself on the very boat, from Fishguard, that had been my hospital-boat twelve years before. That at Limerick I met Old Ireland herself sitting black-shawled and mourning on the station bench and telling of the Fall. And so to the beautiful city of Sligo celebrated in song by my father.

See *RPG 2*, p.80. Graves made the journey to Ireland on 2 April 1929 in search of Geoffrey Phibbs, who had been living in London in a *ménage à quatre* with Laura Riding, Graves and Graves's wife, Nancy Nicholson, at 35A St Peter's Square, Hammersmith ('salmon' (l.21): on the reverse of the Irish two-shilling coin (florin)). Phibbs was not at Lisheen, his family home 'near Sligo' (l.30; see also the following poem, 'Single Fare', l.19), having gone to France to be reunited (temporarily) with his wife. The drama caused by Phibbs's defection culminated in Riding's attempted suicide by throwing herself from a window on 27 April. See *GTAT29*, p.445; and *RPG 2*, pp.71-116.

Text: *P26-30.*
Variants:

l. 4 Liliburlero *P26-30*] *Lilibulero P29* (cf. 'lilli burlero', 'Lillibullero', the nearest forms in the *Oxford English Dictionary*)

Single Fare

Various personal connections with Ireland are alluded to in ll.18-20. Cooper's Hill,[7] near Limerick, was the ancestral home of Jane Cooper (d. 1886), first wife of Graves's father, the poet Alfred Perceval Graves (1846-1931). Lisheen, in County Sligo, was the family home of Geoffrey Phibbs; see the note on 'Return Fare' (*P29*), above. Cloghan Castle, at Lusmagh, south of Banagher, County Offaly, was bought in 1852 by one of Graves's ancestors, Dr Robert James Graves (1796-1853), the Dublin physician who in 1835 identified exophthalmic goitre, named Graves's disease after him. Killua, in Clonmellon, West Meath, was the seat of the Chapman family; Thomas Robert Tighe Chapman (who changed his name to Lawrence) was the father of Graves's friend T.E. Lawrence; see the note on 'The Pier-Glass' (*P-G*), *Complete Poems*, Volume I, p.365.

There is another personal connection in l.14: Nancy Nicholson's great-granduncle was the painter Robert Scott Lauder of the Bass (1803-1869). The Bass Rock was the property of the Lauders from the fourteenth century until it was bought by the government in 1671. (Held by a small group of Jacobites from June 1691 to April 1694, the island was the last place in Britain to surrender to William III.)

Text: *CP75.*
Variants:

l. 1 way of *CP75*] Holyhead or *P29*
the lying devils] the devils

l. 2 back to Holy] now returned to

[7] See *GTAT29*, pp.21-2, 347.

ll. 3-5:

Each took a single fare; it is an island
In the Atlantic north and west of France.
And the dumb devils also into Scotland

l. 8 Eire] Erin
l. 10 from] of
l. 12 to what township did they book,] where exactly did they go,
l. 15 Leagued with] Fronting
l. 18 'Is there no loyalist's country seat in Ireland
l. 19 stands] standing
– as Cooper's] – Cooper's

It Was All Very Tidy

Text: *CP75*.

Emendation:

The space between sts.5 and 6, omitted in error in *CP75* (st.5 ends at the bottom of the page (p.64) in *CP65*) has been restored.

Variants:

st. 2 *l. 5* nodded: *CP75*] laughed. *P29*
st. 4 *l. 3* 'Am I not myself?'
st. 6 *l. 1* not think] consent
st. 7 *l. 2* For shame, to untie
l. 5 whistle, or] whistle and
l. 6 disturbance.] disaster.
l. 7 frozenly,] fearfully,
l. 8 unexceptionable:] not unwelcome.

TEN POEMS MORE (1930)

Ten Poems More was published in Paris by Nancy Cunard's Hours Press in June 1930.[8] There were 200 numbered, signed copies, hand-set and hand-printed, with covers by Len Lye (incorporating photographs of his constructions made with rock and pebbles, plus wire, cement, earthenware and other materials).[9]

[8] In 1963 Nancy Cunard (1896-1965) wrote, 'I do remember you and I made a nice bit of money on the volume – something like £80 in royalties, I think I was able to send you, [. . .] saying to myself, "At last fine poetry seems properly remunerated!"' (Nancy Cunard to Graves, 17 July 1963; Canelluñ).

[9] Len Lye (1901-1980), the New Zealand-born artist, writer, experimental film-maker and kinetic sculptor, was one of Graves's and Riding's circle of friends in Hammersmith. He designed the jacket for Graves's autobiography, *Good-bye to All That* (1929), which Graves dictated to Lye's first wife, Jane. During their stay in Deyá in 1930 Lye designed the covers for four Seizin Press books, including Graves's *To Whom Else?* (1931) (see note), and two Hours Press books by Riding, *Twenty Poems Less* (1930) and *Four Unposted Letters to Catherine* (1930).

The Reader Over My Shoulder

Text: *CP75.*

Previous title: 'To the Reader Over My Shoulder' (*10PM, P26-30*).

Variants:

st. 3 l. 5 proud *CP75*] clean *10PM*

l. 6 clay.] flesh.

In *10PM* the stanzas do not have ll.3 and 6 indented.

History of the Word

Cf. 'In the Beginning Was a Word', *Poetry,* 30 (April 1927), 16; see *Complete Poems,* Volume III, 'Uncollected Poems'.

Text: *CP61.*

Variants:

l. 5 a lax interpretation *CP61*] interpretation's freedom *10PM*

l. 7 These,] Which

l. 8 claim] name

l. 11 day] time

l. 12 its] his

l. 13 knowledge] deafness

l. 14 that hear] where first

Interruption

Text: *CP75.*

Variant:

l. 4 trampling, *CP75*] tramping, *10PM*

New Legends

Text: *CP75.*

Previous title: 'The Age of Certainty' (*10PM, P26-30*).

Variants:

st. 1 l. 2 serene, *CP75*] alone, *10PM*

l. 3 Mistress] Yet queen

st. 3 ll. 2-4:

Invariable she-Proteus
Sole unrecordable
Giving my tablets holiday.

st. 4 l. 3 Of] Sorrow

Saint

Text: *CP59.*

Previous title: 'The Beast' (*10PM*).

In *10PM* and *P26-30* there are three more stanzas at the beginning, omitted in *CP38* and subsequently:

Edmund Spenser loathed the Blatant Beast,
Yet to the history's end withheld the stroke
That must, he knew, provoke
Rancour in men that loved the monster least.

And this was prudence: while the Beast lives
The infamy of his ravage is delight
And to the Red Cross Knight
A fore-won laurel of salvation gives.

But the Beast killed is carrion and a worse
Than carrion: which old Spenser would not tell
Knowing his Faerie well –
Therefore to me it falls to write that curse.

In st.1 l.2 above, a misprint in *10PM*, 'witheld', has been emended to 'withheld', as in *P26-30*.

Other variants:

st. 1 *l. 1* Blatant Beast was *CP59*] foul Beast, then, was *10PM*
l. 2 tourney: wit and fashion] combat: the whole city
l. 3 for compassion] groaned for pity
l. 4 Wept as] To see
Red] Rep (*misprint*)
pushed] urge
st. 2 *l. 1* The people] Duly they
paeans] triumphs
st. 3 *l. 2* who] which
l. 4 yellow] draggled
patched] foul
st. 4 *l. 1* huge rocks,] great stones
l. 2 ashore] to shore
st. 5 *l. 1* sulphur fire:] hot coal-fire:
st. 6 *l. 2* all his] his high
st. 9 *l. 3* mountain-cell] moutain-cell (*misprint*)
st. 11 *l. 1* Would] He would

Tap Room

Text: *P26-30*.

Previous title: 'Cracking the Nut Against the Hammer' (*10PM*).

Variant:

st. 2 *l. 1* impracticable *P26-30*] impraticable *10PM* (*misprint*)

The Terraced Valley

Text: *CP75*.

Emendation:

The space between sts.4 and 5, omitted in error in *CP75* (st.4 ends at the bottom of the page (p.138) in *CP65*) has been restored.

Variants:

st. 1 *l. 2* new *CP75*] strange *10PM*
l. 4 lay] was
l. 5 Broad sunshine ripened the whole skin
l. 6 the round world] ancient earth
st. 3 *l. 6* unyielding] unbreaking
l. 8 out-of-doors] out of doors
st. 4 *l. 2* counter-earth] common earth
st. 5 *l. 1* wide] whole
l. 3 Immediate at my elbow,] Close in the sunshine by me,
l. 4 That antique spell with a doom-echoing shout

Oak, Poplar, Pine

'When I first attended a regimental musketry course the sergeant-instructor informed the class: "In the Army there are only three sorts of tree: oak, poplar, and pine."'[10]

Text: *10PM.*

Act V, Scene 5

Text: *CP61.*

In *10PM* (which does not have the comma in the title) there are also quotation marks around st.1 ll.1-3 and st.2, making the poem a dialogue.

Other variants:

st. 1 *l. 1* call *CP61*] choose *10PM*
l. 3 Each an unnecessary player.'
l. 4 'But where's the tragedy,'] 'No, not unnecessary',
l. 5 Remains] Survive
done?] done

---

[10] Graves to *The Times*, 17 Nov. 1944, p.5. The full text of the letter, headed 'From or To?', is as follows:

Sir, – A lack of literary sensitivity in well-known writers has sometimes prevented the Editors of the Oxford English Dictionary, whose task is to record precedents rather than to lay down principles of English, from differentiating between the shades of meaning conveyed by closely related words. It should, however, be an axiom with conscientious writers that, despite the eloquence of Roget's 'Thesaurus', there are no synonyms in English.

When I first attended a regimental musketry course the sergeant-instructor informed the class: 'In the Army there are only three sorts of tree: oak, poplar, and pine.' Someone coughed and asked politely: 'You mean, sergeant, that oak and elm, for example, are synonymous?' 'Yes, sir, very synonymous!'

'Averse to' and 'averse from' are very-synonymous but not identical in meaning. 'Averse to' expresses passive or polite aversion; with 'averse from' goes an active and ill-mannered turning of the head.

Yours, &c., ROBERT GRAVES.

Galmpton, Brixham, South Devon, Nov. 14.

l. 6 This is no tragedy, but dead men's laughter.
l. 7 purge the soul –] are the purge –

St.2 gained three lines, ll.2-4, in *CP38*. In *10PM* and *P26-30* it has nine, like st.1; the first is

'No purge for my complaint: I'd have them own

followed by l.5.

st. 2 *l. 5* up-stage] on-stage
l. 6 on] in
field of] royal
l. 7 thus:] well:
Oscar! Joy for us!'] Oscar: snug in Hell!' –
l. 10 and pantomime of sin;] in character,
l. 11 let] drive
rage on,] yet futher: (*misprint*; further: *P26-30*)
against] with
l. 12 her thund'rous rolling-pin.] against her sooty cleaver.'

Song: Lift-Boy

Text: *CP75*.

Previous titles: 'Tail Piece:[11] A Song to Make You and Me Laugh' (*10PM*), 'Lift-Boy' (*P26-30*).

Variants:

st. 1 *l. 2* boot-boy *CP75*] knife-boy *10PM*
st. 4 *l. 6* not Old] nor Old

10PM and *P26-30* have a fifth stanza, in italics:

Can a phonograph lie? Can a phonograph lie?
Can a, can a phonograph?
A song very neatly
Contrived to make you and me
Laugh.

POEMS 1926-1930 (1931)

Published by Heinemann on 9 February 1931, *Poems 1926-1930* has the following epigraph:

It is a conversation between angels now
Or between who remain when all are gone.
LAURA RIDING.

[from *Poems:* A Joking Word][12]

[11] So-called, presumably, to avoid its becoming the eleventh poem in *10PM*.

[12] 'It Is Or It Will Be Or It Was', ll.1-2, from *Poems: A Joking Word* (London: Cape, 1930), pp.170-1.

Seven of the forty-five poems in *Poems 1926-1930* were published there for the first time. Of the remaining thirty-eight, Graves's introductory 'Note' specifies the number from each of his three previous volumes: six of the 'Nine Additional Poems' in *Poems (1914-27)* ('The Progress', 'O Jorrocks, I Have Promised' and 'To a Charge of Didacticism' are omitted); twenty-three[13] of the twenty-five poems in *Poems 1929* ('Back Door' and 'A Sheet of Paper' are omitted); and nine from *Ten Poems More* (including 'Tail Piece: A Song to Make You and Me Laugh', re-titled 'Lift-Boy'; 'Survival of Love' and 'Oak, Poplar, Pine' are omitted).

The seven poems 'written since'[14] are indicated with an asterisk in the following list, which gives the complete contents:

I
Thief; Saint; Gardener; Ship Master; Philatelist Royal; Lift-Boy; Brother*

II
Castle; Cabbage Patch; Railway Carriage; Front Door; Repair Shop; Landscape; Bay of Naples*; Tap Room; Sandhills; Pavement; Quayside

III
To the Reader Over My Shoulder; In Broken Images; Flying Crooked*; Hector; Interruption; Act V, Scene 5; Dismissal; Reassurance to the Satyr*

IV
Hell; To Be Less Philosophical; Synthetic Such*; Anagrammagic; Midway; Lost Acres; In No Direction; Guessing Black or White; Warning to Children; Dragons*; History of the Word; Against Kind

V
O Love in Me; Return Fare; Single Fare; It Was All Very Tidy; The Terraced Valley; The Age of Certainty; The Next Time*

Brother

Text: *PS51/CP75*.

Variants:

l. 1 It's *CP75*] It is *P26-30*
l. 2 still] yet
l. 3 of] with
l. 4 puzzled] doubtful
l. 5 though flattened by] through praise and through
l. 6 The] His

Omitted from *CP38* and *CP14-47*, 'Brother' reappears in its final form as one of four 'Revisions' in *PS51*.

---

[13] The 'Note' states twenty-four.

[14] 'Note'.

Flying Crooked

A rejoinder in verse to 'Flying Crooked' by 'a distinguished entomologist' on the 'Ariadne' page of the *New Scientist* on 10 February 1966[15] drew this response:

> Sir, – My poem *Flying Crooked* was written as a satire on the ingenious routineers of poetry, as also on the ingenious routineers of science (as opposed to, say, men like Eratosthenes, Newton, Kekulé,[16] Niels Bohr and my friend the late Norbert Weiner) who fail to understand that the cabbage-white's seemingly erratic flight provides a metaphor for all original and constructive thought.
>
> It is delightful to have my t's crossed, and my i's dotted, by Mr Garrett Jones ('Ariadne', 10 February) as though I did not know why the butterfly acts as it does: by diving like a swift on this bitter poem he exactly proves its main contention.[17]

Text: *CP75*.
Variant:

l. 1 a *CP75*] the *P26-30*

Synthetic Such

Text: *CP75*.
Variants:
The first two lines in *P26-30*:

'The parts of Such composing Such
Amount, in every lifeless scene,

st. 1 *l. 3* Is *CP75*] To
this] that
st. 2 *l. 1* And if unseeking it should find
l. 2 Some] An
l. 3 Which gave] To give
l. 4 Post-scientifically full,
st. 3 *l. 1* Still less even than now, I think,
l. 2 cause unscientific] want of certitude give
l. 3 appalled by thought,] self-analysed
l. 4 To its] Into

The Next Time

Text: *CP75*.
Variants:

st. 1 *l. 3* cramped *CP75*] locked *P26-30*
st. 2 *l. 2* The wheels failing once more] When once more the wheels fail

---

15 *New Scientist*, 29 (10 Feb. 1966), 358.
16 See 'The Marmosite's Miscellany', st.33, *Complete Poems*, Volume I, p.294.
17 *New Scientist*, 29 (24 Feb. 1966), 499.

TO WHOM ELSE? (1931)

Published in Deyá, Mallorca, in July 1931, *To Whom Else?* was Seizin 6, the second and last of Graves's books of poems to be produced by the Seizin Press.[18] There were 200 numbered and signed copies; Len Lye's covers have geometrical patterns in grey, dark blue and silver.

Largesse to the Poor

Text: *CP14-47.*

Variants:

sect. 1 l. 5 condition *CP14-47*] contentment *TWE*
sect. 2 l. 10 grief,] shame,
sect. 3 l. 3 that] all
l. 4 Which] That
l. 5 I place by place foreknew –
l. 6 To] I
l. 10 might-be-worse,] better or worse,

The Felloe'd Year

Text: *P30-33.*

Variants:

l. 8 moved, *P30-33*] move, *TWE*
l. 9 yet – I the same, yet praying] yet, samely, but not I
l. 10 That] For whom
this round-felloe'd] the felloe'd
l. 11 Be a] Are the
a turning] the turning

Time

Text: *CP75.*

Previous title: 'On Time' (*TWE*).

Variants:

st. 2 l. 2 And *CP75*] When *TWE*
st. 3 l. 1 Time,] time,
l. 2 Time,] time,
l. 3 Life-wearied.] Life-weary.
st. 4 l. 1 easy] all too easy
a blowing flower] a flower
l. 3 Time] time
st. 5 l. 1 Time's lapse, the emulsive element coaxing] the lie of lies: sweet oil that eases (Time's ease and the sweet oil that coaxes *P30-33, CP38, CP14-47, CP55, SP58*)
l. 3 To] With

---

[18] For the Seizin Press, see the note on *P29*. A 1931 Seizin Press announcement (evidently worded by Riding) states: '*To Whom Else?* consists of poems and as it were poems in which the problem of dedication is treated without poetic ambiguity.'

st. 6 in *TWE*:

> Time is old age and crafty childhood, both:
> What monster lives heart-whole against
> His innocent vagueness,

st. 7 *l. 1* Or will not render him the accustomed tax,

On Rising Early

Text: *CP75*.

Variants:

st. 1 *l. 3* warming *CP75*] gilding *TWE*
st. 3 *l. 3* an] the
st. 4 *l. 2* Today another, and many not yet past,
l. 3 ruled] rule
had] have
l. 4 was] is
ll. 5-7 in *TWE*:

> And no more tiredness than the recollection
> Of last night's fierce encounter that was relaxed
> In death-like sleep at last.

The Foolish Senses

Text: *CP38*.

Variants:

st. 1 *l. 5* serfdom *CP38*] fealty *TWE*
st. 2 *l. 3* spread] fade
l. 6 What had not yet been.
st. 3 *l. 1* so confound] put shame on
l. 2 your] such
l. 3 That] As
uses] honesty

Devilishly Provoked

Text: *MDC*.

Previous title: 'Devilishly Disturbed' (*TWE, P30-33*).

There are three stanzas in *TWE* and *P30-33;* the version printed in 1962 in *MDC* (where it is dated 1933 instead of 1931) is a reworking of sts.1-2.

Variants:

st. 1 *l. 1* provoked *MDC*] disturbed *TWE*
l. 2 my officious] this unready
l. 3 For every word I write
l. 4 It scrawls me] I scratch out
l. 5 But] And
l. 8 blotted] cancelled

The second and third stanzas in *TWE*:

Devilishly disturbed
  By this unready heart:
The flame staggers and leaps,
  The shadows trip and start,
And far from crying joy
  To watch their lusty play
I loathe the outrageous art
  That turns my hour away.

Devilishly disturbed
  By this unready mind,
Its mouth so halting-dumb
  Its eye so winking-blind –
Yet, once the eye has seen
  And once the mouth has said,
The Devil awhile is numb,
  My heel being on his head.

(The hyphens in st.3 l.3 'halting-dumb' and l.4 'winking-blind' are omitted in *P30-33*.)

Ogres and Pygmies

Text: *CP75*.

Variants:

sect. 1 l. 1 *indent TWE, P26-30*
l. 4 not of *CP75*] of no *TWE*
l. 6 vast] proud
l. 8 hog.] sheep.
l. 11 shadows of their fame;] memory of them.
l. 12 on the hill] in the waste,
l. 13 those] their
l. 14 country-folk salute] king and priest must yearly
l. 15 With May Day kisses, and whose] Buss, and their cold
sect. 2 l. 2 throats] lips
l. 7 pits] holes
huge mounds,] great cairns;
l. 8 wrestled with the bear] slew whole armies,
l. 15 judge] choose
l. 17 marvel] likely
l. 18 Prove his own disproportion and not laugh.

The poem was divided into two sections in *CP38*.

To Whom Else?

Text: *CP38*.

Variant:

st. 1 l. 6 bounded, *CP38*] ended, *TWE*

As It Were Poems

Text: *P30-33.*

Emendations:

II par. 3 Isaiah *TWE*] Isiah *P30-33* (*misprint*)

III par. 1 to whosoever *Ed.*] to to whosoever *P30-33* (*misprint*)

Variants:

I:

sect. 2 For he suborned Trojan captives *P30-33*] certain Trojan captives *TWE*

The next section in *TWE*, omitted in *P30-33*:

> In the legend of Pyramus and Thisbe, where was I?
>
> I was not Pyramus nor was I Thisbe nor the Wall nor the Moon nor a Cruel Parent. Indeed, I am nowhere to be found in that story.

sect. 3 But the natural . . . the part] the self-shaming part

I was the gross fool] the fool

sect. 6 In the legend of that Lucius] the Lucius

I was that impassioned ass in the gold trappings.] golden ass.

sect. 7 In the legend . . . and of Osiris] and Osiris

II:

par. 1 A sick girl . . . fitting people into legends of her own making.] telling people who they were. She put them into legends of her own making.

For you and for me] Coming to this house

You were the Christ-Woman] Christ-woman

with whom King West takes ship to Palestine: to find the Golden Seal.] and she and I were to take ship together to Palestine to find the hidden Golden Seal.

You as of old nursed the souls of the dead; she and I led the living.] And you were to be a comforting angel to the inhabitants of Hell and she and I were to hearten the living.

par. 2 in *TWE*:

But you said that in the legend of the Christ there was no room for further happening – that was a page scrawled over on both sides, and whoever read themselves into it thereby denied themselves.

par. 3 And I scolded angrily: Jesus, the Christ-Man, was a timid plagiarist.] And I said that Jesus, the Christ-man, was such a scheming, timid one.

He made] He had made

fitting himself into them.] to himself, putting himself always into their historic future.

III:
par. 1 in *TWE*:

Dear Name, how shall I call you? The name in which you have taught me of the legends and of my hiding from you in them, and of my hiding you from myself in them, is not the name in which you now go hidden from others according to their bookish reading of you. That open name is the one by which my reason calls you, and in which you reasonably answer me; when, listening to you, I would not have all my fellow level-heads say, 'Look, he has gone mad. He is talking with a familiar spirit.'

The next paragraph in *TWE*, omitted in *P30-33*:

Two-named one, how shall I call you without duplicity?

par. 2 'Call me,' you say,] reply,

you do not call upon any of those false spirits of the legends, those names of travesty.] I may know that you are not calling upon any of those belied spirits of the legends with whom men have ever held stealthy, frightened converse.

For in my . . . be belied in drunken mystifications:] sound of the closed names invoked in the mysteries:

fellows? So let] fellows? I tear away the legends from your unwilling eyes that you may call on me with your willing mind; so may

After par. 2, *TWE* has an additional paragraph:

> These are your very spoken words, not my bookish writing of you. Therefore with spoken words I answer:

par. 3

Instead of the first sentence, *TWE* has the following two sentences:

> 'Those many names with which I hid myself from you, and you from myself, are vanishing into a single name of names. Isis was once the secrecy of the names.

In Egypt she . . . to her people as the manifoldly incomprehensible.] for her people was the plural incomprehensible.

And Lilith, the . . . her lodges were held in stealthy darkness.] her manifold lodges were held under cover of darkness.

At length the . . . whom] who it was that

par. 4 'Now let all . . . Isis, the greatly] Isis. Isis is you, greatly

par. 5 'So likewise Osiris . . . meddling, Osiris the triple-named.] hiding from you. I know this Osiris in me by the many deaths that I have died, fearing death. Osiris the triple-named.

On Portents

Cf. *WG61*, pp.343/334:

[. . .] all original discoveries and inventions and musical and poetical compositions are the result of proleptic thought – the anticipation, by means of a suspension of time, of a result that could not have been arrived at by inductive reasoning – and of what may be called analeptic thought, the recovery of lost events by the same suspension. [. . .]

I wrote about the Muse some years ago in a poem: ['On Portents' quoted, without title]. Poets will be able to confirm this from their own experience. And because since I wrote this poem J.W. Dunne's *Experiment with Time* has prosaicized the notion that time is not the stable moving-staircase that prose men have for centuries pretended it to be, but an unaccountable wibble-wobble, the prose men too will easily see what I am driving at. In the poetic act, time is suspended and details of future experience often become incorporated in the poem, as they do in dreams. This explains why the first Muse of the Greek Triad was named Mnemosyne, 'Memory': one can have memory of the future as well as of the past. Memory of the future is usually called instinct in animals, intuition in human beings.

Text: *CP75*.

POEMS 1930-1933 (1933)

Poems 1930-1933 was published in May 1933 by Arthur Barker.[19] The introductory 'Note' states:

> Some of these poems [15 of the total of 28] appeared in *To Whom Else?* (Seizin Press, a limited edition) but several passages have been changed here: the remainder are printed for the first time.
>
> *Poems* 1930-1933, following on from *Poems* 1914-1926 and *Poems* 1926-1930 (both Heinemann), closes the dated sequence.

In the following contents list, the new poems are indicated with an asterisk:

> The Bards*; Time; Ulysses*; Down, Wanton, Down!*; The Cell*; The Succubus*; Nobody*; Danegeld*; Trudge, Body*; On Rising Early; On Necessity; Ogres and Pygmies; Music at Night*; The Legs; Without Pause*; Devilishly Disturbed; The Clock Men*; The Commons of Sleep*; The Foolish Senses; What Times Are These?*; The Felloe'd Year; Largesse to the Poor; On Dwelling; To Whom Else?; On Portents; As It Were Poems I, II, III

---

[19] *I, Claudius* and *Claudius the God* (both 1934) were also published by the recently established young Arthur Barker, to whom Graves and Riding turned after a dispute with Jonathan Cape, publisher of Graves's two previous best-sellers, *Lawrence and the Arabs* (1927) and *Good-bye to All That* (1929). On 31 January 1933 Graves wrote to Barker: 'I return proofs: the printers have gone quite mad at the end, trying to turn prose [i.e. 'As It Were Poems'] into Free Verse. I also send the blurb. Like the David Copperfield one [i.e. for *The Real David Copperfield* (London: Arthur Barker, 1933)] which pleased you it is largely L.R.'s doing.' The blurb was as follows:

> Poems 1930-1933: by Robert Graves
>
> This is the third concluding volume of a twenty-year dated sequence of poems; the two previous volumes being *Poems* 1914-1926 and *Poems* 1926-1930, published by Messrs. Wm. Heinemann. The author's object has been to explore – with progressive variations of technique – the possible ways of being a poet and yet not losing physical reality. Such an object inevitably leads to an acute sense of divided allegiance; and these poems are a detailed expression of such a crux.

(Carbon ts., Canelluñ. The blurb evidently was not used: Higginson does not mention a dust jacket for *P30-33*.)

The Bards

'I think that poems should supply their own illumination', Graves wrote in the 'Foreword' to *CP38* (see note, p.300), explaining why he had not, for example, annotated this poem with references to 'Celtic legend'; later, nonetheless, he cited 'The Pursuit of the Gilla Dacker' as a source.[20]

Text: *CP75*.
Previous title: 'Lust in Song' (*CP38, CP14-47*).
Variants:

l. 1 The bards falter in *CP75*] Their cheeks are blotched for *P30-33*
l. 3 for their] as they

Ulysses

Text: *CP75*.
Variants:

st. 1 l. 1 the *CP75*] this *P30-33*
l. 2 gowned as] in the gown of
st. 2 l. 4 angry] they were
l. 5 lotus island's drunken] Lotus Orchard's filthy
st. 3 l. 3 to] at
l. 4 ears:] ears,
song] song:
l. 5 groaned] gasped
st. 4 l. 4 afterwards to find] the continuance kind
l. 5 Still] Of
wherewith] with which
st. 5 l. 1 witty] pleasant

The Philosopher

Text: *CP75*.
Previous title: 'The Cell' (*P30-33*).
Variants:

st. 2 l. 1 And, *CP75*] But *P30-33*
l. 3 escape –] escape,
st. 3 l. 2 a] the
st. 4 l. 1 solace] refuge
l. 3 One might] Could one
st. 5 l. 1 a logic] connexion
wall,] wall
l. 2 And floor and ceiling, more attentively
l. 3 cob spider's.] cob-spider –

[20] Graves mentioned it to Douglas Day: see his *Swifter than Reason: The Poetry and Criticism of Robert Graves* (Chapel Hill: University of North Carolina Press, 1963), p.143n., and Daniel Hoffman, *Barbarous Knowledge: Myth in the Poetry of Yeats, Graves and Muir* (New York: Oxford University Press, 1967), pp.166-8.

st. 6 l. 1 Truth captured] Plain logic
increment] benefit
flies:] flies –
st. 7 l. 2 at greater length] more accurately
l. 3 And neatly than at home.

The Succubus

Text: *CP75.*

Variants:

st. 1 l. 3 a *CP75*] that *P30-33*
l. 5 lips] mouth
st. 2 l. 6 halo'd] nippled
st. 3 l. 5 brats on you] you with brats
l. 6 Yet is the fancy grosser] Flesh, is she truly more gross
lusts were] lust is

Nobody

Text: *CP75.*

Variants:

st. 1 l. 1 nobody, *CP75*] nobody *P30-33*
st. 3 l. 1 about the] about in the
st. 6 l. 2 everyone] every man
st. 7 l. 1 envy,] jealousy,

Trudge, Body!

Text: *CP75.*

An exclamation mark was added to the title in *S* (1958), and to the final line of each stanza in *CP59*.

Other variants:

st. 3 l. 1 cooling, warming, *CP75*] cooling or warming, *P30-33*
l. 3 Beyond heat] Beyond the heat
l. 5 With] Here
hours] crowns

In *P30-33* st.3 has two more lines after l.6:

The hills hang above you, they smile or glare,
But shall have dropped behind before you lord it there.

After a space *P30-33* then repeats st.1 (as st.4). The four extra lines were omitted in *S* and subsequently.

Without Pause

Text: *CP14-47.*

Emendation:

l. 5 ash *P30-33, CP38*] asp *CP14-47* (*misprint*)

Variants:

l. 17 heartache: *CP14-47*] heartache, *P30-33*
l. 18 head,] head

l. 32 no: so,] no, so
l. 36 lurch-away.] lurch away.

The Clock Man

Text: *CP14-47.*
Previous title: 'The Clock Men' (*P30-33*).
Variant:
st. 2 l. 5 accept, inured to shame, and *CP14-47*] with wilful shame accept, to *P30-33*

COLLECTED POEMS (1938)

Published in November 1938 by Cassell, Graves's second *Collected Poems* was the culmination of his literary collaboration with Laura Riding. Over more than a decade he had submitted every poem to her as it was written. Most had to be further revised, incorporating her emendations and comments, before she eventually 'passed' them; others were destroyed.[21] Then, in preparing his new collection during April-August 1938, he went over all his work again with her, rewriting and deleting. A week before finishing he noted: 'Only about 10 poems have escaped revision.'[22]

Riding also helped revise the substantial 'Foreword', in which he acknowledges her 'constructive and detailed criticism of my poems in various stages of composition'.[23]

Collected Poems (1938) contains 144 poems, a mere ten more than *Poems (1914-26)*, which is, besides, twenty-six pages longer; only forty-one poems from it are preserved.[24] (For Graves's policy of progressively

[21] Cf. *Focus*, 2 (Feb.-March 1935), 15: 'As for work since last *Focus* [Jan. 1935], I have written eight poems and destroyed three. Two of the survivors passed Laura's scrutiny without a singly [*sic*] query. This is a record.'

[22] Diary, 4 Aug. 1938. Cf. 28 July: 'Rewrote seven poems on lines suggested by Laura.' On 9 Aug. he recorded, 'Going over poems with Laura for last time', but the next day, 'More work on poems with Laura'. Finally on 11 Aug. he was able to write 'Finished *Poems*', and they were sent off two days later. See also the 'Foreword' to *CP14-47*, below.

[23] See Diary, 7 Aug. 1938: 'I rewrote introduction to my poems for the severalth time, to Laura's amendments.'

[24] The figures of 144 and forty-one include two early poems, 'In the Wilderness' (*OB*) and 'To R.N.' (*FF*), which are reprinted in full in the 'Foreword' to *CP38*. He originally intended making 'In the Wilderness' the 'starting-point', as in *Poems (1914-26)* (ms., Carbondale).

suppressing his work, see *Complete Poems*, Volume I, Introduction.)[25] From his six subsequent books – *Poems (1914-27), Poems 1929, Ten Poems More, Poems 1926-1930, To Whom Else?, Poems 1930-1933* – he included fifty poems, out of a total of seventy-eight. The remaining fifty-three poems were new. Of these, seventeen had previously appeared in print: fifteen in *Epilogue* and *Focus* (see the notes below), and – exceptionally – two in anthologies.[26]

Graves divided the book into five 'parts', designated with roman numerals in place of dates (see Introduction); in the 'Foreword', where each part is described, he calls them 'stages of a struggle: the struggle to be a poet in more than a literary sense'.

As one of two epigraphs to the book, he chose a quotation from a poem by Riding, 'The Way It Is':

> As to the common brute it falls
> To see real miracles
> And howl with irksome joy.[27]

For the other epigraph he again took the stanza from Skelton's 'Garlande of Laurell' which he had used for *Poems (1914-26)*:

> But such evydence I thynke for to enduce
> And so largely to lay for myne indempnité,
> That I trust [thereby] to make myne excuse

---

[25] It was Riding, in fact, who formulated the explanation for the omission from *CP38* of 'so much already published work'. Graves had written, 'Briefly: my principle has been to suppress as far as possible all digressions from the main subject, which is poetry.' On the ts. draft (Carbondale) she has cancelled this and substituted, 'I have suppressed poems whenever I felt that they did an injustice to my seriousness at the time. This may seem self-protective; but a book of poems should not be an act of martyrdom to the enjoyment readers take in a poet's mistakes and digressions.' (Cf. the final version in the 'Foreword', par. 9, below.)

[26] 'To Bring the Dead to Life' was first published in *The Faber Book of Modern Verse*, edited by Michael Roberts (London: Faber, 1936), p.233, and 'The Laureate' (as 'The Wretch') in *The Modern Poet*, edited by Gwendolen Murphy (London: Sidgwick and Jackson, 1938), p.81. In 1928 Riding and Graves had published *A Pamphlet Against Anthologies* (London: Cape); as for periodicals, throughout the 1930s Graves contributed poems only to their own *Epilogue* (with one to *Focus*).

[27] From *Poet: A Lying Word* (London: Barker, 1933), p.15; reprinted in *Collected Poems* (London: Cassell, 1938; and Manchester: Carcanet, and New York: Persea Books, 1980), p.156. The complete stanza (st.1):

> It falls to an idiot to talk wisely.
> It falls to a sot to wear beauty.
> It falls to many to be blessed
> In their shortcomings,
> As to the common brute it falls
> To see real miracles
> And howl with irksome joy.

Of what charge soever ye lay ageinst me;
For of my bokis parte ye shall se,
Which in your recordes, I knowe well, be enrolde:
And so Occupacyon, your regester, me tolde.[28]

The complete 'Foreword' is as follows:

FOREWORD

The five parts into which this book is divided are stages of a struggle: the struggle to be a poet in more than a literary sense. Because of anticipations and regressions, however, the order of the poems is not strictly chronological.

The first stage is that of being strongly moved by poetic urgencies but attempting to identify them with the impulses of romance.

In the second stage the discrepancy between romantic and poetic values becomes painfully felt; and the spell of poetry is seen as a protection against the death-curse in which humanity seems entailed.

In the third stage the poetic self has become the critic of the divided human self. Poetry is not a mere mitigation of haunting experiences: it is an exorcism of physical pretensions by self-humbling honesties.

In the fourth stage the criticism is turned outwards upon a world in gloom: poetry is seen not only as a saving personal solution but as a general source of light.

In the fifth stage comes a more immediate sense of poetic liberation – achieved not by mysticism but by practical persistence.

No notes are given; for I think that poems should supply their own illumination – otherwise they are incomplete fancies which no glosses, however numerous, can perfect. I have not, for example, annotated 'The Cuirassiers of the Frontier', 'Lust in Song', 'The Cloak' with references, respectively, to Byzantine military history, Celtic legend and early nineteenth-century memoirs of exile. That would have been to exaggerate trivial and fanciful elements which already qualify the poetic value of these poems: better to face the reader's incomprehension of incidental allusions that have stimulated me in the writing, than to court his favour with a parade of scholarship. Poems either do or do not stand by their poetic meaning: learned explanation cannot give them more than they possess.

The title *Collected Poems* obliges me to explain why (though more than fifty of them have not appeared in any previous volume of mine) I have omitted so much already published work.

---

[28] 'Skelton Poeta to the Quene of Fame', ll.1135-41 in *The Poetical Works of John Skelton*, edited by Alexander Dyce, 2 vols (London: Thomas Rodd, 1843), I, p.407; see *Complete Poems*, Volume I, pp.346-7 and 364.

Briefly: I have suppressed whatever I felt misrepresented my poetic seriousness at the time when it was written. This may seem self-protective; but the publication of poems should not be an act of martyrdom to the pleasure that readers may derive from one's mistakes and digressions. The temptation to digress has always vexed me. Indeed, it was the subject of my first poem, written in 1908 when I was thirteen years old. This was about the mocking interruptions of a poet's privacy by a star, and began:

> I sat in my chamber yesternight,
>   I lit the lamp, I drew the blind
> And I took my pen in hand to write;
>   But boisterous winds had rent the blind
>   And you were peering from behind –
> Peeping Tom in the skies afar,
> Bold, inquisitive, impudent star!

In those days my digressions were chiefly towards difficult technical experiments in prosody and phrasing. In 1909, for example, I tried my hand at a set of translations from Catullus; and also adapted to English the complicated Welsh *englyn* metre, the chief feature of which is matching sequences of consonants. In 1910 I addressed some lines 'To a Pot of White Heather Seen in the Window of a House in a Mean Street':

> Thou, a poor woman's fairing – white heather,
> Witherest from the ending
> Of summer's bliss to the sting
> Of winter's grey beginning. . . .

Here the devices of rhyming unstressed with stressed syllables (the second stanza had *nature, rapture, pure* and *treasure* as its end-rhymes) and of internal assonantal rhyme (*heather, wither*) were derived from the Welsh. I found the strictly matching consonantal sequences of Welsh bardic poetry too crabbed for English, but modified them to cross-alliteration – as in a poem, 'The Dying Knight and the Fauns', written in 1911:

> . . . Woodland fauns with hairy haunches
> Grin in wonder through the branches,
> Woodlands fauns who know not fear:
> Wondering they wander near,
> Munching mushrooms red as coral,
> Bunches, too, of rue and sorrel,
> With uncouth and bestial sounds,
> Knowing naught of war and wounds.
> But the crimson life-blood oozes
> And makes roses of the daisies. . . .

I was preoccupied with the physical side of poetry – the harmonious variation of vowels and the proper balance, in a line or stanza, between syllables difficult and easy to articulate. For the most part I wrote in a romantic vein, of wizards, monsters, ghosts and outlandish events and scenes. One typical poem began:

> Hateful are studied harmonies
> Where screams the parrot as he flies,
> Craning his painted neck . . .

Another ended:

> Green terror ripples through our bones,
> We yearn for careless day.

In August 1914, just after leaving school to join the Army, I wrote 'In the Wilderness', my last Christian-minded poem:

> He, of his gentleness,
> Thirsting and hungering
> Walked in the wilderness;
> Soft words of grace he spoke
> Unto lost desert-folk
> That listened wondering.
> He heard the bittern call
> From ruined palace-wall,
> Answered him brotherly;
> He held communion
> With the she-pelican
> Of lonely piety.
> Basilisk, cockatrice,
> Flocked to his homilies,
> With mail of dread device,
> With monstrous barbèd stings,
> With eager dragon-eyes;
> Great bats on leathern wings
> And old blind broken things
> Mean in their miseries.
> Then ever with him went,
> Of all his wanderings
> Comrade, with ragged coat,
> Gaunt ribs – poor innocent –
> Bleeding foot, burning throat,
> The guileless young scapegoat:
> For forty nights and days
> Followed in Jesus' ways,
> Sure guard behind him kept,
> Tears like a lover wept.

In 1916, while on service in France, I published my first volume of poems, *Over the Brazier*: some of them had been written at school, but most in the trenches and billets – which gave them a dangerously topical reality. The emotion underlying this volume and *Fairies and Fusiliers*, published two years later, was a frank fear of physical death. The digressive quality of the poems included can be judged from the following quotations.

An incident in billets (June 1915):

Back from the Line one night in June
I gave a dinner at Béthune:
Seven courses, the most gorgeous meal
Money could buy or batman steal.
Five hungry lads welcomed the fish
With shouts that nearly cracked the dish;
Asparagus came with tender tops,
Strawberries in cream, and mutton chops.
Said Jenkins, as my hand he shook,
'They'll put this in the history book.'
We bawled Church anthems *in choro*
Of Bethlehem and Hermon snow,
And drinking songs, a mighty sound
To help the good red Pommard round. . . .

My reported death in action (July 24th, 1916) on my twenty-first birthday:

. . . But I *was* dead, an hour or more.
I woke when I'd already passed the door
That Cerberus guards, half-way along the road
To Lethe, as an old Greek signpost showed.
Above me, on my stretcher swinging by,
I saw new stars in the subterrene sky:
A Key, a Rose in bloom, a Cage with bars,
And a barbed Arrow feathered in fine stars.
I felt the vapours of forgetfulness
Float in my nostrils. Oh, may Heaven bless
Dear Lady Proserpine, who saw me wake
And, stooping over me, for Henna's sake
Cleared my poor buzzing head and sent me back
Breathless, with leaping heart along the track. . . .

Nonsense to cheer up a brother-officer, after our experiences in the Somme fighting (September 1916):

Back from the Somme two Fusiliers
Limped painfully home; the elder said,

'Robert, I've lived three thousand years
This Summer, and I'm nine parts dead.'
'But if that's truly so,' I cried, 'quick, now,
Through these great oaks and see the famous bough

'Where once a nonsense built her nest
With skulls and flowers and all things queer,
In an old boot, with patient breast
Hatching three eggs; and the next year
Foaled thirteen squamous young beneath, and rid
Wales of drink, melancholy and psalms, she did . . .'

The effect of untrained drafts on a Line battalion (January 1917):

'Is that the Three-and-Twentieth, Strabo mine,
Marching below, and we still gulping wine?'
From the sad magic of his fragrant cup
The red-faced old centurion started up,
Cursed, battered on the table. 'No,' he said,
'Not that! The Three-and-Twentieth Legion's dead,
Dead in the first year of this damned campaign –
The Legion's dead, dead, and won't rise again.
Pity? Rome pities her brave lads that die,
But we need pity also, you and I,
Whom Gallic spear and Belgian arrow miss,
Who live to see the Legion come to this:
Unsoldierlike, slovenly, bent on loot,
Grumblers, diseased, unskilled to thrust or shoot.
O brown cheek, muscled shoulder, sturdy thigh!
Where are they now? God! watch it straggle by,
The sullen pack of ragged, ugly swine!
Is that the Legion, Gracchus? Quick, the wine!' . . .

A miserable letter from Frise Bend on the Somme (March 1917) to Robert Nichols, who was writing his 'Faun's Holiday' at Bray and wanted me, he said, to feed the faun with cherries:

Here by a snow-bound river
In scrapen holes we shiver,
And like old bitterns we
Boom to you plaintively.
Robert, how can I rhyme
Verses at your desire –
Sleek fauns and cherry-time,
Vague music and green trees,
Hot sun and gentle breeze,
England in June attire,

And life born young again,
For your gay goatish brute
Drunk with warm melody
Singing on beds of thyme
With red and rolling eye,
Waking with wanton lute
All the Devonian plain,
Lips dark with juicy stain,
Ears hung with bobbing fruit?
Why should I keep him time?
Why in this cold and rime
Where even to think is pain?
No, Robert, there's no reason;
Cherries are out of season,
Ice grips at branch and root,
And singing birds are mute.

In contrast with these poems of war occasion I included a number on the subject of childhood. The digression was towards wistfulness, in disregard of the pseudo-adult experience of soldiering.

When the War was over I resumed my education by going up to Oxford University:

This round hat I devote to Mars,
  Tough steel with leather lined.
My skin's my own, redeemed by scars
From further still more futile wars
  The God may have in mind.

Minerva takes my square of black
  Well-tasselled with the same;
Her dullest nurselings never lack
With hoods of scarlet at their back
  And letters to their name. . . .

By this time I was married. My chief theme for three or four years was romantic love in a country setting. I published two more volumes of poems, *Country Sentiment* and *The Pier-Glass*. The following first stanzas indicate the prevailing mood:

Come close to me, dear Annie, while I tie a lover's knot,
To tell of burning love between a kettle and a pot:
The pot was stalwart iron and the kettle trusty tin,
And though their sides were black with smoke they bubbled
    love within. . . .

and:

Henry, Henry, do you love me?
Do I love you, Mary?
Oh can you mean to liken me
To the aspen tree
Whose leaves do shake and vary
From white to green
And back again,
Shifting and contrary? . . .

and:

Tangled in thought am I,
Stumble in speech do I?
Do I blunder and blush for the reason why?
Wander aloof do I,
Lean over gates and sigh,
Making friends with the bee and the butterfly? . . .

and:

Are you shaken, are you stirred
By a whisper of love?
Spell-bound to a word
Does Time cease to move,
Till her calm grey eye
Expands to a sky
And the clouds of her hair
Like storms go by?

With the love-theme went the old fear-theme, sharpened rather than blunted by the experiences of peace. The better poems of this period are included in Part I of the present volume. Poetry to me at this time was neither a formal muse nor a familiar deity, but a hidden Janus (one head benignant, the other malevolent) whose unpredictable behaviour made the poet's task an impossible one.

I now wrote several prose books and pamphlets – *On English Poetry, Poetic Unreason, Another Future of Poetry, Contemporary Techniques of Poetry* – for the most part concerned with the sensuous aspects of poetry. This preoccupation led me to a study of psychology; I was searching for some means of capturing and holding the reader's attention by hypnotic suggestion. I tended to make the test of a poem's worth not its internal coherence and truthfulness but its power to charm a large audience. Equally misguided was my recourse to philosophy to justify such poetic practice. Though I had ceased to be a Christian I was behaving like a Churchman; and anything worth preserving that I wrote between 1922 and 1926 was written in spite of, rather than by the help of, my new theories. Nearly the whole of the *Mock Beggar Hall* and *Feather Bed* volumes has been here omitted, a large part of *Whipperginny* and *Welchman's Hose*, and all but two lines of *The Marmosite's Miscellany*, a long reckless satire. What remains is to be found in Part II.

Occasional stanzas of the discarded poems still stand out for me: such as the following from a poem, called 'The Figure Head', on the death of the Christian God as typified by a farmer:

'Granted,' we said, 'he's no more seen
Tending fat sheep in pastures green,
Or scattering at the break of morn
Largesse, profuse, of corn,

'Master must be assumed to know
Where best his favours to bestow;
He has left us (caring for us still)
To cultivate free-will.

'Himself, from some grand inner room,
Directs the cowman, steward and groom,
Makes up his ledgers, page by page,
In joy or solemn rage.

'Our feeding and our water-time,
Our breeding and our slaughter-time,
The dyke, the hedge, the plough, the cart –
These thoughts lie next his heart.'

The ducks and geese believed this true;
What now, poor poultry, will they do,
Stunned with confusion, when the glum
Gloved undertakers come,

Tilting the coffin past the pond,
The ricks, the clamps, the yard beyond,
Skirting the midden-heap with care,
Then out, they know not where? . . .

and these from 'Virgil the Sorcerer':

Virgil, as the old Germans have related,
  Meaning a master-poet of wide fame –
And yet their Virgil stands dissociated
  From the suave hexametrist of that name,

Maro, whose golden and lick-spittle tongue
   Served Caesar's most un-Roman tyrannies,
Whose easy-flowing Georgics are yet sung
   As declamations in the academies –

Not Mantuan Virgil but another greater
   Who at Toledo first enlarged his spells,
Virgil, sorcerer, prestidigitator,
   Armed with all power that flatters or compels.

and these from 'The Knowledge of God':

So far from praising he blasphemes
   Who says that God has been or is,
Who swears he met with God in dreams
Or face to face in woods and streams,
   Meshed in their boundaries. . . .

The caterpillar years-to-come
   March head to tail with years-that-were
Round and around the cosmic drum;
To time and space they add their sum,
   But how is Godhead there?

But about almost everything that I wrote at this stage I feel as John Skelton felt about his poem 'Apollo Whirléd Up His Chair', which he prayed the god to erase for ever out of the Ragman Rolls of literature. My essays on the psychology of poems gained wide currency and have done corresponding mischief.

In 1925 I first became acquainted with the poems and critical work of Laura Riding, and in 1926 with herself; and slowly began to revise my whole attitude to poetry. (The change begins half-way through Part II.)

That the proportion of what would be called 'unpleasant poems' is so high in this twenty-three-year sequence surprised me on first looking it over. But I see this now not as a furious reaction against the anodynic tradition of poetry in which I was educated but as the blurted confession of a naturally sanguine temperament; that the age into which I was born, in spite of its enjoyable lavishness of entertainment, has been intellectually and morally in perfect confusion. To manifest poetic faith by a close and energetic study of the disgusting, the contemptible and the evil is not very far in the direction of poetic serenity, but it has been the behaviour most natural to a man of my physical and literary inheritances. Other steps remain, and a few have already been taken. I should say that my health as a poet lies in my mistrust of the comfortable point-of-rest. Certainly, this suspicious habit, this dwelling upon discomfort and terror, has brought me good luck: for in the midst of my obstinate stumblings there have come sudden flashes of grace and knowledge –

As to the common brute it falls
To see real miracles
And howl with irksome joy.

I have to thank Laura Riding for her constructive and detailed criticism of my poems in various stages of composition – a generosity from which so many contemporary poets besides myself have benefited.

R.G.

1938.

The following list gives the complete contents (new poems are indicated with an asterisk):

I
The Haunted House; Reproach; The Finding of Love; 'The General Elliott'; Outlaws; One Hard Look; A Frosty Night; Allie; Unicorn and the White Doe; Henry and Mary; Love Without Hope; What Did I Dream?; The Country Dance; The Hills of May; Lost Love; Vain and Careless; An English Wood; The Bedpost; The Pier-Glass; Apples and Water; Wanderings of Christmas*; Pygmalion and Galatea; Down; Mermaid, Dragon, Fiend

II
In Procession; Angry Samson; Warning to Children; Song: To Be Less Philosophical; Alice; Blonde or Dark?; Richard Roe and John Doe; The Witches' Cauldron; Ancestors; Children of Darkness; The Cool Web; Certain Mercies*; The Cuirassiers of the Frontier*; Love in Barrenness; The Presence; The Land of Whipperginny; In No Direction; The Castle; Return; Lust in Song; Nobody; Without Pause; Full Moon; Vanity; Pure Death; Sick Love; It Was All Very Tidy

III
Callow Captain*; Thief; Saint; The Furious Voyage; Song: Lift-Boy; The Next Time; Ulysses; The Succubus; The Stranger*; Trudge, Body; The Clock Man; The Reader Over My Shoulder; The Smoky House*; Green Loving*; The Legs; Gardener; Front Door Soliloquy; In Broken Images; On Rising Early; Flying Crooked; The Foolish Senses; Largesse to the Poor; The Goblet*; Fiend, Dragon, Mermaid*; Fragment of a Lost Poem*

IV
Galatea and Pygmalion*; The Devil's Advice to Story-Tellers*; Sea Side; Lunch-Hour Blues*; Wm. Brazier; Welsh Incident; Vision in the Repair-Shop; Hotel Bed*; Progressive Housing*; Interruption; Act V, Scene 5; Midway; Hell; Leda*; Synthetic Such; The Florist Rose*; Being Tall*; Lost Acres; At First Sight*; Recalling War*; Down, Wanton, Down!; X*; A

Former Attachment; Nature's Lineaments; Time; The Philosopher; On Dwelling; Parent to Children*; Ogres and Pygmies; History of the Word; Single Fare; To Challenge Delight*; To Walk on Hills*; To Bring the Dead to Life*; To Evoke Posterity*; The Poets*; Defeat of the Rebels*; The Grudge*; Never Such Love*; The Halfpenny*; The Fallen Signpost*; The China Plate*; Idle Hands*; The Laureate*; A Jealous Man*; The Cloak*; The Halls of Bedlam*; Or to Perish Before Day*; A Country Mansion*; The Eremites*; The Advocates*; Self-Praise*

V
On Portents; The Terraced Valley; The Challenge*; To Whom Else?; To the Sovereign Muse*; The Ages of Oath*; New Legends; Like Snow*; The Climate of Thought*; End of Play*; The Fallen Tower of Siloam*; The Great-Grandmother*; No More Ghosts*; Leaving the Rest Unsaid*

The Christmas Robin

Text: *CP75*.

Previous title: 'Wanderings of Christmas' (*CP38*).

'The Christmas Robin' first appeared as 'Christmas', one of three poems with this title which Graves, Laura Riding and James Reeves contributed to the December 1935 number of *Focus*, the circle's newsletter.[29] Its eighteen lines became twenty in the revised (and retitled) version in *CP38*, and are grouped into five four-line stanzas, of which the first, omitted in *S* (1958) and subsequently, is as follows:

> The Christmas of this year came soon indeed,
> While yet the name glittered with unfetched holly;
> Now, Christmas morning bells are passing-bells –
> Sadly among mince-pies it lies in state.

Other variants:

st. 1 *l. 1* February had buried *CP75*] January will bury *CP38*
l. 2 woods, where grew self-seeded] woods where grow, untended,
l. 3 yet unknown,] not yet known
l. 4 And too remote for January thought.

---

[29] *Focus*, 4, pp.18, 26, 33. Edited by Riding and printed in Palma, *Focus* ran in 1935 for four issues: Jan. (12pp.), Feb.-Mar. (23pp.), April-May (40pp.), and Dec. (64pp.). The other two Christmas poems were also republished (with few changes): see Laura Riding, *Collected Poems* (London: Cassell, 1938; reprinted Manchester: Carcanet, 1980), p.273, and James Reeves, *Collected Poems 1929-1959* (London: Heinemann, 1960), p.154.

st. 2 l. 2 we] the
paused] pause
l. 3 cried] cry
l. 4 was there] is soon
December.] November.

The last two stanzas in *CP38* (revised in *S*):

Time runs for lovers at a frantic speed:
Already love is velveted in age,
With grandchildren in troops about their knees,
With coloured Christmas candles guttering down.

'And look, the robin! Look!' An all too tardy
Or all too early Merry Christmas token –
The wide-legged robin with his breast aglow,
In the spade-handle, scornful of the snow.

Certain Mercies

Graves wrote 'Certain Mercies' on 28 June 1937 while recovering in St Mary's Hospital, Paddington, from an operation for a fistula, which he underwent on 21 June. Between entering the hospital on 20 June and leaving it on 6 July he also wrote 'Leda', 'The Florist Rose', and 'To Challenge Delight' (all in *CP38*).[30]

Text: *CP75*.

Variants:

st. 1 l. 2 Appear *CP75*] Become *CP38*
st. 7 l. 1 That, with] That with
deference,] deference

The Cuirassiers of the Frontier

In a letter to *The Times* in 1966 Graves explained that

> the 'gaping silken dragon puffed by the wind' [st.4 ll.4-5] reverenced by the Byzantine Roman cataphracts,[31] as well as by the Chinese, had been adopted as their ensign in preference to the customary eagles simply because it was a windsock.
>
> The Byzantine horse and foot archers were able to judge the direction and force of the wind by observing its behaviour and were greatly assisted, as at the Battle of Chettos,[32] when firing rapid volleys at a distance into massed Persians.[33]

---

[30] Diary.
[31] 'The Cataphracts' is the initial title on drafts of 'The Cuirassiers of the Frontier'.
[32] See *Count Belisarius* (1938), Chapter 23.
[33] *The Times*, 23 April 1966, p.11. See also János Makkay, 'The Sarmatian Connection', *Hungarian Quarterly*, 37 (Winter 1996), 113-25.

Text: *CP38/CP75.*

Variables of Green

Text: *CP75.*

Previous title: 'Green Loving' (*CP38, CP14-47*).

'Variables of Green', printed in 1962 in *MDC* and *NP62*, is a revised version of st.1 of a four-stanza, twenty-five-line earlier poem, 'Green Loving'.

'Green Loving' was first published in *Epilogue I* (Autumn 1935), 91-2, as the fourth of five numbered, untitled poems comprising 'To the Sovereign Muse', a 'Poem-Sequence' (pp.87-92).[34] The poems were revised and given individual titles in *CP38*, where they are no longer grouped together and appear in a different order, as follows: 1: 'The Challenge', in section V, p.176; 2: 'Fiend, Dragon, Mermaid', III, p.103; 3: 'To the Sovereign Muse', V, p.180; 4: 'Green Loving', III, p.92; 5: 'Like Snow', V, p.183.

'Green Loving' was reprinted without further change in *CP14-47*, and then suppressed. 'Variables of Green' is dated 1931 in *MDC*,[35] but Graves kept it in section XIII in *CP65* and *CP75*, as in *NP62*, with poems from the early 1960s.

Variants:

In st.1 of 'Green Loving', which has seven lines, ll.1-3 are followed by l.5; the next two lines in *CP38* are:

(The hue
Loyal to beauty below sky seen),

l. 6 my loves *CP75*] my many loves *CP38*

The other three stanzas in *CP38* are as follows:

But clear sky, the clear eye,
Smiling shames
Love to a confusion of muttered names.
True sky was never seen until to-day:
For tinged before with the gross fears of clay

[34] *Epilogue: A Critical Summary* was a hard-bound, book-length periodical edited by Laura Riding and Robert Graves (as 'Associate Editor'). Originally to have been entitled *The Critical Vulgate*, it was published jointly by their Seizin Press and by Constable, in principle twice a year, though there were in fact only two further volumes (Summer 1936 and Spring 1937).

[35] Some of the dates in *MDC* are inaccurate: see the notes on 'The Philatelist-Royal' and 'To Be Less Philosophical' (both *P14-27*).

All skies were, or their mildness burned away
By the sun's lubber flames.

'You in woman's beauty
I shall love till I die,
As living green, earthily,
The immortal sky.'
But death so vaunted is death-memory
And makes of all green loving a told story.

Lover, ungreen yourself, let her far glance
Find yours at her own distance.
Too close your eyes before,
And held no more
Than dreaming images of your own substance.

Fiend, Dragon, Mermaid

Text: *CP38.*

A sequel to 'Mermaid, Dragon, Fiend' (*W*) (see *Complete Poems*, Volume I), 'Fiend, Dragon, Mermaid' was first published in *Epilogue I* (Autumn 1935), 89-90, as the second poem in the sequence 'To the Sovereign Muse'; see the note on 'Variables of Green', above.

Fragment of a Lost Poem

Text: *CP38/CP75.*

See Graves's diary, 6 April 1937:[36] '. . . trying to recover a poem originally called *Moments in Never* that I lost with all my other fair copies in London. Remembered 2 verses & 2 lines out of 3 verses.'

Only one stanza and one half-line appear in *CP38*, reprinted without change through to *CP75*. Nine sheets of ms. and ts. drafts of 'Moments in Never' are, nonetheless, among the material sent to Buffalo in 1959; the latest ts. version, retitled 'Proofs of Royalty', has three seven-line stanzas. There is also a fair copy of 'Fragment of a Lost Poem'.

Like another 'lost poem', 'Gulls and Men' (*CP14-47*) (see note, and 'Foreword' to *CP14-47*), the drafts could have been among the papers Graves found on returning to Mallorca in 1946; at one point in 1935 he was working on both poems. If they were, he evidently decided to leave the 'Fragment' as it was.[37]

---

[36] He was in Switzerland at this time; see the note on 'Hotel Bed at Lugano' (*CP38*).

[37] Graves's diary records four drafts of 'Moments in Never' on 12-13 June 1935, and two of 'Proofs of Royalty' on 10 Oct.; on 11 Oct. he made 'alterations' to 'Gulls and Men'.

Galatea and Pygmalion

Cf. 'Pygmalion to Galatea' (*P14-26*). (See *Complete Poems*, Volume I.)

Text: *CP61.*

Emendation:

st. 1 l. 7 blood. *CP38, CP14-47, CP55*] blood, *CP59, CP61*

Variants:

st. 1 l. 3 Fulfilled, so they say, Pygmalion's *CP61*] Fulfilled, they say, all Pygmalion's *CP38*

l. 4 the] that

st. 2 l. 1 Alas,] Yet young

l. 2 articulation] art-perfection

l. 4 single] famous

Lunch-Hour Blues

Text: *CP38.*

This poem was first published in *Epilogue III* (Spring 1937), 164, as 'At the Marble Table'.

Hotel Bed at Lugano

Graves and Riding stayed in Lugano, Switzerland, from February to June 1937, having left Mallorca on 2 August 1936 after the outbreak of the Spanish Civil War.

Text: *CP61.*

Previous title: 'Hotel Bed' (*CP38*).

This last version of the poem, published in *5PH* (1958) and three subsequent volumes (*S, CP59, CP61*), has two additional lines, sect.2 ll.8-9; it also has a space at the line-break in sect.3 l.5, creating a separate, fourth section.

Other variants:

sect. 4 l. 1 A-bed *CP61*] In bed *CP38*

l. 4 Provokes] Evokes

Leda

See the note on 'Certain Mercies' (*CP38*), above.

Text: *CP75.*

Variant:

st. 3 l. 4 The *CP75*] Stale *CP38*

The Florist Rose

See the note on 'Certain Mercies' (*CP38*), above.

Text: *CP38/CP75.*

At First Sight

Text: *CP75.*

In *CP38* there are three more stanzas, two after st.1, and one after st.2. The poem was revised for *CP14-47* and then reprinted without further change.

Variants:
The second and third stanzas in *CP38*:

To them are born those winsome girls or boys
Whose over-delicate looks discourage
Belief in any bottom of good sense,

Who grow up sad and live absurdly,
Choose boorish and indifferent spouses
Against continuance of the dainty breed.

st. 2 l. 1 But *CP75*] And *CP38*
l. 2 fiercely] hugely

The fifth stanza in *CP38*:

And the issue is plentiful: hardy affections,
Born of a twinned purpose, multiply . . .
But slow untarnishes the name of love.

Recalling War
'Recalling War' was written in 1935, with the title 'Remembering War'.[38]
In 1940 Graves stated: '[. . .] my publishers fastened the war-poet label on me in 1916 when *Over the Brazier*, my first book of verse, appeared; but when twenty years later I published my *Collected Poems*, I found that I could not conscientiously reprint any of my "war poems" – they were too obviously written in the war-poetry boom.'[39]

Text: *CP61*.
Variant:
sect. 3 l. 5 tasty *CP61*] tasteless *CP38*

Parent to Children
Text: *SP58*.
There are three more stanzas in *CP38* (and *Epilogue III* (Spring 1937), 164-5, in which the poem was first published), omitted in *CP14-47* and subsequently.

---

38 The first entry in Graves's February 1935-May 1939 diary records that he gave 'the poem *Remembering War*' to his assistant Karl Gay to type on 22 Feb. 1935. The entry for 25 Feb. begins: 'Altered *Remembering War* (8th version)'. The poem was one of five he 'went over' with Laura Riding on 6 March; it 'had already been seen by her and recast according to her suggestions. She now passed them all with only two emendations.'
39 'War Poetry in This War', *Listener*, 26 (23 Oct. 1940), 566-7, reprinted as 'The Poets of World War II' in *The Common Asphodel: Collected Essays on Poetry 1922-1949* (London: Hamish Hamilton, 1949), pp.307-12 (p.307), and *CWP*, pp.79-83 (p.79).

CP38 has the following stanza between sts.4 and 5:

Yet I envisaged progeny,
And children I begot, to fear;
And these were you, though now are not you.

The seventh and eighth stanzas in *CP38*:

And will you be revenged,
Filially name me
Grandparent to your children – tree of fear?

Or, bolder than I was,
Scorn the consanguine vice,
Reject all loves born of bed-ignorance?

To Challenge Delight

See the note on 'Certain Mercies' (*CP38*), above.
Text: *CP38*.

To Walk on Hills

Text: *CP75*.
This poem was first published in *Epilogue II* (Summer 1936), 145-6.
Variants:
sect. 2 l. 4 bleatings *CP75*] bleating *CP38*
sect. 7 l. 1 cruel] horrid
sect. 8 l. 3 Tell us,] Confess,

To Bring the Dead to Life

Text: *CP75*.
Variant:
st. 4 l. 2 A ring, a purse, a chair: *CP38*

To Evoke Posterity

Text: *CP75*.
Variants:
st. 1 l. 4 hero! *CP75*] hero, *CP38*
st. 2 l. 1 fixed:] known:
st. 5 l. 3 would you] you would

Any Honest Housewife

Text: *CP75*.
Previous title: 'The Poets' (*CP38, NMG, CP14-47*).
Variants:
st. 1 l. 1 could *CP75*] would *CP38*
st. 2 l. 4 liars,] liars

Defeat of the Rebels

Text: *CP61*.

Variants:

st. 2 *l. 1* on us *CP61*] to us *CP38*

l. 3 rocks,] rocks

Never Such Love

Text: *CP75*.

This poem was first published in *Epilogue II* (Summer 1936), 146-7; st.3 l.1 reads 'When more than "love!" is uttered', changed in *CP38* to 'When the name "love" is uttered'.

The Halfpenny

Text: *CP38*.

'The Halfpenny' was first published in *Epilogue III* (Spring 1937), 168-9.

The Fallen Signpost

In his diary Graves records on 19 August 1938: 'James [Reeves] set me a poem to write about a Signpost: he has one to write about Speed. I had great difficulty with mine.' The entry for the following day begins, 'Finished the *Fallen Signpost* in five drafts: no, six. James discussed it with me and found two words <for me> [cancelled].' The poem was inserted in the proofs of *CP38* in place of 'Safe Receipt of a Censored Letter' (eventually published in *MDC* (1962)).[40]

Text: *CP61*.

Variants:

st. 1 *l. 3* may *CP61*] can *CP38*

l. 4 Your] The

The Laureate

'Nor need "The Wretch" [. . .] be particularly identified with any Mr Y or Z. There is poetry, and there is literary gossip.'[41]

Text: *CP38/CP75*.

A Jealous Man

Text: *CP75*.

'A Jealous Man' was first published in *Epilogue III* (Spring 1937), 166-7.

---

40 The poet James Reeves (1909-1978), a close friend since 1935, was visiting Graves and Riding at the Château de la Chevrie, near Rennes, where they lived from July 1938 to April 1939 with Beryl and Alan Hodge. The bound set of proofs (Buffalo) is inscribed 'James with | love from Robert | Sept 26, 1938'.

41 Ms. draft (Carbondale) of the 'Foreword' to *CP38* (cf. par.7, above). 'The Wretch' was the original title.

The Cloak

Text: *CP75.*

This poem was first published as 'The Exile', in *Epilogue III* (Spring 1937), 165-6.

Variants:

l. 7 maybe at *CP75*] at perhaps *CP38*
l. 9 at] with

The Halls of Bedlam

Text: *CP75.*

Variants:

st. 6 l. 2 more *CP75*] money, *CP38*
l. 3 Than] But

A Country Mansion

Text: *CP*75.

Variants:

st. 1 l. 4 demesne. *CP75*] domain. *CP38*
st. 7 l. 4 carnality's] an antique
st. 10 l. 1 the] this

The Eremites

Text: *SP58.*

Variants:

st. 1 l. 1 bearded *SP58*] froward *CP38*
l. 3 Couched] Crouched

Advocates

Text: *CP75.*

Previous title: 'The Advocates' (*CP38, NMG, CP14-47*).

Emendation:

The full stop at the end of sect.2 l.1, faint in *CP65* and barely visible in *CP75*, has been restored.

Variant:

sect. 1 l. 5 those *CP75*] these *CP38*

Self-Praise

Text: *SP58.*

Variants:

st. 1 l. 1 recommend. *SP58*] recommend, *CP38*
l. 2 Nine chances out of nine,
l. 3 When] For
Englishmen] citizens
st. 3 l. 1 But praise] Praise
fellow-creatures] the mouths of others
l. 2 Englishmen] citizens
st. 4 l. 1 Swelling the universal boast
st. 5 l. 1 O,] Then

The Challenge

Text: *SP58.*

This is the first poem in the sequence 'To the Sovereign Muse' in *Epilogue I* (Autumn 1935), 87-9; see the note on 'Variables of Green' (*CP38*), above.

Variants:

st. 13 l. 2 reach *SP58*] stretch *CP38*
st. 18 l. 1 I watched her glide over the mountain peak
l. 2 dumbfoundered] dumbfounded
st. 20 l. 1 Toward] Towards
st. 21 l. 3 Toward] Towards

To the Sovereign Muse

Text: *CP14-47.*

The title was originally given to the sequence in *Epilogue I* (Autumn 1935), in which this is the third poem (pp.90-1); see the note on 'Variables of Green' (*CP38*), above.

Variants:

sect. 1 l. 1 Debating here one night we *CP14-47*] He, he and I in our time *CP38*
l. 3 bore that sacred] erstwhile bore the
l. 7 upon] at
l. 10 they feared to acclaim.] not yet enjoyed.

In sect.2, ll.1-2 replace three lines in *CP38*:

This was to praise ourselves, rebuke ourselves
How we sufficed, fell short, exceeded
In days before you came, you first,

l. 3 pluck] plucked
sect. 3 l. 1 And we confessed that since you came
l. 6 wagged] wag

The Ages of Oath

Text: *CP75.*

Variants:

st. 1 l. 6 earthworks, *CP75*] earthwork, *CP38*
st. 2 l. 6 Later,] At last,
st. 3 l. 3 upright] many
l. 5 true] right
true] right
l. 6 Now] Then

Like Snow

Text: *CP75.*

'Like Snow' was first published in *Epilogue I* (Autumn 1935), 92, as the fifth, concluding poem in the sequence 'To the Sovereign Muse'; see the note on 'Variables of Green' (*CP38*), above.

The Climate of Thought

Text: *CP75*.

This poem was first published in *Epilogue II* (Summer 1936), 147.

Variants:

sect. 2 l. 1 voyage, on; *CP75*] voyage on; *CP38*

l. 6 such] the

l. 7 As] That

End of Play

Text: *CP75*.

'End of Play' was first published in *Epilogue III* (Spring 1937), 167-8.

Variants:

st. 2 l. 4 sky – *CP75*] sun – *CP38*

st. 3 l. 3 mettlesome,] frolicsome,

The Fallen Tower of Siloam

See Luke 13. 4-5.

See also *WG61*, pp.344/335:

> A sense of the equivocal nature of time is constantly with poets, rules out hope or anxiety about the future, concentrates interest detachedly in the present. I wrote about this with proleptic detail in 1934, in a poem 'The Fallen Tower of Siloam'.[42]

Text: *CP75*.

Variants:

st. 1 l. 5 unterrible *CP75*] not terrible *CP38*

st. 2 l. 2 wide] great

l. 5 curled] whirled

No More Ghosts

Text: *CP75*.

Variant:

st. 4 l. 1 ghosts *CP75*] ghost *CP38*

Leaving the Rest Unsaid

Graves's diary entry for 23 May 1937: 'Hot day. Could not settle down to work, somehow, until this evening when I wrote six drafts of *Leaving the Rest Unsaid* as a final poem for the book.'

Text: *CP75*.

The third stanza was added in *P53*.

---

[42] For Graves's concept of 'proleptic thought', see the note on 'On Portents' (*TWE*). 'The Fallen Tower of Siloam' was in fact written in 1937, in Lugano; in his diary Graves records four drafts on 19 March, and a further draft the next day.

Other variants:

st. 1 *l. 2* And garnished with a funeral colophon – *CP38*
l. 3 Must *CP75*] Should
st. 2 *l. 1* ruefully] punctually
st. 4 *l. 1* But no, I will not] Should I then choose to
l. 2 To let your tearful] And let a pious
st. 5 *l. 1* So now,] Therefore,
l. 2 gander's wing] cherub's wings,

NO MORE GHOSTS (1940)

Faber published this selection of Graves's poetry in September 1940, as one of a new series of 'Sesame Books'.[43] Four of the fifty poems were new; all the rest (including ten in *Poems (1914-26)*) were chosen from *Collected Poems* (1938).

The Glutton

Text: *CP61*.

Previous title: 'The Beast' (*NMG, P38-45, CP14-47*).[44]

The second and third lines were added in *CP55*, where the poem is retitled and divided into two sections.

Other variants:

sect. 1 l. 1 glutton *CP61*] love-beast. *NMG*
l. 5 And its] Its

A Love Story

Text: *CP75*.

Emendation:

st. 5 *l. 4* owls, *CP65, PAL*] owls *CP75* (*misprint*)

Variant:

st. 3 *l. 2* chill *CP75*] frozen *NMG*

The Thieves

Text: *CP75*.

---

[43] This series of small books, aimed at introducing the work of twentieth-century poets to a wider public, was launched in the spring of 1940 with four poets from the Faber list: T.S. Eliot, Stephen Spender, W.H. Auden and Louis MacNeice. Graves was then approached as the first of a group of seven with other firms, to be published in the autumn to enlarge the series: Graves, Edward Thomas, Edith Sitwell, Siegfried Sassoon, Ezra Pound, Roy Campbell and Herbert Read. (Geoffrey Faber to Sir Newman Flower, Cassells, 16 April 1940; Canelluñ (copy).) *NMG* was reprinted in 1941, 1945 and 1947 – 8000 copies altogether (Higginson).

[44] 'The Beast' was also the previous title of 'Saint' (*10PM*).

Variant:
st. 1 l. 2 meum-tuum *CP75*] meum-teum *NMG*[45]

To Sleep

Text: *CP75.*

Variants:
st. 1 l. 6 kept *CP75*] been *NMG*
st. 3 l. 5 dawn-birds] dawn birds

WORK IN HAND (1942)

Work in Hand, published by the Hogarth Press on 26 March 1942, contains eighteen poems by Graves, preceded by seventeen poems by Alan Hodge and eleven by Norman Cameron. The 'Authors' Note' states: 'These three small books are published under a single cover for economy and friendship.'[46] Graves's poems include four from *No More Ghosts*; the order is as in *Poems 1938-1945* (see note), but with 'Dream of a Climber' after 'The Shot'.

Dawn Bombardment

Graves gave Laura Riding a five-line poem, 'The Hostage' (an earlier version of st.1), with a letter on her thirty-eighth birthday, 16 January 1939. On 1 March he received her reply:

Dearest Robert

March 1 seems right for answering your letter of January 16. Let's call it a world birthday (the world seems to [have] forgotten that it has one).

About your Hostage poem.

---

[45] James Reeves noticed the error in 1959. Graves wrote to him: 'Meum-teum is really extraordinary – How could it have passed so many scrutinies and proof-readings; and my own eye when I read it from the public platform and into the public microphone, really beats me. I must trace it to its source. Of course I always read it aloud as meum-tuum.' (16 April 1959; *SL 2*, p.180.)

[46] Because of the war, paper was scarce and there were difficulties with printing and binding. Norman Cameron (1905-1953) was one of Graves's closest friends; they first met in 1927. Alan Hodge (1915-1979) was co-author with Graves of *The Long Week-End: A Social History of Great Britain 1918-1939* (London: Faber, 1940), and *The Reader Over Your Shoulder: A Handbook for Writers of English Prose* (London: Cape, 1944); see footnote 40. *WIH* was also to have contained poems by two other friends, James Reeves (see footnote 40) and Harry Kemp (1911-1994), who had worked with Riding and Graves in 1936-38 and contributed to *Epilogue*, but the Hogarth Press refused. (See Graves to Reeves, 4 Sept. [1941]; Texas.)

You're wrong about the guns. You tried to state in this [this in (?)] The Joke – but the joke isn't that you're a hostage in this fortress, I think, but rather:

The fortress fancies it is besieged – the guns are its own. You beg the commander not to fire: 'The enemy is a friend'. You're wrong really to do that: the guns must be *spent*. Then only do they use the fortress windows for looking out of. Don't pretend you haven't had guns of your own tucked away – get them all shot off.

Yours for love and peace to the poor gun-gods and all that bottling up
Laura[47]

St.2 was adapted from a separate six-line ts. poem entitled 'The Child'.

Text: *WIH/CP75.*

The Worms of History

Text: *CP61.*
Variants:

st. 3 l. 3 As for *CP61*] It was *WIH*
l. 5 Which were his mourning for divinity:
l. 6 upon] on the

A Withering Herb

Text: *CP14-47.*
Variants:

sect. 1 l. 4 stemless *CP14-47*] stalkless *WIH*
sect. 2 l. 4 stem,] stalk,

The Shot

Text: *CP75.*
Variant:

sect. 1 l. 4 charmed and *CP75*] charmed, it *WIH*

Dream of a Climber

The climber was the scientist and mathematician Jacob Bronowski (1908-1974), later famous for the 1971-72 television series *The Ascent of Man*, who lived in Deyá for almost a year in 1933-34 and worked with Riding on *Epilogue*. When James Reeves, who was a friend of Bronowski's, objected to an earlier version, Graves wrote reassuring him:

I have { demilitarized / de-nicotinized / de-thinged } the poem, which originally – the first few lines at least – came to me in a dream.[48] I did not recognize Jacob

[47] Diary (the letter from Riding is enclosed in it); see *RPG 2*, pp.295-7.
[48] Recorded in Graves's diary, 15 Feb. 1939.

at first; and I admit it was naughty of me to put sneakers on his feet afterwards. Now it can stand for *all* the aspirants to fame through science. I hope you will be able to read it with an undreary eye, as a new poem. It is better, in any case.[49]

Text: *WIH/CP61*.

Lollocks

Text: *CP75*.

Variant:

st. 8 l. 6 As it falls *CP75*] So soon as it's *WIH*

Frightened Men

Text: *CP75*.

Variants:

The first two lines in *WIH*:

We are not of their kind, nor ever were,
Never having had such claws to our paws

sect. 1 l. 3 half-remembered *CP75*] hypothetic
sect. 2 l. 2 neighbourly to] amiable with
love] hate
least.] most.

Graves used the conclusion ('as who returns . . . his own.') in another poem, 'The Moon Ends in Nightmare', which he did not publish; see *Complete Poems*, Volume III, 'Uncollected Poems'. The third and final section is as follows:

I crept to where my window beckoned warm
Between the white oak and the tulip tree
And rapped – but was denied, as who returns
After a one-hour-seeming century
To a house not his own.[50]

The Oath

Text: *CP75*.

Variant:

st. 2 l. 4 ciphers *CP75*] travellers *WIH*

---

[49] 23 Feb. [1941]; Texas.

[50] 'Frightened Men' was written on 10-11 Feb. 1939 (Diary). Graves inserted 'The Moon Ends in Nightmare' (there is an earlier draft at Buffalo) in his diary before the last entry, for 6 May 1939. The poem was reproduced with a transcript in the *Malahat Review*, 35 (July 1975), 8-9, a special number in celebration of Graves's eightieth birthday.

Language of the Seasons

Text: *CP75.*

Variant:

sect. 2 l. 2 Where, *CP75*] While, *WIH*

The Rock at the Corner

Text: *CP61.*

Variant:

st. 3 l. 2 see it as *CP61*] know it for *WIH*

POEMS 1938-1945 (1945)

'I have been rather amused by the reviews of my poems,' Graves wrote after the publication of *Poems 1938-1945* by Cassell in November 1945.[51] 'Everyone has suddenly decided to "recognize" me as one recognizes a new Govt. of some troublesome country. This is the first really cordial batch I've had since – 1916!'[52]

A revived interest was also reflected in the sales: the initial 3000 copies were supplemented the following April by a second impression of over 4000 more.[53]

Popularity was not, however, presaged – or sought – in the 'Foreword':

> Since poems should be self-explanatory I refrain from more foreword than this: that I write poems for poets, and satires or grotesques for wits. For people in general I write prose, and am content that they should be unaware that I do anything else. To write poems for other than poets is wasteful. The moral of the Scilly Islanders who earned a precarious livelihood by taking in one another's washing is that they never upset their carefully balanced island economy by trying to horn

[51] This is the date given by Higginson. *P39-45* itself states 'First Published 1946'; according to *RPG 3* it was published 'towards the end of January 1946' (p.108).

[52] Graves to Lynette Roberts, n.d. ['c. May' 1946], *Poetry Wales*, 19, no.2 (1983), 92-3; *SL 1*, p.344. Walter Allen, for example, wrote: 'It contains some of the most concentrated poetry of our time, and is unsurpassingly well written. Many of the poems [. . .] are remarkable by any standards, and would be in any age. [. . .] It is the fruit of great talents and complete integrity.' (*Time and Tide*, 27 (23 Feb. 1946), 182.)

[53] Higginson records 4387 copies, on 2 April 1946, with 5500 in the first American edition in June. The English printer, Oliver Simon (1895-1956) of the Curwen Press, Plaistow, produced two more volumes in the 1950s in the same small format as *P38-45*: *PS51* and *P53*. (The Curwen Press had previously printed *WH*, which was published in 1925 by the *Fleuron*, the typographical journal launched the year before by Simon with Stanley Morison (1889-1967).)

into the laundry trade of the mainland; and that nowhere in the Western Hemisphere was washing so well done.

Galmpton-Brixham, R.G.
S. Devon.
1945.

There are thirty-one 'Poems' and thirteen 'Satires and Grotesques' in the book, all written since Graves completed *Collected Poems* (1938), which was now out of print. Eighteen are from *No More Ghosts* (1940) and *Work in Hand* (1942); the other twenty-six poems, including four from *The Golden Fleece* (1944), are indicated with an asterisk in the following contents list:

POEMS
A Love Story; Dawn Bombardment; The Worms of History; The Beast; A Withering Herb; The Shot; The Thieves; Lollocks; To Sleep; Despite and Still; The Suicide in the Copse; Frightened Men; A Stranger at the Party; The Oath; Language of the Seasons; Mid-Winter Waking; The Rock at the Corner; The Beach*; The Villagers and Death*; The Door*; Under the Pot*; Through Nightmare*; To Lucia at Birth*; Death by Drums*; She Tells Her Love While Half Asleep*; Instructions to the Orphic Adept*; Theseus and Ariadne*; Lament for Pasiphaë*; The Twelve Days of Christmas*; Cold Weather Proverb*; To Juan at the Winter Solstice*

SATIRES AND GROTESQUES
Dream of a Climber; The Persian Version*; The Weather of Olympus*; Apollo of the Physiologists*; The Oldest Soldier*; Grotesques i*, ii*, iii*, iv*, v*; The Eugenist*; 1805*; At the Savoy Chapel*

The Door
Text: *CP75.*
Variant:
st. 1 l. 5 Which *CP75*] That *P38-45*

To Lucia at Birth
Graves's sixth child, Lucia, was born on 21 July 1943, in Brixham, South Devon.
Text: *CP75.*
Variant:
sect. 2 l. 2 a royal *CP75*] the Royal *P38-45*

Death by Drums
Ms. drafts of the poem refer to 'olive-gatherers with Morisco wail' – calling to one another across the Deyá valley. Horned devils feature in the ancient Mallorcan folk dances of the *Cossiers.*

Text: *CP75*.
Variant:
l. 3 wholesome bitter *CP75*] pure and wholesome *P38-45*

She Tells Her Love While Half Asleep
This poem first appears in *GF* (1944), p.126, as a song which Orpheus sings of Eurydice one night while the Argonauts are sailing to the island of Lemnos.
Text: *P38-45/CP75*.

Instructions to the Orphic Adept
In *GF* this is Orpheus' song as Jason and his Argonauts return to their ship after being initiated into 'the Great Mysteries of the Goddess' on the island of Samothrace:

> As they went, Orpheus sang them the song of the Cypress and the Hazel. In this he instructed them how to behave when they were dead, if they wished to become oracular heroes rather than perennially live out their existence underground as ignorant and twittering shades.[54]

See also *GM*, 31.*b*,*5*; and *WG61*, pp.218-19/213.

Text: *CP75*.
Variants:
Headnote *Campagno CP75*] *Compagno P38-45*
sect. 2 l. 3 shall] will

Theseus and Ariadne
'Theseus and Ariadne' developed from a directly autobiographical poem in seven ms. drafts entitled 'To Die and Die', about revisiting a house where Graves had once been with Laura Riding;[55] the male and female roles are, however, in reverse. The seventh draft is as follows:

To Die and Die

She was once with me in this gentle house
Crooked with age and overtopped by pines
To which after long years again I come.

---

[54] See *GF*, pp.153-4 (p.153).
[55] The Place, the sixteenth-century house of their friends John Aldridge, the painter, and Lucie Brown, in the village of Great Bardfield, Essex. Graves and Riding stayed there for just over a week from 14 August 1936, visiting it again briefly on 25 October. When he returned from America after his break with her, Graves went to The Place on 24 August 1939 and remained there for eight months; Beryl Hodge joined him in October. See *RPG 2*, pp.249-50, 258, 316-29.

What does she think tonight, dreaming of me,
Snug in her figured couch across the waves
And accurately observing how I walk
Down this clean gravel path bordered with box
And down the strawberry path between the hazels,
Basket on shoulder, battered hat on head?
Is it: 'Long lost in my erroneous past,
He haunts the ruin and its ravaged lawns'?

It is my nature never to remove,
Only to die and die.
Though I walk here in simpler company
And with more constancy of pulse than when
Threat of her hate[56] was thunder in the air
When the pines agonized with flaws of wind
And flowers glared up at me with frantic eyes;
Or though I call a living blessing down
On what for her is rubble now and weed,
I recant nothing of such praise I poured her
From my foreboding, strained, sincere heart.
I am the same man still, revived from death,[57]
And grateful for the horror of her parting
When she had wearied of my obstinacy.[58]

'Theseus and Ariadne' was first printed in *GF*. At a feast in Chapter 23, Orpheus tells the Argonauts how Daedalus outwitted the Minotaur and after escaping from Cnossos helped Theseus to conquer Crete. Then, taking his lyre, he sings 'of Theseus and the princess whom once he courted and deserted upon the island of Naxos'.[59]

See also *GM*, 98.

Text: *CP75*.

Variants:

sect. 1 l. 4 Across *CP75*] And down *P38-45*
below] beneath
vines.] vine.
sect. 2 l. 10 supposes] would have mere

Lament for Pasiphaë

Graves put this poem into Chapter 37 of *GF*: the Argonauts hear Orpheus, delirious with fever, repeat 'the prophetic lament of King Sisyphus for the Goddess Pasiphaë, which he sang in the quarries of

[56] Third and fifth drafts: 'going'.
[57] Third draft: 'revived in love,'.
[58] Cancelled: 'constancy' (other changes in this draft are not recorded here); first draft: 'adoration'.
[59] *GF*, p.192.

Ephyra on the evening before the stone crushed him' (pp.278-9). Sisyphus was made to labour in the marble-quarries as a punishment for his refusal to recognize the new Olympian order substituting worship of Zeus as sovereign deity for that of the Triple Goddess (*GF*, p.61). She appears here as Pasiphaë ('She who shines for all'), the Moon-Goddess whose ritual marriage with Minos the bull-headed Sun-God is enacted in the ritual of the Spring Festival at Cnossos (*GF*, pp.20, 187-92; see also *WG61*, pp.329/319-20, and *GM*, 88.7).

Text: *P38-45/CP75.*

The Twelve Days of Christmas

See *WG61*, pp.190-2/185-6, 194/190, 389/380, 458/449; and *GM*, 7.7, 12.*a*,*1*, 13.

Text: *CP14-47.*

Variant:

st. 1 l. 3 vowed in rage *CP14-47*] fiercely vowed *P38-45*

Cold Weather Proverb

Graves described this poem as 'an attempt to formalise an unrhymed metre for small proverbial poems in the style of the Welsh & Japanese. The ornament is chiasmic alliteration'.[60]

Text: *P38-45/CP61.*

See the note on 'To Poets Under Pisces' (*CP14-47*).

To Juan at the Winter Solstice

Graves provided the following notes on 'To Juan at the Winter Solstice' for an American anthology:[61]

> This was begun just before, and completed just after, the birth of my seventh child[62] on December 21, 1945.[63] The *winter solstice* is the traditional birthday of all the 'Solar Heroes' or 'Demons of the Year' of antiquity, such as the Greek gods Apollo, Dionysus, Zeus, Hermes, Syrian Tammuz, Hercules, the Irish demi-gods Lugh and Cuchulain, the Egyptian Horus, and the Welsh Merlin and Llew Llaw.[64] In Celtic popular mythology they are sometimes represented as poetically gifted infants who confound the bards or magicians of the court where they first appear. Their fate is bound up with that of the Moon Goddess who appears to them in her different characters at different seasons of

[60] Letter to James Reeves, 3 Jan. 1945; Texas.

[61] Kimon Friar and John Malcolm Brinnin, eds, *Modern Poetry: British and American* (New York: Appleton-Century-Crofts, 1951), pp.500-1.

[62] Cf. *WG61*, pp.128/123.

[63] In fact, in the morning of 22 December; see *RPG 3*, p.87. Graves had the poem printed to send as a New Year card.

[64] See *WG61*, pp.111/106, 194-5/190, 318-19/309-10.

the year, that is to say at different years of their life, as successively mother, lover, and layer-out. This poem epitomizes the theme of the Solar Hero's invariable fate, with circumstances deduced from all the relevant mythologies. That this one story and one story only is the central infinitely variable theme of all poetry is the true, firm contention of my *The White Goddess: A Historical Grammar of Poetic Myth* [. . .]. *Boreal Crown* is Corona Borealis, alias the Cretan Crown, which in Thracean-Libyan mythology, carried to Bronze Age Britain, was the purgatory where Solar Heroes went after death: in Welsh it was called 'Caer Arianrhod' (the castle of the goddess Arianrhod – mother of the hero Llew Llaw). The *log* is the Yule log, burned at the year's end. The *great boar* kills practically all the heroes (even Zeus, according to one account) at the fall of the year.

See *WG61*, pp.21/17, 24-5/20-1:

The elements of the single infinitely variable Theme are to be found in certain ancient poetic myths which though manipulated to conform with each epoch of religious change – I use the word 'myth' in its strict sense of 'verbal iconograph' without the derogatory sense of 'absurd fiction' that it has acquired – yet remain constant in general outline. Perfect faithfulness to the Theme affects the reader of a poem with a strange feeling, between delight and horror, of which the purely physical effect is that the hair literally stands on end. A.E. Housman's test of a true poem was simple and practical: does it make the hairs of one's chin bristle if one repeats it silently while shaving? But he did not explain *why* the hairs should bristle. [. . .]

The Theme, briefly, is the antique story, which falls into thirteen chapters and an epilogue, of the birth, life, death and resurrection of the God of the Waxing Year; the central chapters concern the God's losing battle with the God of the Waning Year for love of the capricious and all-powerful Threefold Goddess, their mother, bride and layer-out. The poet identifies himself with the God of the Waxing Year and his Muse with the Goddess; the rival is his blood-brother, his other self, his weird. All true poetry – true by Housman's practical test – celebrates some incident or scene in this very ancient story, and the three main characters are so much a part of our racial inheritance that they not only assert themselves in poetry but recur on occasions of emotional stress in the form of dreams, paranoiac visions and delusions. The weird, or rival, often appears in nightmare as the tall, lean, dark-faced bed-side spectre, or Prince of the Air, who tries to drag the dreamer out through the window, so that he looks back and sees his body still lying rigid in bed; but he takes countless other malevolent or diabolic or serpent-like forms.

The Goddess is a lovely, slender woman with a hooked nose, deathly pale face, lips red as rowan-berries, startlingly blue eyes and long fair hair; she will suddenly transform herself into sow, mare, bitch, vixen, she-ass, weasel, serpent, owl, she-wolf, tigress, mermaid or loathsome hag. Her names and titles are innumerable. In ghost stories she often figures as 'The White Lady', and in ancient religions, from the British Isles to the Caucasus, as the 'White Goddess'. I cannot think of any true poet from Homer onwards who has not independently recorded his experience of her. The test of a poet's vision, one might say, is the accuracy of his portrayal of the White Goddess and of the island over which she rules. The reason why hairs stand on end, the eyes water, the throat is constricted, the skin crawls and a shiver runs down the spine when one writes or reads a true poem is that a true poem is necessarily an invocation of the White Goddess, or Muse, the Mother of All Living, the ancient power of fright and lust – the female spider or the queen-bee whose embrace is death. Housman offered a secondary test of true poetry: whether it matches a phrase of Keats's, 'everything that reminds me of her goes through me like a spear'. This is equally pertinent to the Theme. Keats was writing under the shadow of death about his Muse, Fanny Brawne; and the 'spear that roars for blood' is the traditional weapon of the dark executioner and supplanter.

Sometimes, in reading a poem, the hairs will bristle at an apparently unpeopled and eventless scene described in it, if the elements bespeak her unseen presence clearly enough: for example, when owls hoot, the moon rides like a ship through scudding cloud, trees sway slowly together above a rushing waterfall, and a distant barking of dogs is heard; or when a peal of bells in frosty weather suddenly announces the birth of the New Year.

Despite the deep sensory satisfaction to be derived from Classical poetry, it never makes the hair rise and the heart leap, except where it fails to maintain decorous composure; and this is because of the difference between the attitudes of the Classical poet, and of the true poet, to the White Goddess.[65]

For various versions of the 'story' examined in *WG*, see especially *WG61*, pp.124-36/119-31 and 447-9/438-40; and for another account of its 'central chapters', see pp.386-8/377-80.

See also, for st.1 l.3: *WG61*, pp.28/24. St.2 l.1: *WG61*, Chapters II, X, XI; l.2: *WG61*, Chapter XXIII; l.3: *WG61*, pp.66-7/61-2, 143/138, 370/361, and *GM*, 50.*1,2,5*; ll.4-6: *WG61*, pp.98-100/94-6, 179/174, 379-81/370-2. St. 3 ll.1-2: *WG61*, pp.144-5/139-40, 321/312, and *GM*, 73.*4*, 88.*6*; l.5: *WG61*, pp.201/196, 296/288. St.4 ll.1-2: *WG61*, pp.194/190, 261/253, 394-6/386-7. St.5: *WG61*, pp.248-9/241-2, 480/471, and *GM*, 1.*a,b,c,2*, 4.*5*, 73.*7*, 103.*1,2*, 137.*d,2*. St.6 l.1: *WG61*, pp.111/106,

---

[65] Cf. Graves's slightly revised version of these paragraphs in 'The Personal Muse', *Oxford Addresses on Poetry* (London: Cassell, 1962), pp.60-2, reprinted in *CWP*, pp.338-9.

178/173; l.2: *WG61*, pp.185/180, 211/205-6, 315/306; l.5: *WG61*, pp.397/388. St.7 ll.2-3: *WG61*, pp.183-4/178-9, 210/205, 261/253, and *GM*, 18.7; l.4 ('long ninth wave'): *WG61*, pp.314/305.

Text: *CP75*.
Variants:
st. 2 *l. 2* Or *CP75*] Of *P38-45*
st. 6 *l. 5* confesses:] confesses
st. 7 *l. 4* crested] long ninth[66]
l. 5 sea-grey] sea-blue

The Weather of Olympus
Text: *CP75*.
Variant:
st. 2 *l. 1* his *CP75*] this *P38-45*

Grotesques
Text: *CP75*.
The sixth poem was added to the sequence in *CP55*.
Variants:
III:
st. 1 *l. 11* moving stairs), *CP75*] moving-stairs *P38-45*
l. 13 steel-chairs.] steel chairs.
V:
l. 1 Snake-god] Snake God

The Eugenist
From a letter to James Reeves, 26 Sept. 1942: 'I have also written a poem for Maurice to print in the *Eugenic*[*s*] *Review* beginning "Come, human dogs, interfertilitate."'[67]
Text: *P38-45*/*CP61*.

1805
Nelson was killed in the Battle of Trafalgar on 21 October 1805; his 'lavish funeral' took place on 9 January 1806.
Text: *CP75*.
Variant:
st. 1 *l. 2* St Paul's, *CP75*] the Abbey, *P38-45*
This change was made in *CP14-47* after James Reeves pointed out the mistake; see *SPP*, pp.237-8.

---

[66] Changed in *CP14-47*; cf. 'The Song of Blodeuwedd' (*CP14-47*), ll.18-19: 'Long and white are my fingers / As the ninth wave of the sea.'
[67] Texas. The editor, Dr Maurice Newfield, a friend of Graves's, printed it in the *Eugenics Review*, 34 (Oct. 1942), 84.

COLLECTED POEMS (1914-1947) (1948)

Collected Poems (1914-1947), Graves's third *Collected Poems*, was published by Cassell in April 1948, a month before his 'historical grammar of poetic myth', *The White Goddess*, in which ten of the seventeen new poems also appear.

There are 187 poems in *Collected Poems (1914-1947)*; in the 'Foreword', Graves gives an account of how the contents were established:

> In Egypt in 1926 I collected all the poems I had published during the previous twelve years, discarded most of them, revised and republished the remainder. Twelve years later with the help of Laura Riding – we had long been in close literary partnership – I made a second revision, and a revision of all the poems that I had written meanwhile.[68] Having by then a clearer notion of the poetic course that I was steering I could discard more generously than before, so that the new book was shorter by forty pages.[69]
>
> Here is a list of the volumes (now all out of print) that I drew upon:– [details follow].
>
> Now to make further improvements: the removal of another twenty poems, the revision of several more, the restoration of four early ones from the 1926 edition,[70] and this shortened foreword.

---

[68] See the note on *CP38*.

[69] Twenty-six, if the foreword and the preliminary and final pages are excluded.

[70] 'In the Wilderness' (*OB*) (see footnote 24), 'Rocky Acres' (*CS*), 'The Troll's Nosegay' (*P-G*), and 'Song of Contrariety' (*W*). All four were included in the selection of thirty-one poems in *RG43*. When the editor of the Augustan Poets series, Edward Thompson, proposed reprinting *RG25*, Graves objected that he 'couldn't possibly consent to be represented in 1943 by work done so long ago' (Graves to Thompson, 8 March 1943; the letters to Thompson cited in this footnote are in the Bodleian Library, Oxford.) He relented, though, and offered to revise the 1925 booklet, explaining: 'I like my early work, in its way, and have no objection to other people's liking of it; but I had to put it well behind me in 1924 before getting on to other things. The period when you & I were together at Islip [1923-25] was a transition period in my poetry, and no good: but it made the break. I know that I had very queer views, and do not stand by them' (12 March). The selection he sent contained in fact only eight of the original twenty-three. 'What I have done,' he wrote on 20 March, 'is to remove the uncomfortably didactic poems [. . .] and replace with others of the same rather romantic quality as the remainder'. This still left the booklet four pages short, so Graves, albeit reluctantly, suggested (12 April) four more titles, among them 'The Troll's Nosegay' and 'Song of Contrariety'. In his introduction Thompson wrote: 'Since Robert Graves made a selection of his poems for the Augustan Series in 1925 he has been writing in an altogether different vein, as may be seen from his *Collected Poems* (*1938*, Cassell) and from *Work in Hand* (*1941*, Hogarth Press). But there is a quality in his early work which is not to be found in his later, and the present volume, a corrected edition of the Augustan selection, is therefore published

The order is roughly chronological. At the end come forty-four poems from *Poems:* 1938-45 (Cassell, 1946) [*sic*]; seventeen more recent ones, including translations of magical texts from the Welsh, Irish and Greek which are discussed in my forthcoming *White Goddess* (Faber & Faber); and a stray poem, *Gulls and Men* (1936), which I left behind in my Majorcan home when I went off in a hurry at the outbreak of the Spanish Civil War, and found waiting for revision on my work-table when I returned ten years later.[71]

R.G.

Deyá, Majorca,
1947.

The twenty poems omitted, all in *Collected Poems* (1938), were:

I: Wanderings of Christmas; Pygmalion and Galatea. II: Song: To Be Less Philosophical; Blonde or Dark? III: The Stranger; The Smoky House; The Foolish Senses; The Goblet; Fiend, Dragon, Mermaid. IV: Lunch-Hour Blues; Hotel Bed; Progressive Housing; Being Tall; X; To Challenge Delight; The Grudge; The Halfpenny; Idle Hands. V: To Whom Else?; Leaving the Rest Unsaid

The complete contents of *Collected Poems (1914-1947)* are as follows (new poems are indicated with an asterisk):

I
In the Wilderness; The Haunted House; Reproach; The Finding of Love; 'The General Elliott'; Rocky Acres; Outlaws; One Hard Look; A Frosty Night; Allie; Unicorn and the White Doe; Henry and Mary; Love Without Hope; What Did I Dream?; The Country Dance; The Troll's Nosegay; The Hills of May; Lost Love; Vain and Careless; An English Wood; The Bedpost; The Pier-Glass; Apples and Water; Angry Samson; Down; Mermaid, Dragon, Fiend

II
In Procession; Warning to Children; Alice; Richard Roe and John Doe; The Witches' Cauldron; Ancestors; Children of Darkness; The Cool Web; Love in Barrenness; Song of Contrariety; The Presence; The Land of Whipperginny; In No Direction; The Castle; Return; Lust in

without apologies [. . .].' Graves's dedication reads, 'To | Edward Thompson | in happy memory of the Islip village football team, canoeing on the Ray, and the children who have now grown up.' (Two of these, David Graves and Frank Thompson, died heroically in World War II.) Returning the proofs, Graves wrote (on 8 Sept.), 'I have read it with disinterested pleasure! An odd book!'

[71] Graves's diary records it in 1935: see note, below.

Song; Nobody; Without Pause; Full Moon; Vanity; Pure Death; Sick Love; It Was All Very Tidy

III
Callow Captain; Thief; Saint; The Furious Voyage; Song: Lift-Boy; The Next Time; Ulysses; The Succubus; Trudge, Body; The Clock Man; The Reader Over My Shoulder; Green Loving; The Legs; Gardener; Front Door Soliloquy; In Broken Images; On Rising Early; Flying Crooked; Largesse to the Poor; Fragment of a Lost Poem

IV
Galatea and Pygmalion; The Devil's Advice to Story-Tellers; Sea Side; Wm. Brazier; Welsh Incident; Vision in the Repair-Shop; Interruption; Act V, Scene 5; Midway; Hell; Leda; Synthetic Such; The Florist Rose; Lost Acres; At First Sight; Recalling War; Down, Wanton, Down!; A Former Attachment; Nature's Lineaments; Time; The Philosopher; On Dwelling; Parent to Children; Ogres and Pygmies; History of the Word; Single Fare; To Walk on Hills; To Bring the Dead to Life; To Evoke Posterity; The Poets; Defeat of the Rebels; Never Such Love; The Fallen Signpost; The China Plate; Certain Mercies; The Cuirassiers of the Frontier; The Laureate; A Jealous Man; The Cloak; The Halls of Bedlam; Or to Perish Before Day; A Country Mansion; The Eremites; The Advocates; Self-Praise

V
On Portents; The Terraced Valley; The Challenge; To the Sovereign Muse; The Ages of Oath; New Legends; Like Snow; The Climate of Thought; End of Play; The Fallen Tower of Siloam; The Great-Grandmother; No More Ghosts

VI
A Love Story; Dawn Bombardment; The Worms of History; The Beast; A Withering Herb; The Shot; The Thieves; Lollocks; To Sleep; Despite and Still; The Suicide in the Copse; Frightened Men; A Stranger at the Party; The Oath; Language of the Seasons; Mid-Winter Waking; The Rock at the Corner; The Beach; The Villagers and Death; The Door; Under the Pot; Through Nightmare; To Lucia at Birth; Death by Drums; She Tells Her Love While Half Asleep; Theseus and Ariadne; The Twelve Days of Christmas; Three Short Poems: Cold Weather Proverb, To Poets Under Pisces*, June*; 1805; At the Savoy Chapel; The Last Day of Leave (1916)*; To Be Named a Bear*

VII
SATIRES AND GROTESQUES
Dream of a Climber; The Persian Version; The Weather of Olympus; Apollo of the Physiologists; The Oldest Soldier; Grotesques i, ii, iii, iv, v; The Eugenist; A Civil Servant*; Gulls and Men*

MAGICAL POEMS
To Juan at the Winter Solstice; The Allansford Pursuit*; The Alphabet Calendar of Amergin*; The Sirens' Welcome to Cronos*; Dichetal do Chennaib*; The Battle of the Trees*; The Song of Blodeuwedd*; Intercession in Late October*; Instructions to the Orphic Adept; Lament for Pasiphaë; The Tetragrammaton*

Nuns and Fish*; The Destroyer*; Return of the Goddess*[72]

To Poets Under Pisces

Text: *CP14-47.*

In *CP14-47* 'Cold Weather Proverb' (*P38-45*), 'To Poets Under Pisces' and 'June' are grouped on one page (p.199) under the title 'Three Short Poems', with smaller individual titles in italics. Though 'Cold Weather Proverb' remained in the canon to *CP61*, the other two poems were not reprinted.

June

Text: *CP14-47.*

See the previous note.

The Last Day of Leave

Text: *CP61.*

Although first published in November 1947, and included in Section VI of *CP14-47*, in subsequent collections – *CP55, CP59* and *CP61* – 'The Last Day of Leave' is placed in Section III, with poems from the late 1920s and early 1930s.

In *CP14-47* the date '1916' is printed as part of the title, both above the poem and in the 'Contents' list; from *CP55* it appears below the title and is omitted in the 'Contents'.

Variant:

st. 13 l. 3 Not *CP61*] No *CP14-47*

To Be Called a Bear

See *WG61*, pp.179/174.

Text: *CP75.*

Previous title: 'To Be Named a Bear' (*CP14-47*).

Variants:

st. 2 l. 2 called *CP75*] named *CP14-47*

l. 3 it is] is it

A Civil Servant

In a letter to James Reeves, 30 March 1946, Graves wrote: 'The "Civil Servant" thing is to be broadcast in "New Poems" soon. It was really

[72] In *CP14-47* there is a space separating these last three titles from the eleven above them.

written about the B.B.C. as a matter of fact. I have changed a few words to increase the "bite".'[73]

Text: *CP14-47/CP61.*

Gulls and Men

Text: *CP61.*

After his return to Mallorca in 1946 Graves wrote to Martin Seymour-Smith: 'I found a lost poem of mine about the Bass Rock here among my papers, quite nice'.[74]

Variant:

st. 2 l. 2 by design, *CP61*] by design *CP14-47*

The Allansford Pursuit

For 'the fragmentary seventeenth-century text',[75] with Graves's account of the origins of the poem and its relation to 'the myth of the sexual chase', see *WG61*, pp.400-2/391-3; the 'whole song' – 'easy to restore in its original version' – is on p.402/393.

Text: *SP58.*

Emendations:

st. 2 l. 1 Yet *mss, WG*] Yet, *CP14-47, CP55, SP58*

st. 3 l. 2 thee, *mss, WG*] thee *CP14-47, CP55, SP58*

These are the only differences in punctuation in *WG*; they have been adopted in the present edition to make the stanzas consistent.

WG has one substantive variant: 'merry' in place of 'crooked' (*CP14-47, CP55, SP58*) in st.2 l.3. The poem is printed without the title, although it appears in the index. *'Cunning and art, etc.'* comes immediately after l.8 of each stanza, without an intervening space.

The poem is also printed in the 'Introduction' to *English and Scottish Ballads*, edited by Robert Graves, revised edition (London: Heinemann, 1957), p.ix; the version is the same as in *WG*, except that it gives the refrain in full after l.8 of st.1, and not at the beginning of the poem.

Amergin's Charm

Cf. *WG61*, 'Introduction', pp.12-13/9:

> English poetic education should, really, begin not with the *Canterbury Tales*, not with the *Odyssey*, not even with *Genesis*, but with the *Song of Amergin*, an ancient Celtic calendar-alphabet, found in several purposely garbled Irish and Welsh variants, which briefly summarizes the prime poetic myth.

---

[73] Texas.

[74] Graves to Martin Seymour-Smith, 25 July 1946; *SL 2*, p.30. Although Graves dates it as 1936 in the 'Foreword' to *CP14-47*, his diary records 'First draft of poem *Gulls and Such*' (the previous title) on 20 Sept. 1935; three more drafts are recorded on 21 Sept., and 'alterations' on 11 Oct.

[75] See headnote.

This is followed by the text of the poem, 'tentatively restored' by Graves. See Chapter XII, 'The Song of Amergin' (especially pp.205-16/200-11).

Text: *CP61.*
Previous title: 'The Alphabet Calendar of Amergin' (*CP14-47*).
Variants:
st. 2 *l. 1* roars *CP61*] rears *CP14-47* (*misprint*)
l. 5 renowned] ruthless
WG has 'ruthless' in st.2 l.5, and 'tomb' in place of 'grave' in st.3 l.5.

The Sirens' Welcome to Cronos

With the poem – the Sirens' song, 'reconstructed [. . .] on the model of similar songs in ancient Irish literature' – Graves gives an account of the Sirens, Cronos and Odysseus in *WG61*, pp.417-19/408-10. See also, for Cronos, *WG61*, pp.65-7/60-2, 171/166, 186/180-1, and *GM*, 6, 7, 28.*1*, 31.*2*; and for the Sirens, *GM*, 154.*d*, *3*, 170.*q*, *r*, *s*, *7*.

Text: *CP61.*
Emendation:
st. 3 *l. 2* egg, *CP14-47, CP55, SP58*] egg *CP59, CP61*
Variants:
Title Sirens' *CP61*] Siren's *CP14-47* (*misprint*)
st. 1 *l. 1* the Ruddy,] Odysseus,
st. 5 *l. 2* the Ruddy,] Odysseus,
WG prints the *CP14-47* version (with four differences in punctuation).

Dichetal do Chennaib

In *WG61* Graves explains that 'the *Dichetal do Chennaib* ("recital from the finger-ends")' was 'an Irish poetic rite', and suggests that 'the poets induced a poetic trance by treating their finger-tips as oracular agents'.[76] ('At this point my own finger-tips began to itch and when I gave them a pen to hold they reconstructed the original incantation': the poem follows.)[77] See Chapters X and XI, especially pp.195-9/190-4.

Text: *CP14-47.*
Variants:
The main differences in *WG*:
st. 2 *l. 4* knocks the heart. *CP14-47*] the heart knocks. *WG*
st. 4 *l. 3* Weather-wise,] Weatherwise,
st. 6 *l. 1* earfinger,] ear finger,
(There are four further differences in punctuation.)

---

[76] *WG61*, pp.198/193-4.
[77] *WG61*, pp.198-9/194 (interpolated within square brackets).

The Battle of the Trees

The poem is 'reassembled and restored'[78] from a 'mid-Victorian translation, said to be unreliable but the best at present available',[79] in *WG61*, Chapter II. Graves argues that it describes 'not a frivolous battle, or a battle physically fought, but a battle fought intellectually in the heads and with the tongues of the learned'. For 'in all Celtic languages *trees* means *letters*'[80] (or *learning*),[81] and the poet, '"Gwion", a North Welsh cleric of the late thirteenth century, whose true name is not known',[82] was 'clearly familiar' with the ancient Irish tree-alphabet, the Beth-Luis-Nion ('Birch-Rowan-Ash').[83] Its eighteen letters referred to a 'sequence of forest trees' serving both as an alphabet and as a sacred calendar, 'a calendar which can be proved, by a study of the festal use of trees throughout Europe, to have been observed in the Bronze Age (and earlier) from Palestine to Ireland, and to have been associated everywhere with the worship of the pre-Aryan Triple Moon-goddess – sometimes called Leucothea, the White Goddess.' The tree-alphabet can be regarded as 'a Celtic counterpart of the eighteen-letter Greek Orphic alphabet, associated with moving trees'.[84]

The myth of the Battle of the Trees (Câd Goddeu) records 'a battle for religious mastery'[85] which took place in Britain 'early in the fourth century B.C.' following an invasion by Belgic tribes.[86] The victors 'instituted a new religious system, and a new calendar, and new names of letters':[87] this entailed the 'suppression of the Lunar Mother-goddess's inspiratory cult, and its supersession [. . .] by the busy, rational cult of the Solar God Apollo', as in Greece – 'the most important single fact in the early history of Western religion and sociology'.[88]

Graves provides a succinct account of the central arguments of *WG* in his 1957 New York lecture, 'The White Goddess' (quoted above).[89] For summaries of his findings on the Beth-Luis-Nion and other alphabets, see *S*, pp.86-90/489-92, and *WG61*, pp.123-4/118-19, 244/237, 340-1/331-2; see also *GM*, 52, 132.3.

---

[78] See headnote.

[79] *WG61*, pp.30/26; the translation, from D.W. Nash's *Taliesin, or The Bards and Druids of Britain* (London: John Russell Smith, 1858), is reprinted on pp.30-6/26-31.

[80] *WG61*, pp.38/33.

[81] 'The White Goddess: A Lecture for the Y.M.H.A. Center, New York, February 9, 1957', in *5PH*, pp.54-72, and *S*, pp.86-105 (p.88); the text in *S* is reprinted in the 1997 edition of *WG61*, pp.489-504 (p.490).

[82] *WG61*, pp.123/118.

[83] *WG61*, pp.40/35, 38/33.

[84] 'The White Goddess', *S*, p.88, and *WG61* (1997 edition), p.491.

[85] *WG61*, pp.50/45.

[86] *WG61*, pp.124/119.

[87] *WG61*, pp.286/278.

[88] 'The White Goddess', *S*, p.89, and *WG61* (1997 edition), p.492.

[89] See footnote 81.

Text: *CP61*.
Variants:
st. 4 l. 1 With *CP61*] For with *CP14-47*
Between sts.8 and 10, *CP14-47* has the following two stanzas:

At a battle raging
  Under each tongue root
Of a hundred-headed thing,
  A monstrous brute,

A toad with a hundred claws
  Armed at his thighs;
And in his head-recesses
  Raging likewise.

These stanzas also appear in *WG48* and *WG52*, which print the *CP14-47* version of the poem (but with a comma after 'Maelderw' in l.3 of the third last stanza).

In his library copy of the American edition (1958) of *WG52*, which contains the revisions and additions for *WG61*, Graves has cancelled these stanzas, changed the comma at the end of st.8 l.4 to a semi-colon, and written st.9 – a reworking of ll.1-2 of the first stanza and ll.3-4 of the second – in the margin.[90]

The Song of Blodeuwedd

According to Graves, 'The Song of Blodeuwedd' is one of 'four or five' poems 'mixed' with the title poem 'The Battle of the Trees' in 'Câd Goddeu' (see the previous note).[91] See *WG61*, Chapter II, especially pp.39-42/34-7; for the story of Blodeuwedd's betrayal of Llew Llaw Gyffes (from the *Mabinogion*), see pp.304-16/296-307.

---

[90] With the remaining four lines, and others from the original 'poem-medley', Graves builds up a 'toad-serpent' sequence in *WG61* which he relates to 'the ancient toadstool mysteries' involving the ritual eating of hallucinogenic toadstools (pp.44-5/40):

Indifferent bards pretend,
They pretend a monstrous beast,
With a hundred heads,
A spotted crested snake,

A toad having on his thighs
A hundred claws,

With a golden jewel set in gold
I am enriched;
And indulged in pleasure
By the oppressive toil of the goldsmith.

[91] *WG61*, pp.36/32.

Text: *CP14-47/CP75.*

Until *CP65* the poem followed 'The Battle of the Trees' (*CP14-47*) and had the headnote which appears in the present edition. 'The Battle of the Trees' was then suppressed and its headnote, shortened,[92] was transferred to 'The Song of Blodeuwedd'.

WG (*WG61*, pp.41-2/37) prints the poem with the title 'Hanes Blodeuwedd'; instead of 'earthy' in l.12 it has 'earthly' (as in the translation: see *WG61*, pp.34/30, l.150, and Nash, *Taliesin*, p.232).

Intercession in Late October

See *GM*, 83.*c,g,2,3*, and *WG61*, pp.183/178, 210/205, 278/270, 394/385.

Text: *CP14-47/CP61.*

The Tetragrammaton

See *WG61*, pp.92/88 ('the "tetragrammaton" was the cryptogrammic Hebrew way of spelling the secret Name [of God] in four letters as JHWH'), 338-9/329-30, and 462-73/453-64 (especially pp. 468-72/458-62).

Text: *CP14-47.*

The poem appears, untitled, in *WG* (*WG61*, pp.471-2/462), with 'my', 'I' and 'me' throughout in place of 'his', 'he' and 'him', 'is' in place of 'was' in st.1 l.2, and 'law' spelt with a capital 'L' in st.2 l.1; it is not divided into stanzas.

Nuns and Fish

See *WG*, Chapter XX, 'A Conversation at Paphos – A.D. 43'. (The chapter starts with ll.1-3 (there is a comma after 'fish' in l.1), and the two speakers, 'Theophilus, a well-known Syrian-Greek historian and Lucius Sergius Paulus, a Roman Governor-General of Cyprus under the Emperor Claudius', conclude their conversation with (respectively) ll.4 and 5.)

Text: *CP14-47.*

The Destroyer

In the first and second editions of *WG* 'The Destroyer' follows 'Return of the Goddess' (*CP14-47*) – both untitled – and ends the book. (The third edition has a further chapter, 'Postscript 1960'.) Graves prefaces it thus:

> And we owe her [i.e. the Goddess] a satire on the memory of the man who first tilted European civilization off balance, by enthroning the

---

92 'Text reassembled and restored' became 'Reassembled', and 'Welsh' (and the hyphen) were deleted in 'medieval Welsh poem-medley'.

restless and arbitrary male will under the name of Zeus and dethroning the female sense of orderliness, Themis. The Greeks knew him as Pterseus the Destroyer, the Gorgon-slaying warrior-prince from Asia, remote ancestor of the destroyers Alexander, Pompey and Napoleon.[93]

See also *WG61*, pp.64/59, 229-30/223-4, 324-34/315-25, and *GM*, 73.
Text: *CP14-47/CP61*.
In st.4 l.3 *WG52* and *WG61* have 'unnoble' in place of 'ignoble'.

Return of the Goddess

This is the last poem in *CP14-47*. Its title is given in *WG61* to Chapter XXVI, which was elaborated from the final paragraphs of *WG48* and added in *WG52*; the poem comes at the conclusion to Graves's argument. There seems no escape from the plight of Western patriarchal civilization until the industrial system breaks down and 'nature reasserts herself with grass and trees among the ruins':[94]

> [. . .] I forsee no change for the better until everything gets far worse. Only after a period of complete religious and political disorganization can the suppressed desire of the Western races, which is for some practical form of Goddess-worship, with her love not limited to maternal benevolence and her after-world not deprived of a sea, find satisfaction at last. [. . .]
>
> But the longer her hour is postponed, and therefore the more exhausted by man's irreligious improvidence the natural resources of the soil and sea become, the less merciful will her five-fold mask be, and the narrower the scope of action that she grants to whichever demi-god she chooses to take as her temporary consort in godhead. Let us placate her in advance by assuming the cannibalistic worst: [the poem follows].[95]

See Graves's analysis of the poem in *Poetry: A Critical Supplement* (April 1948), 18-20:[96]

> The poem, which like all my poems is written for poets, is staged in an alder thicket because cranes nest in alders, and because the crane is sacred to Artemis, and because cranes feed on frogs. It may be read as a critical comment on Aesop's moral, which you quote, 'Better no rule than cruel rule'; namely, better cruel rule than no rule – the fact

---

[93] *WG61*, pp.486/477.
[94] *WG61*, pp.482/472-3.
[95] *WG61*, pp.484-6/475-7.
[96] Written in response to an analysis by John Frederick Nims which was published with the poem (sts.1-3, entitled 'Return of the Goddess Artemis') in *Poetry*, 71 (Oct. 1947), 14-16, 22.

being that Artemis, the Lady of Wild Things, the Triple Moon-Goddess, the Most Beautiful, whose seat was at the hinge of the grid-iron around which her two bears revolved, whose milk spurts across the sky near the galaxy, and who lived independent of male gods until about 2000 B.C., had been deposed by Zeus, the patriarchal Aryan newcomer to Greece, and her ancient civilization destroyed and remodelled. Zeus, like all Father-gods, presently grew senile and the law and order which he had established on a basis of force, began to collapse under headless, undirected individualism. Zeus's prime oracle was the Oak, which he shared with various thunder gods, such as Allah whose name means 'Oak', and what is an oak but a log?

The crane represents the Goddess because her colours are red, white and black; these were the three colours sacred to the moon (the three colours that the moon assumes) as in Suidas's riddle about the mulberry and the three-coloured moon-heifer. She also has a habit of laying the fish she spears in a silver circle on the bank when she is at work, so that she is sometimes called Arianrhod, the Goddess of the Silver Wheel, which is understood as the turning universe. As crane she is the Goddess of literature; the Greek myth quoted by Hyginus is that the alphabet was formed from watching the flight of cranes. The same connection with letters is found in Irish literature; the crane-bag of Manannan which held the secrets of the people of the Sea, and in Egyptian sacred history – Thoth the inventor of the alphabet was symbolized by a crane.

The alder has always been associated with the Goddess; because it was the first tree used for making boats – the Moon-Goddess's symbol is a boat – and because it yields a red dye and because it is a water-tree (the moon is the giver of water) and because its buds grow in a spiral of immortality. It was planted around all oracular islands.

Artemis had a thousand names at least. One of them was Themis, the Goddess of Order or Neatness, as opposed to the petulant caprice of Zeus with his oak club and his thunderbolt; but this order was founded on religious awe of her magic.

The owl was another of her birds; the warning, oracular aspect – but it got associated with Athene in a period when Artemis and Athene had ceased to be the same Goddess.

'To fetch them home again' is a line from a Scottish seventeenth-century witch ballad in honour of the same Goddess; it refers to her pursuit of the runaway who tries to escape her power.[97]

See also *WG61*, pp.85/81, 172/166, 179/174, 211/205-6, 224/218, 227/221, 233-4/226-8, 483/474.

---

[97] St.3 l.5; cf. l.4 of each stanza of 'The Allansford Pursuit' (*CP14-47*), and see *WG61*, pp.401-2/392-3.

In a letter to a friend Graves explained that the Latin 'charm' means '"the five feasts are enough for us, Artemis of the Nut-tree, when you are about" (i.e. the working week, excluding the Sabbath and Sunday both of which Jehovah appropriated to himself). The formula *S.T.C.D.Q.* can also be represented with willow, holly, nut, oak, apple.'[98] See *WG61*, pp.259-60/251-2, and 462-73/453-64 (especially 464-5/454-6 and 471/462).

Text: *CP75*.
Emendation:
st. 2 l. 3 wing, *ms., WG, CP61*] wing *CP75*

The version in *WG* (*WG61*, p.486/477) has 'the' for 'your' in st.1 l.4; ll.3 and 4 in st.2 in the reverse order, with 'Dark waters bubble' in place of 'Dark water bubbles' in l.4; and 'She' for 'You' in st.3 l.3. It does not have the Latin conclusion.

Graves changed st.3 l.2 'red-leggèd' to 'red-wattled' in *WG52* (and *WG61*) after the poet John Heath-Stubbs wrote to him pointing out that cranes did not have red legs (they were either black or 'very dark grey'). In the poetry volumes, nevertheless, the legs remain red.[99]

POEMS AND SATIRES 1951 (1951)

> The Goddess has been plaguing me lately, very cruelly, and I have managed to satisfy her by two or three poems written in red arterial blood; she appeared in person in Deyá during the last full moon, swinging a Cretan axe, but is now away again. Put into historical terms the story isn't really interesting: no liaison dangerous or alteration of the local ebbs & flows. But there are the poems; their publication in my new collection is the only impingement of poetic on historical truth [. . .].[100]

The 'new collection', *Poems and Satires 1951*, was published by Cassell on 30 November 1951. 'The White Goddess' is the first of the seventeen 'Poems', which are followed by eight 'Satires'; in the third section, 'Revisions', are four earlier poems: 'The Progress' (*P14-27*), 'Traveller's Curse After Misdirection' (*WH*), 'Sergeant-Major Money' (*WH*), and 'Brother' (*P26-30*).

---

[98] Graves to George Simon, 15 April 1946; *SL 2*, p.48.

[99] See John Heath-Stubbs, *Hindsights: An Autobiography* (London: Hodder and Stoughton, 1993), pp.174-5. See also *WG48*, p.211 ('her red legs denote her relation with the Underworld, red being the colour of death'); cf. *WG61*, pp.233/227..

[100] Graves to Reeves, 14 Dec. 1950; *SL 2*, p.83. He refers to Judith Bledsoe, then aged 17, his Muse during the next two years, whom he met in November 1950.

Graves revised the 'Foreword' in a proof copy of the book sent to his American agent (Willis Kingsley Wing, New York; it was not, however, published in the U.S.): these changes (in ink) are recorded below.

FOREWORD

Nine poets out of every ten are content to die young; the mortality is highest when they leave their universities to take up careers. Many of the survivors who do not turn playwrights – which, however, is to temper poetry with rhetoric – try to prolong their lives by philosophical or ecclesiastical studies or the writing of occasional verse; continuing moribund until the time comes to rally their strength for a poetic testament, or until physical dissolution mercifully overtakes them. Thus popular imagination conceives of the poet as either a doomed gallant struggling in the toils of romantic love; or a blind, white-bearded prophet; or, if he is ever middle-aged (as I am now), a paunchy Horace-Herrick, jocosely celebrating the trim servant-girl who carries the drinks out to his garden retreat. For Keats and Shelley were never old; Homer was never young; and Milton was all but silent between *Lycidas* and the literary epics of his blindness.

I once suggested that no poet could hope to write more than twenty pages in his lifetime that were really worth preserving; yet, though for conscience' sake I have suppressed hundreds of my own, both written and printed, *Collected Poems*, 1947, still contains an ambitiously large number, and here are more.[101] 'Do I contradict myself?' I ask, and cannot answer with Walt Whitman: 'Very well, then, I do contradict myself', because truth and tidiness are both debts owed by a poet to his readers. So I try to remember for whom I meant that those twenty pages might be worth preserving. Was it for posterity? I must have been thinking of myself as the posterity of certain posterity-conscious heavy-weights, of the last three centuries, who have always bored and depressed me.

Personally, I have little regard for posterity or, at least, make no attempt to anticipate their literary tastes. Whatever view they may take of my work, say a hundred years hence, must necessarily be a mistaken one, because this is my age, not theirs, and even with my help they will never fully understand it. Can I imagine myself sympathizing with their reasons for selecting this or that poem of mine to print in their anthologies? They may even choose to revive verses which, because I know that they are in some way defective, I have done my best to suppress. I write for my contemporaries.[102]

A volume of collected poems should form a sequence of the intenser moments of the poet's spiritual autobiography, moments for which

101 '[. . .] preserving; then why so many here?'

102 Sentence cancelled.

prose is insufficient: as in the[103] ancient Welsh and Irish prose tales the lyric is reserved for the[104] emotional crises. Such an autobiography, by the way, does not always keep chronological step with its historical counterpart: often a poetic event anticipates or succeeds the corresponding physical event by years.[105]

What, in fact, I was trying to say about the poets who bored me, was that either their spiritual autobiographies did not seem to have been tidily and truthfully recorded – but then, of course, it was their age, not mine – or that they were as good as dead after the first few pages. If my argument is sound so far, a poet's test for fixing the canon of his poems will be: 'Am I still alive, and is such-and-such a poem an integral part of the poetic sequence? And if so, has it reached its final version? Or is it merely a marginal rhyme? Or should it, perhaps, have been left in prose?' When those questions have been honestly settled, the only qualitative distinction between whatever poems happen to survive should be one of greater or lesser intensity, corresponding with the rise and fall of narrative interest. I disagree with the popular anthologist's view that a composite spiritual biography can be formed from the best work of a number of poets, and that a poem's worth is judged by the ease with which it lends itself to this treatment. The proper place for any but a fugitive and anonymous poem is with all the others written by one particular hand.

It may be some little time before I can be quite certain how much of the present volume forms a relevant part of my story.[106] Nothing is easier for a poet than to convince himself after working for several days on a short poem – and I am still unable to finish one in less than five or six drafts – that he has not been wasting time. However, if it happens to be faultily constructed, or written for the wrong reasons, or simply dull, he will usually recognize this by the way it fades on the page after a few months.[107] The longer one lives and the more poems accumulate, the easier it is to discard doubtful ones.

I am including here a revised version of the Dedication to *The White Goddess* and four poems, all of them more than twenty years old, omitted from the 1947 collection, but now recast.[108]

R.G.

Deyá, Majorca, Spain.

---

[103] Word cancelled.

[104] Word cancelled.

[105] '[. . .] years, and the order of poems in the present sequence is only roughly chronological.'

[106] 'I cannot be certain yet how much of the latter part of this collection forms a relevant part of my autobiography.'

[107] 'years.'

[108] Sentence cancelled.

The White Goddess

Compare the evocation of the Goddess in the first chapter of *WG61*, pp.24-5/20-1 ('The Goddess is a lovely, slender woman with a hooked nose, deathly pale face, lips red as rowan-berries, startlingly blue eyes and long fair hair'), quoted in the note on 'To Juan at the Winter Solstice' (*P38-45*).

For the implications of 'white', see *WG61*, pp.67-70/62-5, and 434-5/425-6: 'The whiteness of the Goddess has always been an ambivalent concept. In one sense it is the pleasant whiteness of pearl-barley, or a woman's body, or milk, or unsmutched snow; in another it is the horrifying whiteness of a corpse, or a spectre, or leprosy.'[109]

WG examines a multiplicity of mythological types of the Goddess; see in particular *WG61*, Chapters IV, XXII and XXIV. 'The most comprehensive and inspired account of the Goddess in all ancient literature', in Apuleius's *The Golden Ass*, is reproduced in Chapter IV (pp.70-3/65-8).[110] Among the portrayals of the White Goddess in poetry in Chapter XXIV (see pp.426-35/417-26, 439/430), Keats's 'La Belle Dame Sans Merci' is given 'detailed consideration in the light of the Theme',[111] while Coleridge's description in 'The Rime of the Ancient Mariner' of the woman dicing with Death is judged to be 'as faithful a record of the White Goddess as exists'.[112]

See also the notes on 'To Juan at the Winter Solstice' (*P38-45*) and 'The Battle of the Trees' (*CP14-47*); *GM*, pp.13-15; and for st.1 l.2, *WG61*, pp.390-2/381-3, and *GM*, 21; st.2 l.5, *GM*, 100.*g*, 131.*d*; l.6, *WG61*, pp. 433-5/424-6; l.7 ('rowan-berry'), *WG61*, pp.167-8/162-3; st.3 l.2, *WG61*, pp.374/365, 385-6/376-7.

Text: *CP75*.

Variants:

st. 3 *l. 1* Green *CP75*] The *PS51*

l. 2 the Mountain] with green the

---

[109] *WG61*, pp.434/425.

[110] In a 1566 translation by William Adlington, revised by S. Gaselee (London: Heinemann, 1915), pp.541-7; Graves published his own translation of *The Golden Ass* (Harmondsworth: Penguin, 1950).

[111] *WG61*, pp.427/418; cf. st.4 (in the version printed in *WG61*):

> I met a Lady in the Meads
> Full beautiful, a faery's child
> Her hair was long, her foot was light
> And her eyes were wild –

[112] *WG61*, pp.433/424; Part III, ll.190-4, are quoted:

> *Her* lips were red, *her* looks were free,
> *Her* locks were yellow as gold:
> Her skin was white as leprosy,
> The Night-mare LIFE-IN-DEATH was she,
> Who thicks man's blood with cold.

In the 'Foreword' to *PS51* (see above) Graves writes: 'I am including here a revised version of the Dedication to *The White Goddess*'. In *WG* the poem is headed (in large capitals) 'In Dedication'; the ten-line version in *WG48* is as follows:

Your broad, high brow is whiter than a leper's,
Your eyes are flax-flower blue, blood-red your lips,
Your hair curls honey-coloured to white hips.

All saints revile you, and all sober men
Ruled by the God Apollo's golden mean;
Yet for me rises even in November
(Rawest of months) so cruelly new a vision,
Cerridwen, of your beatific love
I forget violence and long betrayal,
Careless of where the next bright bolt may fall.

WG52 prints the *PS51* 'revised version', but has 'I' and 'my' throughout in place of 'we' and 'our', and keeps 'Careless' in st.3 l.8. This *WG52* version is printed in *WG61*, with the changes to st.3 ll.1-2 as shown above (they first appear in *CP59*).[113]

The Chink

Text: *CP75*.

In subsequent collections 'The Chink' is placed in Section V with poems from the 1930s.[114]

---

[113] The first (?), heavily revised draft of st.1 has ll.3-6 in near-final form, starting 'When I was young', with, after l.4,

And later, sobered, in my own village
My own house even, the familiar rooms.
But never found you,

These lines are cancelled and the following (with further revisions) substituted:

She is not here, they said, nor ever was[.]
Return to your village; there[,] they said
She will be hiding where you never searched.

Other lines on the sheet include the cancelled phrase 'Grown gaunt and grey'.

[114] 'The Chink' was first published in 1949 in *Poetry Review*, 40 (June-July), 172; the corrected text was printed with an apology in the next number (Aug.-Sept.), 298, below this letter to the editor:

Sir,

Will you please assure my readers that the mysterious 'writhing' in the last line of my poem *The Chink* is the work of a printer's devil with a lisp. I wrote 'rising', and should be obliged if you filled his mouth with soap.

Yours,

ROBERT GRAVES.

Variants:

st. 1 l. 6 *indent suppressed CP75*] *indent PS51*

st. 2 l. 5 *indent*] *no indent*

The Jackals' Address to Isis

This poem appears in *WG52* and *WG61* in Chapter XVIII, 'The Bull-Footed God' (*WG61*, pp.317/308). See *WG61*, pp.275/267, 277-8/269-70, 316-17/307-8, 321/312, 388/379; and *SL 1*, pp.333-4.

Text: *CP61.*

The Death Room

Text: *CP75.*

Emendation:

l. 7 lame, *CP61*] lame. *CP75* (*misprint*)

The Young Cordwainer

See 'the mysterious twelfth-century French ballad of the Young Shoemaker', and Graves's interpretation, in *WG61*, pp.322-3/313-14; see also pp. 305-6/297-8 and 485/475-6.

Text: *PS51/CP75.*

Your Private Way

The first draft was written in pencil on a piece of board which Graves picked up on the Deyá beach.[115]

Text: *PS51/CP75.*

My Name and I

Exceptionally, this poem started as a series of reflections in prose.[116]

Text: *PS51/CP75.*

The Portrait

See Graves's letter to James Reeves, 15 Dec. 1951, quoted in the note on 'Darien' (*PS51*), below.

Text: *PS51/CP75.*

Darien

See Graves's letter to James Reeves, 14 Dec. 1950, quoted in the note on *PS51.*

After publication of the book, Graves wrote to Reeves:

> Why 'Darien'? Because that was his name. Judith (the subject of 'The Portrait') had named him so prophetically even before I met her; and that incident in my spiritual autobiography was recorded a year ago at

[115] Buffalo.

[116] Mss, Buffalo.

Deyá. Spiritual as opposed to physical autobiography; my physical head is still firmly fixed between my shoulder-blades and 'the damage is irreparable because there is none' (quotation from Laura).[117]

See also *WG61*, pp.157-8/152-3 and 318-19/309-10, and 99/95, 186-8/181-3, 192/187-8; *GM*, 31.*b*,*2*, 88.*8*; and the notes on 'To Juan at the Winter Solstice' (*P38-45*) and 'The White Goddess' (*PS51*), above.

Text: *CP75*.
PS51 does not have a line break in sect.9 l.6.

The Survivor

See 'Escape' (*GD*) and the note on the poem (pp.342-3), *Complete Poems*, Volume I.
Text: *CP75*.

The Dilemma

There is another poem with this title in *P70-72* and *CP75*; see *Complete Poems*, Volume III.
Text: *PS51*.

'¡Wellcome, to the Caves of Artá!'

Text: *CP61*.
Emendations:

Epigraph thier *New Yorker*[118]] their *CP61* (cf. st.4 l.6)
st. 1 l. 3 thier *ms., New Yorker, PS51, CP55, SP58*] their *CP61*
l. 6 stregnth *ms., New Yorker, PS51*] strength *CP61*

In *PS51* the title, 'The Spider' in the epigraph and the names in st.3 are in *guillemets*, thus: « ». 'Artá' (in the title and st.2 l.3) has no accent.

To a Poet in Trouble

Text: *PS51*.
Emendation:

l. 5 patroness), *PS51 proofs*[119]] patroness) *PS51*

---

[117] Graves to Reeves, 15 Dec. 1951; *SL 2*, p.103. See 'Fragments', 6, in Riding's *Poems: A Joking Word* (London: Cape, 1930), p.124: 'But the damage is irreparable, / For there is none.'
[118] *New Yorker*, 26 (9 Dec. 1950), 42.
[119] Sent to Graves's American agent (see the note on *PS51*, above).

POEMS 1953 (1953)

'I have just sent off a slim volume to Cassell's,' Graves wrote to Reeves, 'only half the size of yours, & also dripping with heather honey & black gall; to mark the close of an epoch.'[120]

Poems 1953 was published by Cassell on 24 September 1953; on the same day they issued a limited edition of 260 signed copies (250 of them for sale). The book contains twenty-seven new poems – 'I have written more poems in the last two years than in the previous ten'[121] – and concludes with 'Leaving the Rest Unsaid' (*CP38*), restored to the canon after being omitted from *Collected Poems (1914-1947).*

Graves introduces the 'slim volume' thus:

FOREWORD

Is a foreword really necessary? Poems, if they are any good, ought to tell their own story. If they are not, why publish them? Nor need one nowadays list the periodicals in which each poem first appeared, as most poets continue to do in forewords. Grateful though one may be to the editors, the copyright does not remain theirs, and to boast of having caught their interest is not quite seemly.

Is a foreword really necessary? Even as an assurance that the poet can express himself decently in prose? And though I have written more poems in the last two years than in the previous ten, must I apologize for having been more than usually plagued?

R.G.

Deyá, Mallorca, Spain.

To Calliope

Text: *CP61.*

This 'brief aside' (l.1) to 'the original Muse'[122] is printed (in italics) as a dedication at the beginning of *CP55, SP58, CP59* and *CP61.*

The Foreboding

Text: *P53/CP75.*

Together with 'Lovers in Winter' and 'With Her Lips Only', Graves placed this poem in Section IV in subsequent volumes of *Collected Poems,* not Section IX.

Cry Faugh!

Text: *CP75.*

---

[120] Graves to Reeves, 11 Dec. 1952; *SL 2,* p.112. Reeves's *The Password and Other Poems* (London: Heinemann, 1952) appeared in the autumn.

[121] See the 'Foreword', below.

[122] *WG61,* pp.391/382.

Variant:
st. 4 l. 2 Tell me, *CP75*] Confess, *P53*

Hercules at Nemea

See *GM*, 123.
Text: *CP75*.
Variants:
st. 1 l. 2 Fierce as *CP75*] Maned like *P53*
seized] held

Lovers in Winter

Text: *P53/CP75*.
See the note on 'The Foreboding' (*P53*), above.

Esau and Judith

For Graves's interpretation of the story of Esau, Jacob and Judith, see *Adam's Rib* (London: Trianon Press, 1955), pp.16-17, and *WG61*, pp.159-62/154-7, 218-19/213-14. See also Robert Graves and Raphael Patai, *Hebrew Myths: The Book of Genesis* (London: Cassell, 1964), 26, 37, 40-2.

Text: *P53*.
The poem appeared some three months after *P53* in the *New Statesman*, 46 (12 Dec. 1953), 765, with 'the' in place of 'a' in st.1 l.5, a full stop instead of a dash at the end of st.2 l.5, and 'Yet' in place of 'For' in st.3 l.1. (The dash at the end of st.3 l.3 was omitted apparently through lack of space.) Judging by ts. drafts, this version is earlier than the one in *P53*.

With the Gift of a Ring

For Graves's interpretation of 'the *Genesis* story of Adam and Eve', see *WG61*, pp.257/249-50.

Text: *CP59*.
Emendation:
l. 4 that *SP58*] than *CP59* (*misprint*)

Liadan and Curithir

Graves examines the relationship between Liadan of Corkaguiney, 'a brilliant young Irish *ollamh* (or master-poet) of the seventh century A.D.', and the *ollamh* Curithir in the 1953 essay 'Juana de Asbaje', in *CrP*, pp.166-84 (pp.166-8), reprinted in *CWP*, pp.119-33 (pp.119-20); and in *WG61*, pp. 449-50/440-1.
Text: *P53/CP75*.

The Sea Horse

Text: *CP75.*

Sect.1, a revised version of a ms. poem entitled 'After Love', and sect. 2 ll.6-7 were added in *CP55*.

Other variants:

sect. 2 l. 1 Do as I do: *CP75*] Tenderly *P53*
unquiet] secret
l. 2 *not in parentheses in P53*
owed] pledged
l. 8 Make much of him in your despair, and shed
l. 9 Tears on] Salt tears to bathe

The Devil at Berry Pomeroy

Graves told James Reeves that when he visited Berry Pomeroy Castle in Devonshire in September 1942, he 'identified' it as 'my nightmare castle of many years [*sic*] standing', and referred Reeves to 'The Castle' (*P29*).[123]

The visit and its sequel are described in 'Reincarnation', in *The Crane Bag and Other Disputed Subjects* (London: Cassell, 1969), pp.75-87 (pp.84-6). In this 1967 piece Graves states that 'The Castle'

> recorded a childhood nightmare of being unable to escape from a ruined castle court. [. . .] As a child, I had spent most of my summer holidays in North Wales, near Harlech Castle, [. . .] an immense, scary, moated pile, closely resembling Berry Pomeroy. We children were always afraid of getting locked up there at nightfall by the deaf old castle-keeper, Mr Richard Jones, while we were playing hide-and-seek in its towers and dungeons (pp.84, 86).

Text: *P53/SP58.*

When 'The Devil at Berry Pomeroy' was reprinted in *CP55* and *SP58*, it was placed in Section III, among poems mainly from the late 1920s and early 1930s.

Dethronement

See *WG61*, pp.216-17/211-12; *GM*, 22.*1*; and the note on 'To Juan at the Winter Solstice' (*P38-45*).

Text: *CP61.*

Variants:

st. 2 l. 4 shall *CP61*] will *P53*
st. 5 l. 4 domain] demesne

Cat-Goddesses

This poem was printed on Graves's 1951 Christmas card.

Text: *P53/CP75.*

[123] Graves to James Reeves, 26 Sept. 1942; Texas.

Rhea

See *GM*, 7, especially *6, 7, 8.*

Text: *P53/CP75.*

The Hero

See 'Instructions to the Orphic Adept' (*P38-45*), sect.8, and note; and *WG61*, pp.111/106-7, 182/176-7, 254/246-7, 256-8/249-50, 321/312, 432/423.

Text: *P53.*

Another poem with this title was first published in *PBFS* (1968), and reprinted in *BG, P68-70,* and *CP75.*

The Encounter

Text: *P53.*

There is another poem with this title in *P70-72* and *CP75.*

I'm Through with You For Ever

Text: *CP61.*

Variant:

st. 4 l. 3 of *CP61*] to *P53*

With Her Lips Only

Text: *P53/CP75.*

See the note on 'The Foreboding' (*P53*), above.

The Blotted Copy-Book

Text: *MDC.*

Emendations:

Title Copy-Book *Ed.*] Copy Book *MDC* (cf. st.3 l.2; Copy-book *P53*)

st. 2 l. 6 Prize-medals *P53*] Prize medals *MDC*

The Sacred Mission

The mission was held in Palma, 1-15 November 1951.

Text: *P53/CP61.*

Sirocco at Deyá

Text: *CP75.*

Headnote in *P53, CP55, SP58*: '(*for Will Price*)'.[124]

Variants:

l. 7 blinding the eyes with sand; *CP75*] blowing sand in the eyes; *P53*

l. 9 limestone] granite

---

[124] A Hollywood director and producer, Will Price collaborated with Graves in 1952 on a film script, 'The World's Delight', based on a story from the *Arabian Nights*. See Martin Seymour-Smith, *Robert Graves: His Life and Work*, revised edition (London: Bloomsbury, 1995), pp.438-40.

COLLECTED POEMS 1955 (1955)

Collected Poems 1955 was published only in the United States, by Doubleday, on 30 June 1955.

Graves's first two volumes of *Collected Poems*, *Poems (1914-26)* (1927) and *Collected Poems* (1938), were followed by American editions in 1929 and 1939, respectively. In the case of *Collected Poems (1914-1947)*, however, his then American publishers, Creative Age Press, wanted to postpone publication for several years, on the grounds that it included the same poems they had already published in their 1946 edition of *Poems 1938-1945*.[125] Thus it was not until 1955 that, after further difficulties with Creative Age, a somewhat different volume was brought out by Doubleday, who also published the first American editions of the 1959 and 1975 *Collected Poems*.

Collected Poems 1955 contains 221 poems. Graves omitted thirteen of the 174 poems in *Collected Poems (1914-1947)*:

> II: Without Pause. III: Trudge, Body; The Clock Man; Green Loving; Largesse to the Poor. V: To the Sovereign Muse. VI: A Withering Herb; The Twelve Days of Christmas; To Poets Under Pisces; June. VII: Dichetal do Chennaib; The Tetragrammaton; Nuns and Fish.

Twenty-one poems of the twenty-nine in *Poems and Satires 1951* are included (among them the four revised versions of earlier poems), and twenty-three of the twenty-eight in *Poems 1953*. There are eight new poems.

Graves made various changes to the arrangement of the poems. Section VII, divided in *Collected Poems (1914-1947)* into 'Satires and Grotesques' and 'Magical Poems', becomes an augmented selection of lighter poems, while the 'Magical Poems' form Section VIII (with two additions, 'The White Goddess' and 'The Jackals' Address to Isis', three omissions (see above), and 'To Juan at the Winter Solstice' transferred to Section VI).

In the 'Foreword' Graves refers to his Anglo-Irish background:

> These poems are printed in roughly chronological order. The first was written in the summer of 1914, and shows where I stood at the age of nineteen before getting caught up in the First World War, which permanently changed my outlook on life. Since then I have made a living as a writer; but my novels, biographies, short stories, historical and critical works of various sorts – some sixty or seventy titles – have always been subordinated to an inveterate profession of poetry. I published my *Collected Poems* in 1926, 1938 and 1947, and on each occasion suppressed anything in previous volumes that no

---

[125] W.P. Watt to Graves, 22 Dec. 1947; Canelluñ.

longer satisfied me. I now do the same thing again, with the result that *Collected Poems 1926* [*sic*] and *Collected Poems 1955* do not differ greatly in bulk. And though I have found it increasingly less difficult to discard old poems on which weeks of thought were spent, and which seemed sound enough when completed, but no longer pass muster, critics may decide that the benefit of the doubt has still been too generously conceded. They will be right, of course. At any rate, I can promise that no silver spoons have been thrown out with the waste, and that I have been fair to my younger and middle selves.

Some sixteen years of the forty represented here were spent in England, fifteen in Spain – which has become my permanent home – the rest mostly in Wales, France, Egypt, Switzerland and the United States. I visited Ireland only briefly during the period; but, my family traditions being Anglo-Irish, I am often reckoned as a member of that fast disappearing race which Giraldus Cambrensis centuries ago described as *Hiberniis ipsis Hiberniores* – 'more Irish than the Irish themselves.' My spiritual restlessness and love of rhythmic variety, my preoccupation with craftsmanship and accuracy of statement, the satiric edge I give even to love-poems, are considered enough to place me nationally, for better or worse; and, since somehow I have never taken the colour of my geographical environment, or belonged to any regional school of poetry, why should I argue the point? How I am labelled does not make much odds, so long as I can still go my own way.

This should suffice by way of a foreword.

R.G.

Deyá,
Majorca,
Spain

In 1958 Doubleday published a paperback (Anchor Books) called *The Poems of Robert Graves: Chosen by Himself*. The 'Foreword' to this book states: 'The selection is made from *Collected Poems, 1955*, and *Five Pens in Hand* (1958) [*sic*]': in fact all the poems from *Collected Poems 1955* were included and five were selected from *5 Pens in Hand*. Penguin published their first selection, *Robert Graves: Poems Selected by Himself*, in 1957: 161 of the 221 in *Collected Poems 1955*, in the same order.[126]

The complete contents of *Collected Poems 1955* are as follows (new poems are indicated with an asterisk):

I

In the Wilderness; The Haunted House; Reproach; The Finding of Love; 'The General Elliott'; Rocky Acres; Outlaws; One Hard Look; A Frosty Night; Allie; Unicorn and the White Doe; Henry and Mary; Love Without Hope; What Did I Dream?; The Country Dance; The Troll's Nosegay;

[126] Higginson records 24,600 copies of *SP57* and 25,000 of *SP58*.

The Hills of May; Lost Love; Vain and Careless; An English Wood; The Bedpost; The Pier-Glass; Apples and Water; Angry Samson; Down; Mermaid, Dragon, Fiend

II

In Procession; Warning to Children; Alice; Richard Roe and John Doe; The Witches' Cauldron; Ancestors; Children of Darkness; The Cool Web; Love in Barrenness; Song of Contrariety; The Presence; The Land of Whipperginny; In No Direction; The Castle; Return; The Bards; Nobody; The Progress; Full Moon; Vanity; Pure Death; Sick Love; It Was All Very Tidy

III

Callow Captain; Thief; Saint; The Furious Voyage; Song: Lift-Boy; Traveller's Curse After Misdirection; The Last Day of Leave; The Next Time; Ulysses; The Succubus; The Reader Over My Shoulder; The Legs; Gardener; Front Door Soliloquy; In Broken Images; The Devil at Berry Pomeroy; On Rising Early; Flying Crooked; Fragment of a Lost Poem; Brother

IV

Galatea and Pygmalion; The Devil's Advice to Story-Tellers; Sergeant-Major Money; Sea Side; Wm. Brazier; Welsh Incident; Vision in the Repair-Shop; Interruption; Act V, Scene 5; Midway; Hell; Leda; Synthetic Such; The Florist Rose; Lost Acres; At First Sight; Recalling War; Down, Wanton, Down!; A Former Attachment; Nature's Lineaments; Time; The Philosopher; On Dwelling; Parent to Children; Ogres and Pygmies; History of the Word; Single Fare; To Walk on Hills; To Bring the Dead to Life; To Evoke Posterity; Any Honest Housewife; Defeat of the Rebels; Never Such Love; The Fallen Signpost; The China Plate; Certain Mercies; The Cuirassiers of the Frontier; The Laureate; A Jealous Man; The Cloak; The Foreboding; With Her Lips Only; The Halls of Bedlam; Or to Perish Before Day; A Country Mansion; The Eremites; Lovers in Winter; Advocates; Self-Praise

V

On Portents; The Terraced Valley; The Challenge; The Chink; The Ages of Oath; New Legends; Like Snow; End of Play; The Climate of Thought; The Fallen Tower of Siloam; The Great-Grandmother; No More Ghosts

VI

A Love Story; Dawn Bombardment; The Worms of History; The Glutton; A Stranger at the Party; The Shot; The Thieves; Lollocks; To Sleep; Despite and Still; The Suicide in the Copse; Frightened Men; The Oath; Language of the Seasons; Mid-Winter Waking; The Rock at the Corner; The Beach; The Villagers and Death; The Door; Under the Pot; Through Nightmare; To Lucia at Birth; Death by Drums; She Tells Her Love While

Half Asleep; Theseus and Ariadne; Penthesileia*; Cold Weather Proverb; The Death Room; To Juan at the Winter Solstice; To Be Called a Bear

VII
My Name and I; 1805; At the Savoy Chapel; Dream of a Climber; The Persian Version; The Weather of Olympus; Apollo of the Physiologists; The Oldest Soldier; Grotesques i, ii, iii, iv, v, vi*; The Eugenist; A Civil Servant; Gulls and Men; Conversation Piece; Queen-Mother to New Queen; General Bloodstock's Lament for England; '¡Wellcome, to the Caves of Artá!'; I'm Through with You For Ever; The Sacred Mission; Poets' Corner*; Coronation Address*; Beauty in Trouble*; Sirocco at Deyá; From the Embassy

VIII
The White Goddess; The Allansford Pursuit; Amergin's Charm; The Battle of the Trees; The Song of Blodeuwedd; Instructions to the Orphic Adept; Lament for Pasiphaë; The Sirens' Welcome to Cronos; Intercession in Late October; The Jackals' Address to Isis; The Destroyer; Return of the Goddess

IX
With the Gift of a Ring; Counting the Beats; The Young Cordwainer; Your Private Way; The Survivor; Questions in a Wood; Darien; The Portrait; Prometheus; The Straw; Cry Faugh!; Hercules at Nemea; Dialogue on the Headland; The Mark; Liadan and Curithir; The Sea Horse; Reproach to Julia; Dethronement; Cat-Goddesses; The Blue-Fly; A Lost Jewel*; The Window Sill*; Spoils*; Rhea; Leaving the Rest Unsaid

Penthesileia

See *GM*, 164.*a,b,1,3*. The first, incomplete draft of the poem is written on the back of a sheet from the revised typescript of *GM*, part of an earlier chapter (160) on the Trojan War.[127]

Text: *CP55/CP75.*

'Penthesileia' appeared in the same month as *CP55* in the *London Magazine*, 2 (June 1955), 36, with the headnote: '(*according to the* Excidium Troiae)' [misprinted 'Troial'].

Poets' Corner

A headnote stating that the poem was 'translated from a seventeenth-century epitaph at Haarlem' appears on ms. and ts. drafts above the Latin (the wording of the Latin has been revised); this headnote is cancelled on the latest draft.

Text: *CP55/CP61.*

[127] It includes a note on how Achilles, hiding disguised as a girl, is brought to reveal his identity and join the expedition to Troy (*GM*, 160.5).

Coronation Address

This poem was first published with the title 'To the Queen' to mark the coronation of Queen Elizabeth II on 2 June 1953.[128]

Text: *CP55/SP58.*

Beauty in Trouble

Text: *CP75.*

Variants:

st. 2 l. 4 Asking how *CP75*] Asking her how *CP55*

st. 7 l. 2 guineas] dollars

The Window Sill

Graves was familiar with the legend according to which the Catalan poet, theologian and philosopher Ramon Llull (1232-1316) was converted when a lady whom he had been pursuing exposed a breast eaten away by cancer. In the version Graves preferred, Llull followed her on horseback into the church of Santa Eulalia in Palma, Mallorca; in another version she allowed him to come to her rooms.

Text: *CP75.*

Variant:

st. 4 l. 3 She said, *CP75*] Said she, *CP55*

Spoils

Text: *CP75.*

Variant:

st. 2 l. 3 these *CP75*] those *CP55*

---

[128] *Time and Tide*, 34 (6 June 1953), 747. Graves wanted to have the poem sold as a broadsheet to the crowds, but this proved impracticable. See Graves to James Reeves, 14 May 1953, *SL 2*, p.115; and W.P. Watt to Graves, 28 May 1953; Canelluñ.

THE CROWNING PRIVILEGE (1955)

In 1955-60 Graves produced no 'slim volumes' of new poems: instead, he included them in four books of prose pieces. The first of these was *The Crowning Privilege*, published by Cassell on 22 September 1955; it contains the text of the 1954-55 annual Clark Lectures, sponsored by Trinity College, which Graves delivered at Cambridge in October 1954.

'At the close of the book, fattened with nine miscellaneous essays on poetry,' he writes in the 'Foreword', 'I include sixteen new poems for good measure.' One of them is a longer version of 'The Sea Horse', from *Poems 1953*; another seven were published in the United States three months earlier in *Collected Poems 1955*: 'A Lost Jewel', 'The Window Sill', 'Spoils', 'Beauty in Trouble', 'Poets' Corner', 'Penthesileia', and 'Coronation Address'.

The complete list is as follows (an asterisk indicates that this is the first appearance in a book):

> The Clearing*; A Lost Jewel; The Three Pebbles*; The Question*; The Window Sill; The Sea Horse; Spoils; Beauty in Trouble; Poets' Corner; End of the World*; Penthesileia; To a Pebble in My Shoe*; The Tenants*; Coronation Address; My Moral Forces*; Interview*

The Three Pebbles

The epigraph (part quotation, part résumé) is from a report on the examination of a barrow, evidently dating from the Early Bronze Age, in Birkrigg, 'a moory height of carboniferous limestone' two and a quarter miles south of Ulverston, Cumbria, in August 1912.[129]

Text: *CrP*.

Emendation:

Epigraph intentional. *ts., ms.*] intentional *CrP*

Possibly

Text: *CP75*.

Previous title: 'The Question' (*CrP, 5PH*).

Variants:

st. 1 l. 1 not a *CP75*] no *CrP*
st. 2 l. 1 not a] no

To a Pebble in My Shoe

The 'pebble' was M.J.C. Hodgart, of Pembroke College, Cambridge:

---

[129] Charles Gelderd, James Randall and John Dobson, 'Some Birkrigg Barrows', Art. XXIII, *Transactions of the Cumberland and Westmorland Antiquarian and Archaeological Society*, XIV, new series, edited by W.G. Collingwood (Kendal: 1914), 466-79 (p.466); see pp.469, 471, 472, 476.

'He is an enemy of mine, gone out of his way to injure me'.[130] (The title was previously 'To a Spiteful Critic'.)[131] Hodgart wrote (anonymously) a hostile review of *The Nazarene Gospel Restored* in the *Times Literary Supplement*.[132] The editor published a reply by Graves and Podro,[133] but refused to reopen the correspondence after a further attack from Hodgart which Graves (and his lawyer) considered libellous.[134] Legal proceedings were started; eventually the case was settled out of court, with the *TLS* apologising in an editorial and paying Graves's costs.[135] See *SL 2*, pp.134-5, 137, 138-40, 142-3.

Text: *CrP.*

The Tenants

Text: *CrP.*

Emendation:

st. 1 *l. 4* fro, *ts., mss*] fro. *CrP*

5 PENS IN HAND (1958)

Besides *The Crowning Privilege*, Graves also included poems in three miscellanies: *5 Pens in Hand, Steps* (1958), and *Food for Centaurs* (1960). The poems in one book overlap with those in the next, as do the lectures, essays, and stories (American volumes alternating with English).

There are twenty poems in 'Poems 1955-1957', the sixth and final section of *5 Pens in Hand*, which was published in the United States by Doubleday on 20 March 1958. Three are from *The Crowning Privilege*: 'The Clearing', 'End of the World', and 'The Question'; and there is a revised version of an earlier poem, 'Hotel Bed at Lugano' (*CP38*). The remaining sixteen poems are new.

The complete list is as follows:

The Face in the Mirror; Forbidden Words; Song for New Year's Eve; A Ballad of Alexander and Queen Janet; The Coral Pool; Gratitude for a Nightmare; Friday Night; The Naked and the Nude; Woman and Tree;

---

130 Graves to James Reeves, 6 Jan. 1956; Texas.

131 *Punch*, 229 (21 Sept. 1955), 327.

132 Robert Graves and Joshua Podro, *The Nazarene Gospel Restored* (London: Cassell, 1953; New York: Doubleday, 1954); *TLS*, 19 Feb. 1954, 125.

133 *TLS*, 5 March 1954, 153.

134 Hodgart accused Graves and Podro of unethical misuse of a text concerning St Paul and 'a thorn in the flesh' (cf. the title, 'a Pebble in My Shoe'); *TLS*, 2 April 1954, 217.

135 *TLS*, 22 July 1955, 413. The *Manchester Guardian* had likewise been obliged to print an apology for libel in its review and pay legal costs in February 1954; see *SL 2*, p.135.

Destruction of Evidence; Hotel Bed at Lugano; The Clearing; The Second-Fated; End of the World; Bitter Thoughts on Receiving a Slice of Cordelia's Wedding Cake; The Question; A Plea to Boys and Girls; A Bouquet from a Fellow Roseman; Yes; The Outsider

The poems are preceded by 'Prologue to a Poetry Reading at the Massachusetts Institute of Technology, Boston', given on 7 February 1957.

Forbidden Words

Text: *CP75.*

Variants:

st. 2 l. 1 Concepts *CP75*] Words that are *5PH*

l. 2 word of] one from

Alexander and Queen Janet

Text: *CP61.*

Previous title: 'A Ballad of Alexander and Queen Janet' (*5PH*).

In *CP59* and *CP61* the poem is placed, like 'The Chink', in Section V, with poems from the 1930s.

Friday Night

Text: *5PH/CP75.*

Another poem entitled 'Friday Night' was first published in the English edition of *P70-72*. Both are in *CP75*.

The Naked and the Nude

'A verse from a wistful poem of mine written 1916, suppressed 1917, has been used to caption a luscious nude in the pornographic New York *Modern Man*. This provoked a poem from me called *The Naked & the Nude* which I hope will soon be published somewhere'.[136]

Text: *5PH/CP75.*

The Second-Fated

For Graves's reported death in the Battle of the Somme in July 1916, see the note on 'Escape' (*GD*), *Complete Poems,* Volume I, pp.342-3.

See also *GM*, p.23; 1.*a,b,1,3,4*, 4.*c,2,3,5*, 21.*1-4*.

Text: *CP75.*

Emendations:

sect. 3 l. 3 victory?' *CP65*] victory. *CP75* (*misprint*)

In *CP65* sect.4 l.6 is at the bottom of the page (p.249), and evidently

---

[136] Graves to James Reeves, 14 Nov. 1955; *SL 2*, p.151. 'The Naked and the Nude' was first published in the *New Yorker*, 32, no.52 (16 Feb. 1957), 99; st. 1 of 'A Pinch of Salt' (*GD* (1916) and *FF* (1917): see *Complete Poems*, Volume I, p.27) appeared in *Modern Man*, 5, no. 3 (Nov. 1955), 27 (with Graves's name).

as a consequence *CP75* has a space after this line, indicating a new section; the space has been suppressed in the present edition.

Variant:

sect. 1 l. 2 Denote *CP75*] Betray *5PH*

5PH does not have a space between the sections, which are indicated by indenting the first line of sects.2, 3 and 4.

A Slice of Wedding Cake

Text: *CP75.*

Previous title: 'Bitter Thoughts on Receiving a Slice of Cordelia's Wedding Cake' (*5PH, SP58*).

A Bouquet from a Fellow Roseman

Text: *SP58.*

Emendation:

The quotation marks around st.3 l.4, omitted in *SP58* (misprint), have been restored.

STEPS (1958)

In *Steps*, the second of Graves's miscellanies, which was published by Cassell on 13 November 1958, twenty-two poems are printed together with stories, 'talks', essays, and 'studies in history'.

Seven of the poems are new. There are revised versions of two earlier poems (not designated as such), 'Trudge, Body!' (*P30-33*) and 'The Christmas Robin' (*CP38*) (see notes, above); the other thirteen poems are from the first miscellany, *5 Pens in Hand* (published in the United States the same year, in March).

The complete list is as follows (new poems are indicated by an asterisk):

> The Face in the Mirror; Song for New Year's Eve; Alexander and Queen Janet; The Coral Pool; Gratitude for a Nightmare; Friday Night; The Naked and the Nude; Woman and Tree; Forbidden Words; Hotel Bed at Lugano; The Enlisted Man*; A Slice of Wedding Cake; A Plea to Boys and Girls; Trudge, Body!; Mike and Mandy*; The Christmas Robin; Nothing*; Call It a Good Marriage*; Read Me, Please!*; The Second-Fated; The Twin of Sleep*; Around the Mountain*

The poems are in the fourth of five sections in *Steps*, between 'Essays' and 'Studies in History'. They follow a 'Preface to a Reading of New

Poems at the University of Michigan', given on 12 February 1958, in which Graves expresses some misgivings about the poems he was now writing:

> And here I am, arrived at the discreet age of sixty-three, explaining how difficult it is to be an old poet: even more difficult, in a sense, than to be a young poet. The young poet does not understand the problems but charges his five-barred gates without fear. Sometimes he contrives to get over, not very gracefully: splintering the top bar perhaps, but still keeping his seat. Sometimes he comes a purler. . . . The old poet, on the other hand, knows too much; he prefers to take Pegasus around through a gap in the hedge, or along by a lane; yet keeps up with the hounds, and is usually in at the death. But this cannot be called hard riding; and the poet should, I think, either ride hard or not at all. In fact, the poems I now write tend to be far too cunning. Not that, like most poets who have reached my age, I resort to rhetoric, traditional forms, musical metres, and Classical references; but I have become such an obsessionist about getting a poem right, that the product is usually too much of a *tour de force*. I would have welcomed a little exuberant inexperience – short of galloping rudely ahead of the pack and trampling the fox to death.
>
> When a young poet writes verses for the wrong reasons – for vainglory, for experiment, or merely to keep his hand in – they soon reveal themselves as failures. They have neither the sacred impulse that will carry them through to poetic truth, nor enough technical skill to invest them with virtuosity. Only an old, cunning poet can disguise the initial falseness of a poem. Myself, I have never learned to be absolutely honest at the moment of composition: to throw down my pen, exclaiming 'No good will come of this!' Instead, I usually say: 'I'll give it a chance.' Thus, as a rule, fewer than two poems in every ten still satisfy my nagging conscience after they have appeared in print; and sometimes I am bitterly ashamed of work that I should have known, from the first, was below standard.
>
> 'Below standard' does not mean, I hasten to add, 'below academic standard'. Most anthologies of Great English Poems, current in schools and colleges, contain a very high percentage of rubbish without even technical cunning to recommend it. By 'below standard' I mean: below the standard I set for my own collected poems, which are the main justification I can offer for my existence; and which must not contain a single unnecessary line, if my ghost is to find peace when I die. That is a measure of my craziness.[137]

The Enlisted Man

Text: *CP59*.

[137] *S*, pp.231-8 (pp.235-6).

Variants:

l. 1 Corporal *CP59*] Colonel Corporal *S*

l. 8 Reasons' *CP59*] Reason's *S*

Mike and Mandy

The original 'Mike' and 'Mandy' were childhood playmates of Graves's son Tomás.

Text: *S*.

Emendation:

st. 6 l. 1 Wife, *AHH*] Wife *S*

A revised version entitled 'Caroline and Charles' was published in 1964 as one of the 'Poems for Children' in *AHH*.

Variants:

st. 1 l. 1 Rug *S*] Rag Rug *AHH*
l. 3 In] Of
st. 2 l. 1 the Rug,] a Rag Rug,
l. 2 Hard] Birch
l. 3 scratch you] brush you hard
st. 3 l. 1 the Hard] a Birch
l. 2 a] the
st. 4 l. 2 Farmer] Farmer's Boy
st. 5 l. 1 the Farmer,] a Farmer's Boy,
l. 2 his] the Farmer's
l. 3 strike] beat
st. 6 l. 1 his] a Farmer's
l. 2 Constable] Bailiff
l. 3 grab] seize
st. 7 l. 1 the Constable,] a Bailiff –
l. 2 Rug,] Rag Rug
l. 3 Lying] Basking
l. 4 In] Of
farm-house] same
l. 6 bang] knock
l. 7 the corner] a corner
firegrate] faggot box

Call It a Good Marriage

Text: *CP75*.

Variant:

st. 3 l. 7 upon *CP75*] on *S*

Read Me, Please!

Text: *FC*.

Variant:

st. 5 l. 4 please!' *FC*] please?' *S* (*misprint*)

The Twin of Sleep

'Drew my Will with Enid's help[.][138] Poem: Death's Twin' (Graves's 1956-66 diary (Canelluñ), 21 May 1958).[139]

Text: *S/CP75.*

Around the Mountain

'Today I have just finished a poem about walking around a mountain, which I think is so-called typical Graves, and serious; after four or five short jokeish ones. I was wondering whether I had reached my menopause.'[140]

Text: *CP75.*

Variant:

st. 7 l. 2 truth, *CP75*] fact, *S*

COLLECTED POEMS 1959 (1959)

Published by Cassell on 23 April 1959, this is Graves's only *Collected Poems* in which there are no poems making their first book appearance. It has a new, tenth section; the sixteen additional poems in it are from *5 Pens in Hand* (ten) and *Steps* (six). Of the thirty-one new poems in those two books and *The Crowning Privilege*, Graves omitted fifteen; he included three revised versions of earlier poems, 'Trudge, Body!' (*P30-33*) and 'The Christmas Robin' (*CP38*), from *Steps*, and 'Hotel Bed at Lugano' (*CP38*), from *5 Pens in Hand*.

Collected Poems 1959 contains 237 poems, compared with 226 in *Collected Poems 1955*. The following nine in *Collected Poems 1955* were omitted:

> III: The Devil at Berry Pomeroy. IV: Parent to Children; The Eremites; Self-Praise. V: The Challenge. VI: A Stranger at the Party. VII: Queen-Mother to New Queen; Coronation Address. VIII: The Allansford Pursuit.

The complete contents of *Collected Poems 1959* are as follows:

Sections I and II are identical to those in *Collected Poems 1955.*

III

Callow Captain; Thief; Saint; The Furious Voyage; Song: Lift-Boy; Traveller's Curse After Misdirection; The Last Day of Leave; The Next

---

[138] Enid Pritchard, Graves's sister-in-law, a solicitor.

[139] Graves worked on the poem on 22 and 24 May, and the entry for 27 May ends, 'Finished Twin of Sleep in 9 drafts'.

[140] Graves to James Reeves, 4 Dec. 1957; *SL 2*, p.172.

Time; Ulysses; The Succubus; The Reader Over My Shoulder; The Legs; Gardener; Front Door Soliloquy; In Broken Images; Trudge, Body!; The Christmas Robin; On Rising Early; Flying Crooked; Fragment of a Lost Poem; Brother

IV
Galatea and Pygmalion; The Devil's Advice to Story-Tellers; Sergeant-Major Money; Sea Side; Wm. Brazier; Welsh Incident; Vision in the Repair-Shop; Interruption; Act V, Scene 5; Midway; Hell; Leda; Synthetic Such; The Florist Rose; Lost Acres; At First Sight; Recalling War; Down, Wanton, Down!; A Former Attachment; Nature's Lineaments; Time; The Philosopher; On Dwelling; Hotel Bed at Lugano; Ogres and Pygmies; History of the Word; Single Fare; To Walk on Hills; To Bring the Dead to Life; To Evoke Posterity; Any Honest Housewife; Defeat of the Rebels; Never Such Love; The Fallen Signpost; The China Plate; Certain Mercies; The Cuirassiers of the Frontier; The Laureate; A Jealous Man; The Cloak; The Foreboding; With Her Lips Only; The Halls of Bedlam; Or to Perish Before Day; A Country Mansion; Lovers in Winter; Advocates

V
On Portents; The Terraced Valley; Alexander and Queen Janet; The Chink; The Ages of Oath; New Legends; Like Snow; End of Play; The Climate of Thought; The Fallen Tower of Siloam; The Great-Grandmother; No More Ghosts

VI
A Love Story; Dawn Bombardment; The Worms of History; The Glutton; The Shot; The Thieves; Lollocks; To Sleep; Despite and Still; The Suicide in the Copse; Frightened Men; The Oath; Language of the Seasons; Mid-Winter Waking; The Rock at the Corner; The Beach; The Villagers and Death; The Door; Under the Pot; Through Nightmare; To Lucia at Birth; Death by Drums; She Tells Her Love While Half Asleep; Theseus and Ariadne; Penthesileia; Cold Weather Proverb; The Death Room; To Juan at the Winter Solstice; To Be Called a Bear

VII
My Name and I; 1805; At the Savoy Chapel; Dream of a Climber; The Persian Version; The Weather of Olympus; Apollo of the Physiologists; The Oldest Soldier; Grotesques i, ii, iii, iv, v, vi; The Eugenist; A Civil Servant; Gulls and Men; Conversation Piece; General Bloodstock's Lament for England; '¡Wellcome, to the Caves of Artá!'; I'm Through with You For Ever; The Sacred Mission; Poets' Corner; Beauty in Trouble; Sirocco at Deyá; From the Embassy

VIII
The White Goddess; Amergin's Charm; The Battle of the Trees; The Song of Blodeuwedd; Instructions to the Orphic Adept; Lament for

Pasiphaë; The Sirens' Welcome to Cronos; Intercession in Late October; The Jackals' Address to Isis; The Destroyer; Return of the Goddess

IX
With the Gift of a Ring; Counting the Beats; The Young Cordwainer; Your Private Way; The Survivor; Questions in a Wood; Darien; The Portrait; Prometheus; The Straw; Cry Faugh!; Hercules at Nemea; Dialogue on the Headland; The Mark; Liadan and Curithir; The Sea Horse; Reproach to Julia; Dethronement; Cat-Goddesses; The Blue-Fly; A Lost Jewel; The Window Sill; Spoils; Rhea

X
The Face in the Mirror; The Coral Pool; Gratitude for a Nightmare; Friday Night; The Naked and the Nude; Woman and Tree; Forbidden Words; The Enlisted Man; A Slice of Wedding Cake; A Plea to Boys and Girls; Nothing; Call It a Good Marriage; Read Me, Please!; The Second-Fated; The Twin of Sleep; Around the Mountain; Leaving the Rest Unsaid

In the 'Foreword', a revised and updated version of the one in *Collected Poems 1955* (that volume itself is not mentioned), Graves affirms that the poems 'remain true to the Anglo-Irish poetic tradition into which I was born':

> These poems follow a roughly chronological order. The first was written in the summer of *1914*, and shows where I stood at the age of nineteen before getting caught up by the First World War, which permanently changed my outlook on life.
>
> Sixteen years of the forty-five that have since elapsed were spent in England; nineteen in Spain – which has become my permanent home – most of the rest in Wales, France, Egypt, Switzerland and the United States. But somehow these poems have never adopted a foreign accent or colouring; they remain true to the Anglo-Irish poetic tradition into which I was born.
>
> I published three successive collections in *1926, 1938* and *1947*, and on each occasion suppressed all poems that no longer passed muster. I now do the same again, with the result that *Collected Poems, 1959* is not much larger than *Collected Poems, 1926*. Critics may decide that benefit of the doubt is being too generously conceded. They will be right, of course. At any rate, I can promise that no silver spoons have been thrown out with the refuse, and that I have been fair to my younger, middle and elder selves. The survival rate has kept fairly even throughout the period, at five poems a year.
>
> *Deyá*
> *Majorca* R.G.

Graves was invited in May 1959 to accept the Gold Medal of the Poetry Society of America, which was presented to him in New York on 21 January 1960. On 3 March that year he received the Foyle Poetry Award in London for *Collected Poems 1959*.[141]

[141] The award was also for *The Anger of Achilles* (New York: Doubleday, 1959; London: Cassell, 1960), his translation of Homer's *Iliad*.

INDEX OF TITLES